Rick Steves'
SNAPSHOT

Bruges & Brussels

Including Antwerp & Ghent

Rick Steves & Gene Openshaw

CONTENTS

INTRODUCTION

This Snapshot guide, excerpted from my guidebook *Rick Steves' Amsterdam, Bruges & Brussels,* introduces you to Belgium's top destinations.

Bruges—once mighty, now mighty cute—comes with fancy beers in fancy glasses, lilting carillons, and lacy Gothic souvenirs of a long-gone greatness. Brussels—the capital of Europe with a Parisian ambience—has a joie de vivre, famous cuisine, a passion for comic books, and the truly grand Grand Place (Main Square), lined with cafés, chocolate shops, and Belgians living the good life. I also cover the funky, fashion-forward port of Antwerp and the thriving urban scene of Ghent—site of the biggest university in Belgium.

Whether you're sipping a beer or sampling a heavenly praline, rattling on your bike over the cobbles, diving into a steaming cone of Flemish (not "french") fries, gliding along a tranquil canal under fairytale spires, or pondering the quirky Belgian sense of humor while watching the *Manneken-Pis,* Belgium delights.

You'll find the following topics in this book:

• **Planning Your Time,** with advice on how to make the most of your limited time

• **Orientation,** including tourist information (abbreviated as TI), tips on public transportation, local tour options, and helpful hints

• **Sights** with ratings:

   ▲▲▲—Don't miss

   ▲▲—Try hard to see

   ▲—Worthwhile if you can make it

   No rating—Worth knowing about

• **Self-Guided Walks** of colorful neighborhoods, and **Self-Guided Tours** of major attractions

• **Sleeping** and **Eating,** with good-value recommendations in every price range

• **Connections,** with tips on train and air travel

Practicalities, near the end of this book, has information on money, phoning, hotel reservations, transportation, and other helpful hints, plus Flemish and French survival phrases.

To travel smartly, read this little book in its entirety before you go. It's my hope that this guide will make your trip more meaningful and rewarding. Traveling like a temporary local, you'll get the absolute most out of every mile, minute, and euro.

Thanks, and have a *goede vakantie!*

Rick Steves

BELGIUM

BELGIUM

Belgium falls through the cracks. It's nestled between Germany, France, and Netherlands, and it's famous for waffles, sprouts, and a statue of a little boy peeing. No wonder many travelers don't even consider a stop here. But visitors find that Belgium is one of Europe's best-kept secrets. There are tourists—but not as many as the country's charms merit. After all, Belgium produces some of Europe's best beer, creamiest chocolates, most beloved comic strips, and tastiest french fries. From funky urban neighborhoods to tranquil *begijnhofs*, from old-fashioned lace to cutting-age Euro-fashions, from cows mooing in a pastoral countryside to gentrified Hanseatic cityscapes bristling with spires...Belgium delights.

Ten and a half million Belgians are packed into a country only a little bigger than Maryland. With nearly 900 people per square mile, it's the second most densely populated country in Europe (after the Netherlands). This population concentration, coupled with a well-lit rail and road system, causes Belgium to shine at night when viewed from space—a phenomenon NASA astronauts call the "Belgian Window."

Belgium is divided—linguistically, culturally, and politically—between Wallonia in the south, where they speak French, and Flanders in the north, where they speak Flemish—an old sailors' dialect that's even more guttural than textbook Dutch (insert your own "phlegmish" pun here). There's also a small minority of German-speakers, in a far-eastern region that once belonged to Germany. Even though about 60 percent of the population speaks Flemish, French-speakers have politically dominated the nation for most of its history—a source of much resentment for the Flemish. Talk to locals to learn how deep the cultural rift is (for starters, read the sidebar on page 4).

Though mostly French-speaking, Belgium's capital, Brussels,

is officially bilingual. Because of Brussels' international importance as the capital of the European Union, more than 25 percent of its residents are foreigners.

It's here in Belgium that Europe comes together: where Romance languages meet Germanic languages; Catholics meet Protestants; and the BeNeLux union was established 40 years ago, planting the seed that today is sprouting into the unification of Europe. Belgium flies the flag of Europe more vigorously than any other place on the Continent.

That could be, in part, because history hasn't been very kind to little Belgium—surrounded, as it is, by much bigger and more powerful nations: France, Germany, the Netherlands, and Britain, each of which has at one time or another found Belgium a barrier on its march to empire. After putting up with tyrants from Charlemagne to the Austrian Habsburgs to Napoleon, Belgium paid the costliest price in both World Wars—most notably at Flanders Fields near Ypres (Ieper) in World War I, and at the Battle of the Bulge near Bastogne in World War II. But its crossroads location has also made Belgium stronger: Belgians are savvy businesspeople, excellent linguists, and talented chefs who've learned how to blend together delicious culinary influences from various cultures.

Belgians have a directness that some find refreshing (and

The Battle for Belgium: Flemish vs. French

Although little, peace-loving Belgium—whose capital, Brussels, is also the capital of the European Union—seems like a warm and cozy place, its society is split right down the middle by a surprisingly contentious linguistic divide with roots dating back to the nation's inception: the Flemish people of Flanders versus the French-speakers of Wallonia.

In 1830, Belgium's Francophone (French-speaking) aristocracy led the drive for independence from the Netherlands. They said, "Belgium will be French, or will not be." And so it was: Linguistic and cultural oppression ruled the day, as the Flemish language was suppressed as unworthy of higher thinking. Even in Flanders, where Flemish people are the majority, most power has traditionally been in the hands of the Francophone bourgeoisie. Education at prestigious universities, for example, was only in French.

The Flemish often feel they'd have been better off had Belgium remained part of the Netherlands...which would have respected their native tongue in their homeland. That's why most Flemish people are not particularly nationalistic about their language—rather than being blinded by Flemish pride, they readily acknowledge that Flemish and Dutch are essentially the same.

Today's Flemish baby boomers remember feeling picked on by their Francophone classmates. To travelers, it almost seems as if Flanders and Wallonia are different countries. For example,

others term brusque), and revel in their sardonic sense of humor. They're not particularly romantic or melodramatic, and—with the wry glimmer in their eye—it can be hard to tell whether they're putting you on. This ties in with their appreciation for a good comic strip. The "ninth art" of comics is deeply respected in Belgium. Some of the world's most beloved comic characters—including the Smurfs and Tintin—were created by Belgians. If you ask a twentysomething Belgian what career they're pursuing, and he or she says "comic books," nobody snickers.

From an accommodations point of view, the Flemish forte is its variety of cozy, funky, affordable B&Bs well-run by gregarious entrepreneurs and typically located up a flight or two of steep, narrow stairs. I've listed my favorite B&Bs in each town (except in Brussels, where they're rare).

Bruges and Brussels are the best two first bites of Belgium. Bruges is a wonderfully preserved medieval gem that expertly nurtures its tourist industry, bringing the town a prosperity it hasn't enjoyed for 500 years, when—as one of the largest cities in the world—it helped lead northern Europe out of the Middle Ages.

each region has its own "national" tourist office, which effectively ignores the other half of the country.

In 1970, Belgium began a gradual process of decentralizing its government (loosely following the Swiss cantonal model), and giving more administrative autonomy to its three regions: Flemish-speaking Flanders, French-speaking Wallonia, and the bilingual city-state of Brussels. Incremental reforms over the last 40 years have separated the Flemish and the Francophones more and more. Each group can now more closely pursue its own agenda, but the flipside is that the country is not as effortlessly bilingual as before. A generation ago, virtually every Belgian spoke both Flemish and French. Today, Flemish students can choose whether to take French or English as a second language... and many choose English. On my last visit to Brussels, I saw a sign in a shop window saying, "Bilingual staff wanted." What used to be commonplace is becoming a rarity.

Despite all the reforms, the longstanding Flemish-Francophone rivalry has flared up again in the last couple of years. Of Belgium's many political parties, the Nieuw-Vlaamse Alliantie (N-VA), which advocates for the secession of Flanders from Belgium altogether, won the highest percentage of the vote in 2010 elections (both in Flanders and in Belgium over-all). It's conceivable that a day may come in the not-too-distant future when a unified "Belgium" no longer exists on the map of Europe.

Brussels is simply one of Europe's great cities. With the finest town square in the country (if not the Continent), a chocolate shop on every corner, a French taste for class and cuisine, and a smattering of intriguing museums, it's equally ideal for a quick stopover as it is for a multiday visit.

With more time, two other Belgian cities are worth visiting. Historic, Old World Ghent—with a proud history as an important trading and university town—is well-preserved and picturesque, packed with charming little museums. And big, bustling Antwerp—with a port that rivals Rotterdam as Europe's largest—has recently enjoyed a dramatic renaissance. It's gone from being a dirty, dangerous, and depressing city to a trendy, newly spiffed-up mecca with fun boutiques, lively neighborhoods, fine museums, and a youthful vibe. To round out your Belgian experience, spend a few hours in the Flemish countryside around the town of Ypres—both for the pastoral scenery, and to visit World War I's Flanders Fields.

While not "undiscovered" (especially popular Bruges), Belgium is certainly underrated. Those who squeeze in a day or two

Belgium Almanac

Official Name: Royaume de Belgique/Koninkrijk België, or simply Belgique in French and België in Flemish.

Population: Of its 10.5 million people, 58 percent are Flemish, 31 percent are Walloon, and 11 percent are "mixed or other." About three-quarters are Catholic, and the rest are Protestant or other.

Latitude and Longitude: 50°N and 4°E. The latitude is similar to Alberta, Canada.

Area: With only 12,000 square miles, it's slightly smaller than the state of Maryland and one of the smallest countries in Europe.

Geography: Belgium's flat coastal plains in the northwest and central rolling hills make it easy to invade (just ask Napoleon or Hitler). There are some rugged mountains in the southeast Ardennes Forest. The climate is temperate.

Biggest Cities: The capital city of Brussels has about 1.8 million people, followed by Antwerp's 950,000.

Economy: With few natural resources, Belgium imports most of its raw materials and exports a large volume of manufactured goods, making its economy unusually dependent on world markets. It can be a sweet business—Belgium is the world's number-one exporter of chocolate. It's prosperous, with a Gross Domestic Product of $383 billion and a GDP per capita of $36,800. As the "crossroads" of Europe, Brussels is the headquarters of NATO and the capital of the European Union.

Government: A parliamentary democracy, Belgium's official head of state is King Albert II. Regional tensions dominate politics: Flemish-speaking, entrepreneurial Flanders wants more autonomy, while the French-speaking "rust belt" of Wallonia is reluctant to give it. The division has made it increasingly difficult for the Belgian Parliament to form a stable coalition government. One prime minister recently said that Belgians are united only by the king, a love of beer, and the national soccer team. Voting is compulsory. More than 90 percent of registered voters participated in the last general election (compared with approximately 62 percent in the US).

Flag: Belgium's flag is composed of three vertical bands of black, yellow, and red.

The Average Belgian: The average Belgian is 42 years old—five years older than the average American—and will live to be 79. He or she is also likely to be divorced—Belgium has the highest divorce rate in Europe, with 60 for every 100 marriages. Beer is the national beverage: on average, Belgians drink 26 gallons a year, just behind the Austrians and just ahead of the Brits.

for Belgium wish they had more time. Like sampling a flavorful praline in a chocolate shop, that first enticing taste just leaves you wanting more. Go ahead, it's OK...buy a whole box of Belgium.

Belgian Cuisine

Belgians brag that they eat as much as the Germans and as well as the French. They are among the world's leading carnivores and beer consumers. Belgium is where France meets northern Europe, and you'll find a good mix of both Flemish and French influences here. The Flemish were ruled by the French and absorbed some of the fancy cuisine and etiquette of their overlords. (The Dutch, on the other hand, were ruled by the Spanish for 80 years and picked up nothing.) And yet, once Belgian, always Belgian: Instead of cooking with wine, Belgians have perfected the art of cooking with their own unique beers, imbuing the cuisine with a hoppy sweetness.

Belgians eat lunch when we do, but they eat dinner later (if you dine earlier than 19:30 at a restaurant, you'll eat alone or with other tourists). Tax and service are always included in your bill (though a 5-10 percent tip is appreciated). You can't get free tap water; Belgian restaurateurs are emphatic about that. Tap water comes with a smile in the Netherlands, France, and Germany, but that's not the case in Belgium, where you'll either pay for water, enjoy the beer, or go thirsty.

Belgian Specialties

Although this book's coverage focuses on the Flemish part of the country, people speak French first in Brussels—so both languages are given below (Flemish/French); if I've listed only one word, it's used nationwide. While the French influence is evident every-where, it's ratcheted up around Brussels.

Traditional Dishes

Stoofvlees/Carbonnade: Rich beef stew flavored with onions, beer, and mustard. It's often quite sweet (sweetened with brown sugar or gingerbread). It's similar to the French beef bourgui-gnon, but made with beer instead of red wine.

(Gentse) Waterzooi: Creamy soup made with chicken, eel, or fish; originated in Ghent.

Konijn met pruimen/lapin à la flamande: Marinated rabbit braised in onions and prunes.

Filet américain: Beware—for some reason, steak tartare (raw) is called "American."

Biersoep/soupe à la bière: Beer soup—though remember that beer can be included in just about any dish.

...à la flamande: Anything cooked in the Flemish style, which generally means with beer.

Seafood

Mosselen/moules: Mussels are served everywhere, either cooked plain *(natuur/nature)*, with white wine *(witte wijn/vin blanc)*, with shallots or onions *(marinière)*, or in a tomato sauce *(provençale)*. You get a big-enough-for-two bucket and a pile of fries. Go local by using one empty shell to tweeze out the rest of the *mosselen*. When the mollusks are in season, from about mid-July through April, you'll get the big Dutch mussels (most are from the coastal area called Zeeland, just north of Belgium). Locals take a break from mussels in May and June, when only the puny Danish kind are available.

Noordzee garnalen/crevettes: Little gray shrimp, generally served in one of two ways: inside a carved-out tomato or in croquettes (minced and stuffed in breaded, deep-fried rolls).

Paling in het groen/anguilles au vert: Eel in green herb sauce. Although a classic dish, this is less common these days, as good-quality eel is in short supply.

Caricoles: Sea snails. Very local, seasonal, and (like eel) hard to find, these are usually sold hot by street vendors.

Vegetables and Side Dishes

Rode kol/chou rouge à la flamande: Red cabbage with onions and prunes.

Asperges: White asparagus, available only for a short time in spring, and usually served in cream sauce.

Witloof/chicoree or *chicon:* Endive, the classic Belgian vegetable, usually served as a side dish. This coarse, bitter green is eaten both raw and cooked.

Spruitjes/choux de Bruxelles: Brussels sprouts (in cream sauce).

Stoemp: Mashed potatoes and vegetables, most common in Brussels.

Snacks

Friets/frites: Belgian-style fries taste so good because they're deep-fried twice—once to cook, and once to brown. The natives eat them with mayonnaise or other flavored sauces, but not ketchup. The Dutch call them *Vlaamse frites*—"Flemish fries"—but the Flemish just call them *friets*. Look for a *frituur* (fry shop) or a *frietkot* (fry wagon).

Cheeses: While the French might use wine or alcohol to rub the rind of their cheese to infuse it with flavor, the Belgians use (surprise, surprise) beer. There are 350 types of Belgian cheeses. From Flanders, look for Vieux Brugge ("Old Bruges") and

Chimay (named for the beer they use on it); from Wallonia, Remoudou and Djotte de Nivelles are good.

Croque monsieur: Grilled ham-and-cheese sandwich.

Tartine de fromage blanc: Open-face cream-cheese sandwich, often enjoyed with a cherry Kriek beer and found mostly in traditional Brussels bars.

Desserts and Sweets

Chocolates: The two basic types of Belgian chocolates are **pralines** (what we generally think of as "chocolates"—a hard chocolate shell with various fillings) and **truffles** (a softer, crumblier shell, often spherical, and also filled).

Wafels/Gaufres: Belgians recognize two general types of waffles: **Liège-style** (dense, very sweet—with a sugary crust, and heated up) and **Brussels-style** (lighter and fluffier, dusted with powdered sugar and sometimes topped with marmalade). And though Americans think of "Belgian" waffles for break-  fast, Belgians generally have them (or pancakes, *pannenkoeken*) as a late-after-noon snack (around 16:00)—though the delicious Liège-style waffles are sold 'round the clock to tourists as an extremely tempting treat. You'll see little windows, shops, and trucks selling these *wafels,* either plain (for Belgians and purists) or topped with fruit, jam, chocolate sauce, ice cream, or whipped cream (for tourists). You'll find the Brussels-style waffles mostly in teahouses, and only in the afternoon (14:00-18:00).

Speculoos: Spicy gingerbread biscuits served with coffee.

Dame blanche: Chocolate sundae.

Pistolets: Round croissants.

Chocolade mousse: Just what it sounds like.

Belgian Beers

Belgium has about 120 different varieties of beer and 580 different brands, more than any other country—the locals take their beers as seriously as the French do their wines. Even small café menus include six to eight varieties. Connoisseurs and novices alike can be confused by the many choices, and casual drinkers probably won't like every kind offered, since some varieties don't even taste like beer. Belgian beer is generally yeastier and higher in alcohol content than beers in other countries.

In Belgium, certain beers are paired with certain dishes. To

BELGIUM

bring out their flavor, different beers are served at cold, cool, or room temperature, and each has its own distinctive glass. Whether wide-mouthed, tall, or fluted, with or without a stem, the glass is meant to highlight the beer's qualities. A memorable Belgian beer experience is drinking a Kwak beer in its traditional tall glass. The glass, which widens at the base, stands in a wooden holder—you pick the whole apparatus up—frame and glass—and drink. As you near the end, the beer in the wide bottom comes out at you quickly, with a "Kwak! Kwak! Kwak!" Critics say this gimmick distracts drinkers from the fact that Kwak beer is mediocre at best.

To get a draft beer in Bruges, where Flemish is the dominant language, ask for *een pintje* (ayn pinch-ya; a pint); in Brussels, where French prevails, request *une bière* (oon bee-yair). Don't insist on beer from the tap. The only way to offer so many excellent beers fresh is to serve them bottled, and the best varieties generally are available only by the bottle. "Cheers" is *proost* or *gezondheid* in Flemish, and *santé* (sahn-tay) in French. The colorful cardboard coasters make nice, free souvenirs.

Here's a breakdown of types of beer, with some common brand names you'll find either on tap or in bottles. (Some beers require a second fermentation in the bottle, so they're only available in bottles.) This list is just a start, and you'll find many beers that don't fall into these neat categories. For encyclopedic information on Belgian beers, visit www.belgianstyle.com.

Ales (Blonde/Red/Amber/Brown): Ales are easily recognized by their color. Try a blonde or golden ale (Leffe Blonde, Duvel), a rare and bitter sour red (Rodenbach), an amber (Palm, De Koninck), or a brown (Leffe Bruin).

Lagers: These are light, sparkling, Budweiser-type beers. Popular brands include Jupiler, Stella Artois, and Maes.

Lambics: Perhaps the most unusual and least beer-like, *lambics* are stored for years in wooden casks, fermenting from wild yeasts that occur naturally in the air. Tasting more like a dry and bitter farmhouse cider, pure *lambic* is often blended with fruits to counter the sour flavor. Some brand names include Cantillon, Lindemans, and Mort-Subite ("Sudden Death").

Fruit *lambics* include those made with cherries *(kriek)*, raspberries *(frambozen)*, peaches *(pêche)*, or blackcurrants *(cassis)*. The result for each is a tart but sweet beer, similar to a dry pink champagne. People who don't usually enjoy beer tend to like these fruit-flavored varieties.

White *(Witte):* Based on wheat instead of hops, these are milky-yellow summertime beers. White beer, similar to a Hefeweizen, is often flavored with spices such as orange peel or coriander.

Trappist Beers: For centuries, between their vespers and matins, Trappist monks have been brewing heavily fermented, malty beers. Three typical Trappist beers (from the Westmalle monastery) are Trippel, with a blonde color, served cold with a frothy head; Dubbel, which is dark, sweet, and served cool; and Single, made especially by the monks for the monks, and considered a fair trade for a life of celibacy. Other Trappist monasteries include Rochefort, Chimay, and Orval. Try the Trappist Blauwe Chimay—extremely smooth, milkshake-like, and complex.

Strong Beers: The potent brands include Duvel (meaning "devil," because of its high octane, camouflaged by a pale color), Verboten Vrucht ("forbidden fruit," with Adam and Eve on the label), and the not-for-the-fainthearted brands of Judas, Satan, and Lucifer. Gouden Carolus is good, and Delerium Tremens speaks for itself.

Mass-Produced Beers: Connoisseurs say you should avoid the mass-produced labels (Leffe, Stella, and Hoegaarden—all owned by InBev, which owns Budweiser in America) when you can enjoy a Belgian microbrew (like Chimay) instead.

BRUGES
Brugge

ORIENTATION TO BRUGES

With pointy gilded architecture, stay-a-while cafés, vivid time-tunnel art, and dreamy canals dotted with swans, Bruges is a heavyweight sightseeing destination, as well as a joy. Where else can you ride a bike along a canal, munch mussels and wash them down with the world's best beer, savor heavenly chocolate, and see Flemish Primitives and a Michelangelo, all within 300 yards of a bell tower that jingles every 15 minutes? And do it all without worrying about a language barrier?

The town is Brugge (BROO-ghah) in Flemish, and Bruges (broozh) in French and English. Its name comes from the Viking word for wharf. Right from the start, Bruges was a trading center. In the 11th century, the city grew wealthy on the cloth trade.

By the 14th century, Bruges' population was 35,000, as large as London's. As the middleman in the sea trade between northern and southern Europe, it was one of the biggest cities in the world and an economic powerhouse. In addition, Bruges had become the most important cloth market in northern Europe.

In the 15th century, while England and France were slugging it out in the Hundred Years' War, Bruges was the favored residence of the powerful Dukes of Burgundy—and at peace. Commerce and the arts boomed. The artists Jan van Eyck and Hans Memling had studios here.

But by the 16th century, the harbor had silted up and the economy had collapsed. The Burgundian court left, Belgium became a minor Habsburg possession, and Bruges' Golden Age abruptly ended. For generations, Bruges was known as a mysterious and dead city. In the 19th century, a new port, Zeebrugge, brought renewed vitality to the area. And in the 20th century, tourists discovered the town.

Today, Bruges prospers because of tourism: It's a uniquely

well-preserved Gothic city and a handy gateway to Europe. It's no secret, but even with the crowds, it's the kind of place where you don't mind being a tourist.

Bruges' ultimate sight is the town itself, and the best way to enjoy it is to get lost on the back streets, away from the lace shops and ice-cream stands.

Planning Your Time

Bruges needs at least two nights and a full, well-organized day. Even nonshoppers enjoy browsing here, and the Belgian love of life makes a hectic itinerary seem a little senseless. With one day—other than a Monday, when the three museums are closed—the speedy visitor could do the Bruges blitz described below (also included in my Bruges City Walk):

9:30	Climb the bell tower on the Markt (Market Square).
10:00	Tour the sights on Burg Square.
11:30	Tour the Groeninge Museum (reopened June of 2011).
13:00	Eat lunch and buy chocolates.
14:00	Take a short canal cruise.
14:30	Visit the Church of Our Lady and see Michelangelo's *Madonna and Child.*
15:00	Tour the Memling Museum.
16:00	Catch the De Halve Maan Brewery tour (note that their last tour runs at 15:00 in winter on weekdays).
17:00	Relax in the Begijnhof courtyard.
18:00	Ride a bike around the quiet back streets of town or take a horse-and-buggy tour.
20:00	Lose the tourists and find dinner.

If this schedule seems insane, skip the bell tower and the brewery—or stay another day.

Bruges Overview

The tourist's Bruges—and you'll be sharing it—is less than one square mile, contained within a canal (the former moat). Nearly everything of interest and importance is within a convenient cobbled swath between the train station and the Markt (Market Square; a 20-minute walk). Many of my quiet, charming, recommended accommodations lie just beyond the Markt.

Tourist Information

The main tourist office, called **In&Uit** ("In and Out"), is in the big, red concert hall on the square called 't Zand (daily 10:00-18:00, take a number from the touch-screen machines and wait, 't Zand 34, tel. 050-444-646, www.brugge.be). The other TI is at the train

Bruges Museum Tips

Admission prices are steep, but they include great audioguides—so plan on spending some time and really getting into it. For information on all the museums, call 050-448-711 or visit www .brugge.be.

Museum Passes: The 't Zand TI and city museums sell a **museum combo-ticket** (any five museums for €15, valid for 3 days). Because the Groeninge and Memling museums cost €8 each, art lovers will save money with this pass.

The **Brugge City Card** is a more extensive pass covering entry to 22 museums, including all the major sights (€34/48 hours, €39/72 hours, sold at TIs and many hotels). If you'll be doing some serious sightseeing, this card can save you money. Its long list of bonuses and discounts includes a free canal boat ride (March-Nov), a visitors' guide, and discounts on bike rental, parking, and some performances.

Blue Monday: In Bruges, nearly all museums are open Tuesday through Sunday year-round from 9:30 to 17:00 and are closed on Monday. If you're in Bruges on a Monday, the following attractions are open: bell-tower climb on the Markt, Begijnhof, De Halve Maan Brewery Tour, Basilica of the Holy Blood, City Hall's Gothic Room, and chocolate shops and museum. You can also join a boat, bus, or walking tour, or rent a bike and pedal into the countryside.

station (Mon-Fri 10:00-17:00, Sat-Sun 10:00-14:00).

The TIs sell the €2.50 *Love Bruges Visitors' Guide*, which comes with a map (costs €0.50 if bought separately), a few well-described self-guided walking tours, and listings of all the sights and services (free with Brugge City Card). You can also pick up a free monthly English-language program called *events@brugge* and a free, fun map/guide "made by locals for young travelers." The TIs have information on train schedules and tours (see "Tours in Bruges," later). Many hotels give out free maps with more detail than the map the TIs sell.

Arrival in Bruges

By Train: Coming in by train, you'll see the bell tower that marks the main square (Markt, the center of town). Upon arrival, stop by the train station TI to pick up the *Love Bruges Visitors' Guide* (with map). The station has ATMs and lockers (€3-4).

The best way to get to the town center is by **bus.** Buses #1-9, #11-17, and #25 go to the Markt (all marked *Centrum*). Simply hop on, pay €1.60 (€1.20 if you buy in advance at Lijnwinkel shop just outside the train station), and you're there in four minutes (get off at third stop—either Markt or Wollestraat). Buses #4 and #14

continue to the northeast part of town (to the windmills and recommended accommodations on and near Carmersstraat, stop: Gouden Handstraat). If you arrive after 20:30, when the daytime bus routes end, you can still take the bus, but the "evening line" buses run much less frequently (buses marked *Avondlijn Centrum, Avondlijn Noord*—#91, *Avondlijn Oost*—#92, and *Avondlijn Zuid*—#93 all go to the Markt).

The **taxi** fare from the train station to most hotels is about €8.

It's a 20-minute **walk** from the station to the center—no fun with your luggage. If you want to walk to the Markt, cross the busy street and canal in front of the station, head up Oostmeers, and turn right on Zwidzandstraat. You can rent a **bike** at the station for the duration of your stay, but other bike-rental shops are closer to the center (see "Helpful Hints," below).

By Car: Park in front of the train station in the handy two-story garage for just €2.50 for 24 hours. The parking fee includes a round-trip bus ticket into town and back for everyone in your car. There are pricier underground parking garages at the square called 't Zand and around town (€9/day, all of them well-marked). Paid parking on the street in Bruges is limited to four hours. Driving in town is very complicated because of the one-way system. The best plan for drivers: Park at the train station, visit the TI at the station, and rent a bike or catch a bus into town.

Helpful Hints

Market Days: Bruges hosts markets on Wednesday morning (on the Markt) and Saturday morning ('t Zand). On good-weather Saturdays, Sundays, and public holidays, a flea market hops along Dijver in front of the Groeninge Museum. The Fish Market sells souvenirs and seafood Tuesday through Saturday mornings until 13:00.

Shopping: Shops are generally open from 10:00 to 18:00. Grocery stores usually are closed on Sunday. The main shopping street, Steenstraat, stretches from the Markt to 't Zand Square. The **Hema** department store is at Steenstraat 73 (Mon-Sat 9:00-18:00, closed Sun).

Internet Access: Punjeb Internet Shop, just a block off the Markt, is the most central of the city's many "telephone shops" offering Internet access (€1.50/30 minutes, €2.50/hour, daily 9:00-20:00, Philipstockstraat 4). **Bean Around the World** is a cozy coffeehouse with imported Yankee snacks and free

Wi-Fi for customers (€1/15 minutes on their computers, Thu-Mon 10:00-19:00, Wed 11:30-19:00, closed Tue, Genthof 5, tel. 050-703-572, run by American expat Olene).

Post Office: It's on the Markt near the bell tower (Mon-Fri 9:00-18:00, Sat 9:30-15:00, closed Sun, tel. 050-331-411).

Laundry: Bruges has three self-service launderettes, each a five-minute walk from the center; ask your hotelier for the nearest one.

Bike Rental: Bruges Bike Rental is central and cheap, with friendly service and long hours (€3.50/hour, €5/2 hours, €7/4 hours, €10/day, show this book to get student rate—€8/day, no deposit required—just ID, daily 10:00-22:00, free city maps and child seats, behind the far-out iron facade at Niklaas Desparsstraat 17, tel. 050-616-108, Bilal). **Fietsen Popelier Bike Rental** is also good (€4/hour, €8/4 hours, €12/day, 24-hour day is OK if your hotel has a safe place to store bike, no deposit required, daily 10:00-19:00, sometimes open later in summer, free Damme map, Mariastraat 26, tel. 050-343-262). **Koffieboontje Bike Rental** is just under the bell tower on the Markt (€4/hour, €9/day, €20/day for tandem, these prices for Rick Steves readers, daily 9:00-22:00, free city maps and child seats, Hallestraat 4, tel. 050-338-027).

Other rental places include the less-central **De Ketting** (cheap at €6/day, Mon-Fri 9:00-12:15 & 13:30-18:30 except Mon opens at 10:00, Sat 9:30-12:15, closed Sun, Gentpoortstraat 23, tel. 050-344-196, www.deketting.be) and **Fietspunt Brugge** at the train station (€9.50/day, €6.50/half-

day after 14:00, €13 deposit, Mon-Fri 7:00-19:30, closed Sat-Sun, just outside the station and to the left as you exit, tel. 050-302-329).

Best Town View: The bell tower overlooking the Markt rewards those who climb it with the ultimate town view.

Getting Around Bruges

Most of the city is easily walkable, but you may want to take the bus or taxi between the train station and the city center at the Markt (especially if you have heavy luggage).

By Bus: A bus ticket is good for an hour (€1.20 if you buy in advance at Lijnwinkel shop just outside the train station, or €1.60 on the bus). And though you can buy various day passes, there's really no need to buy one for your visit. Nearly all city buses go directly from the train station to the Markt and fan out from there;

they then return to the Markt and go back to the train station. Note that buses returning to the train station from the Markt also leave from the library bus stop, a block off the square on nearby Kuiperstraat (every 5 minutes). Your key: Use buses that say either *Station* or *Centrum*.

By Taxi: You'll find taxi stands at the station and on the Markt (€8/first 2 km; to get a cab in the center, call 050-334-444 or 050-333-881).

Tours in Bruges

Bruges by Boat—The most relaxing and scenic (though not informative) way to see this city of canals is by boat, with the cap-

tain narrating. The city carefully controls this standard tourist activity, so the many companies all offer essentially the same thing: a 30-minute route (roughly 4/hour, daily 10:00-17:00), a price of €7 (cash only), and narration in three or four languages. Qualitative differences are because of individual guides, not companies. Always let them know you speak English to ensure you'll understand the spiel. Two companies give the group-rate discount to individuals with this book: Boten Stael (just over the canal from Memling Museum at Katelijnestraat 4, tel. 050-332-771) and Gruuthuse (Nieuwstraat 11, opposite Groeninge Museum, tel. 050-333-393).

Bruges by Bike—**QuasiMundo Bike Tours** leads daily five-mile English-language bike tours around the city (€25, €3 discount with this book, 2.5 hours, departs March-Oct at 10:00, in Nov only with good weather, no tours Dec-Feb). For more details and contact info, see their listing under "Near Bruges," later.

City Minibus Tour—City Tour Bruges gives a rolling overview of the town in an 18-seat, two-skylight minibus with dial-a-language headsets and video support (€14.50, 50 minutes, pay driver). The tour leaves hourly from the Markt (10:00-20:00 in summer, until 19:00 in spring, until 18:00 in fall, less in winter, tel. 050-355-024, www.citytour.be). The narration, though clear, is slow-moving and a bit boring. But the tour is a lazy way to cruise past virtually every sight in Bruges.

Walking Tour—Local guides walk small groups through the core of town (€9, 2 hours, daily July-Aug, Sat-Sun only mid-April-June and Sept-Oct, depart from TI on 't Zand Square at 14:30—just drop in a few minutes early and buy tickets at the TI desk). Though earnest, the tours are heavy on history and given in two languages,

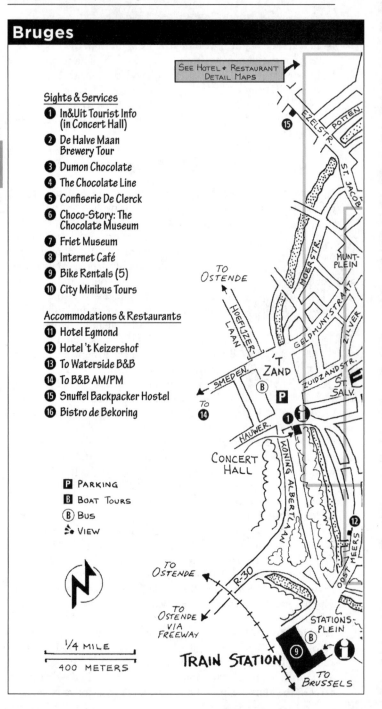

Bruges

See Hotel & Restaurant Detail Maps

Sights & Services
1. In&Uit Tourist Info (in Concert Hall)
2. De Halve Maan Brewery Tour
3. Dumon Chocolate
4. The Chocolate Line
5. Confiserie De Clerck
6. Choco-Story: The Chocolate Museum
7. Friet Museum
8. Internet Café
9. Bike Rentals (5)
10. City Minibus Tours

Accommodations & Restaurants
11. Hotel Egmond
12. Hotel 't Keizershof
13. To Waterside B&B
14. To B&B AM/PM
15. Snuffel Backpacker Hostel
16. Bistro de Bekoring

P Parking
B Boat Tours
B Bus
View

1/4 MILE
400 METERS

TO OSTENDE

'T ZAND

CONCERT HALL

TO OSTENDE
TO OSTENDE VIA FREEWAY

R-30

STATIONS-PLEIN

TRAIN STATION

TO BRUSSELS

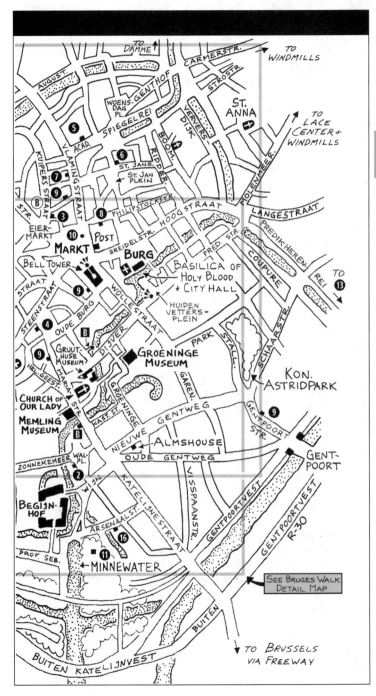

so they may be less than peppy. Still, to propel you beyond the pretty gables and canal swans of Bruges, they're good medicine. In the off-season, "winter walks" leave from the same TI four evenings a week (€9, Nov-Feb Sat-Mon and Wed at 17:00).

Local Guide—A private two-hour guided tour costs €50 (reserve at least one week in advance through TI, tel. 050-448-686). Or contact Christian Scharlé and Daniëlle Janssens, who give two-hour walks for €70, three-hour guided drives for €150, and full-day tours of Bruges and Brussels for €200 (Christian's mobile 0475-659-507, Daniëlle's mobile 0476-493-203, www.tourmanagement belgium.be, tmb@skynet.be).

Horse-and-Buggy Tour—The buggies around town can take you on a clip-clop tour (€36, 35 minutes; price is per carriage, not per person; buggies gather in Minnewater, near entrance to Begijnhof). When divided among four or five people, this can be a good value.

Near Bruges

Popular tour destinations from Bruges are Flanders Fields (famous WWI sites about 40 miles to the southwest; see that chapter for more information) and the picturesque town of Damme (4 easy-to-bike miles to the northeast).

Quasimodo Countryside Tours—This company offers those with extra time two entertaining, all-day, English-only bus tours through the rarely visited Flemish countryside. The "Flanders Fields" tour concentrates on WWI battlefields, trenches, memorials, and poppy-splattered fields (Tue-Sun at 9:15, no tours Mon or in Jan, 8 hours, visit to In Flanders Fields Museum not included). The other tour, "Triple Treat," focuses on Flanders' medieval past and rich culture, with tastes of chocolate, waffles, and beer (departs Mon, Wed, and Fri at 9:15, 8 hours). Be ready for lots of walking.

Tours cost €60, or €50 if you're under 26 (cash preferred, €10 discount on second tour if you've taken the other, includes sandwich lunch, 9- or 30-seat bus depending on demand, non-smoking, reservations required—call 050-370-470, www.quasimodo.be). After making a few big-hotel pickups, the buses leave town from the Park Hotel on 't Zand Square (arrange for pickup when you reserve).

Flanders Fields Battlefield Daytours by Nathan—Nathan (or his right-hand man, Karl) leads small groups on minibus day trips to the WWI sights between here and Ypres (Ieper). While pricier than Quasimodo's tour (listed above), Nathan's are more intimate: eight travelers on a minibus rather than a big busload (allowing your guide to tailor the tours to passengers' interests and nationalities); pickup from any hotel or B&B (because the small bus is allowed in the town center); and an included restaurant lunch instead of

a picnic. Nathan's tours also include free time at the excellent museums in Ypres and Passchendaele (€65, €3 discount when booked direct using this book, price includes admissions, cash only, departs Tue-Sun around 8:45 from your hotel or B&B, 8.5 hours, call 050-346-060 or toll-free 0800-99133 to reserve, www.visitbruges.org, info@visitbruges.org). In the evening, Nathan offers a shorter **Last Post Evening Tour,** with a stop at Tyne Cot Cemetery en route to the moving 20:00 bugle call at the Menin Gate in Ypres (€40, no discounts, departs Tue-Sun around 18:15 from your B&B/hotel, returns to Bruges around 21:15).

Bike Tours—QuasiMundo Bike Tours, which runs bike tours around Bruges (listed earlier), also offers a daily "Border by Bike"

tour through the nearby countryside to Damme (€25, €3 discount with this book, March-Oct, departs at 13:00, 15 miles, 4 hours, tel. 050-330-775, www.quasimundo.com). Both their city and border tours include bike rental, a light raincoat (if necessary), water, and a drink in a local café. Meet at the metal "car wash" fountain on Burg Square 10 minutes before departure. If you already have a bike, you're welcome to join either tour for €15. Jos, who leads most departures, is a high-energy and entertaining guide.

Charming Mieke of **Pink Bear Bike Tours** takes small groups

on an easy and delightful 3.5-hour guided pedal along a canal to the historic town of Damme and back, finishing with a brief tour of Bruges. English tours go daily through peak season and nearly daily the rest of the year (€22, €2 discount with this book, €15 if you already have a bike, meet at 10:25 under bell tower on the Markt, tel. 050-616-686, mobile 0476-744-525, www.pinkbear.freeservers.com).

For a do-it-yourself bike tour, see page 31. For bike rental shops in Bruges, see page 18.

SIGHTS IN BRUGES

These sights are listed in walking order, from the Markt (Market Square), to Burg Square, to the cluster of museums around the Church of Our Lady, to the Begijnhof (10-minute walk from beginning to end, without stops). For a self-guided walk and more information on the major sights, see the Bruges City Walk chapter.

▲**Markt (Market Square)**—Ringed by a bank, the post office, lots of restaurant terraces, great old gabled buildings, and the iconic bell tower, this square is the modern heart of the city (most city buses run from near here to the train station—it's a block down Kuiperstraat at the library bus stop). Under the bell tower are two great Belgian-style french-fry stands, a quadrilingual Braille description of the old town, and a metal model of the tower. In Bruges' heyday as a trading center, a canal came right up to this square. Geldmuntstraat, just off the square, is a delightful street with many fun and practical shops and eateries.

▲▲**Bell Tower (Belfort)**—Most of this bell tower has presided over the Markt since 1300, serenading passersby with carillon music. The octagonal lantern was added in 1486, making it 290 feet high—that's 366 steps. The view is worth the climb and probably even the €8 (daily 9:30-17:00, 16:15 last-entry time strictly enforced—best to show up before 16:00, €0.30 WC in courtyard).

▲▲**Burg Square**—This opulent square is Bruges' civic center, the historic birthplace of Bruges, and the site of the ninth-century castle of the first count of Flanders. Today, it's an atmospheric place to take in an outdoor concert while surrounded by six centuries of architecture.

▲**Basilica of the Holy Blood**—Originally the Chapel of Saint Basil, this church is famous for its relic of the blood of Christ, which, according to tradition, was brought to Bruges in 1150

after the Second Crusade. The lower chapel is dark and solid—a fine example of Romanesque style. The upper chapel (separate entrance, climb the stairs) is decorated Gothic. An interesting treasury museum is next to the upper chapel (treasury-€1.50; April-mid-Oct daily 9:30-12:00 & 14:00-18:00; mid-Oct-March Thu-Tue 10:00-12:00 & 14:00-16:00, Wed 10:00-11:45 only; Burg Square, tel. 050-336-792, www.holyblood.com).

▲**City Hall**—This complex houses several interesting sights. Your €2 ticket includes an audioguide; access to a room full of old town maps and paintings; the grand, beautifully restored **Gothic Room** from 1400, starring a painted and carved wooden ceiling adorned with hanging arches (daily 9:30-17:00, last entry 30 minutes before closing, Burg 12); and the less impressive **Renaissance Hall** (Brugse Vrije), basically just one ornate room with a Renaissance chimney (same hours, separate entrance—in corner of square at Burg 11a).

▲▲▲**Groeninge Museum**—This recently renovated museum, which reopened in June of 2011, houses a world-class collection of mostly Flemish art, from Memling to Magritte. While there's plenty of worthwhile modern art, the highlights are the vivid and pristine Flemish Primitives. ("Primitive" here means "before the Renaissance.") Flemish art is shaped by its love of detail, its merchant patrons' egos, and the power of the Church. Lose yourself in the halls of Groeninge: Gaze across 15th-century canals, into the eyes of reassuring Marys, and through town squares littered with leotards, lace, and lopped-off heads (€8, more for special exhibits, Tue-Sun 9:30-17:00, closed Mon, Dijver 12, tel. 050-448-743, www.brugge.be).

○ See the Groeninge Museum Tour chapter.

Gruuthuse Museum—Once a wealthy brewer's home, this 15th-century mansion is a sprawling smattering of everything from medieval bedpans to a guillotine. As it's undergoing an extensive restoration, the museum is only partially open until October of 2011; after that it closes completely until the end of 2012 (if open: €6, includes entry to apse in Church of Our Lady, Tue-Sun 9:30-17:00, closed Mon, Dijver 17, Bruges museums tel. 050-448-711, www.brugge.be).

▲▲**Church of Our Lady (Onze-Lieve-Vrouwekerk)**—The church stands as a memorial to the power and wealth of Bruges in its heyday. A delicate *Madonna and Child* by Michelangelo is near the apse (to the right if you're facing the altar). It's said to be the only

Bruges at a Glance

▲▲▲Groeninge Museum Top-notch collection of mainly Flemish art. **Hours:** Tue-Sun 9:30-17:00, closed Mon. See page 25.

▲▲Bell Tower Overlooking the Markt, with 366 steps to a worthwhile view and a carillon close-up. **Hours:** Daily 9:30-17:00. See page 24.

▲▲Burg Square Historic square with sights and impressive architecture. **Hours:** Always open. See page 24.

▲▲Memling Museum/St. John's Hospital Art by the greatest of the Flemish Primitives. **Hours:** Tue-Sun 9:30-17:00, closed Mon. See page 26.

▲▲Church of Our Lady Tombs and church art, including Michelangelo's *Madonna and Child*. **Hours:** Church open Mon-Fri 9:30-17:00, Sat 9:30-16:45, Sun 13:30-17:00 only; museum and apse closed Mon. See page 25.

▲▲Begijnhof Benedictine nuns' peaceful courtyard and Beguine's House museum. **Hours:** Courtyard always open, museum open Mon-Sat 10:00-17:00, Sun 14:30-17:00, shorter hours off-season. See page 27.

▲▲De Halve Maan Brewery Tour Fun tour that includes beer. **Hours:** April-Oct daily on the hour 11:00-16:00, Sat until 17:00; Nov-March Mon-Fri at 11:00 and 15:00 only, Sat-Sun on the hour 11:00-16:00. See page 28.

SIGHTS IN BRUGES

Michelangelo statue to leave Italy in his lifetime (thanks to the wealth generated by Bruges' cloth trade). If you like tombs and church art, pay to wander through the apse (Michelangelo viewing is free, art-filled apse-€2, covered by Gruuthuse admission; church open Mon-Fri 9:30-17:00, Sat 9:30-16:45, Sun 13:30-17:00; museum and apse closed Mon, last entry 30 minutes before closing, Mariastraat, www.brugge.be).

▲▲Memling Museum/St. John's Hospital (Sint Janshospitaal)—The former monastery/ hospital complex has a fine museum in what was once the monks' church. It contains six much-loved paintings by the greatest of the Flemish Primitives, Hans Memling. His *Mystical Wedding of St. Catherine* triptych is a highlight, as is the miniature, gilded-oak shrine to St. Ursula (€8,

▲▲Biking Exploring the countryside and pedaling to nearby Damme. **Hours:** Rental shops generally open daily 9:00-19:00. See page 30.

▲Markt Main square that is the modern heart of the city, with carillon bell tower (described on opposite page). **Hours:** Always open. See page 24.

▲Basilica of the Holy Blood Romanesque and Gothic church housing a relic of the blood of Christ. **Hours:** April-mid-Oct daily 9:30-12:00 & 14:00-18:00; mid-Oct-March Thu-Tue 10:00-12:00 & 14:00-16:00, Wed 10:00-11:45 only. See page 24.

▲City Hall Beautifully restored Gothic Room from 1400, plus the Renaissance Hall. **Hours:** Daily 9:30-17:00. See page 25.

▲Chocolate Shops Bruges' specialty, sold at Dumon, The Chocolate Line, Confiserie De Clerck, and on and on. **Hours:** Shops generally open 10:00-18:00. See page 28.

Gruuthuse Museum 15th-century mansion displaying an eclectic collection that includes furniture, tapestries, and lots more. **Hours:** Tue-Sun 9:30-17:00, closed Mon, partly open until October of 2011, then closed entirely through end of 2012. See page 25.

Choco-Story: The Chocolate Museum The whole delicious story of Belgium's favorite treat. **Hours:** Daily 10:00-17:00. See page 29.

includes fine audioguide, Tue-Sun 9:30-17:00, closed Mon, last entry 30 minutes before closing, across the street from the Church of Our Lady, Mariastraat 38, Bruges museums tel. 050-448-713, www.brugge.be).

○ See the Memling Museum Tour chapter.

▲▲Begijnhof—Inhabited by Benedictine nuns, the Begijnhof courtyard (free and always open) almost makes you want to don a habit and fold your hands as you walk under its wispy trees and whisper past its frugal little homes. For a good slice of Begijnhof life, walk through the simple Beguine's House museum (€2, Mon-Sat 10:00-17:00, Sun 14:30-17:00, shorter hours off-season,

English explanations, museum is left of entry gate).

Minnewater—Just south of the Begijnhof is Minnewater, an idyllic world of flower boxes, canals, and swans.

Almshouses—As you walk from the Begijnhof back to the town center, you might detour along Nieuwe Gentweg to visit one of about 20 almshouses in the city. At #8, go through the door marked *Godshuis de Meulenaere 1613* into the peaceful courtyard (free). This was a medieval form of housing for the poor. The rich would pay for someone's tiny room here in return for lots of prayers.

Bruges Experiences: Beer, Chocolate, Windmills, and Biking

▲▲**De Halve Maan Brewery Tour**—Belgians are Europe's beer connoisseurs, and this handy tour is a great way to pay your respects. The brewery makes the only beers brewed in Bruges: Brugse Zot ("Fool from Bruges") and Straffe Hendrik ("Strong Henry"). The happy gang at this working-family brewery gives entertaining and informative 45-minute tours in three languages. Avoid crowds by visiting at 11:00 (€6 includes a beer, lots of very steep steps, great rooftop panorama; tours run April-Oct daily on the hour 11:00-16:00, Sat until 17:00; Nov-March Mon-Fri 11:00 and 15:00 only;

Sat-Sun on the hour 11:00-16:00; Walplein 26, tel. 050-444-223, www.halvemaan.be).

During your tour, you'll learn that "the components of the beer are vitally necessary and contribute to a well-balanced life pattern. Nerves, muscles, visual sentience, and healthy skin are stimulated by these in a positive manner. For longevity and life-long equilibrium, drink Brugse Zot in moderation!"

Their bistro, where you'll drink your included beer, serves quick, hearty lunch plates. You can eat indoors with the smell of hops, or outdoors with the smell of hops. This is a good place to wait for your tour or to linger afterward.

▲**Chocolate Shops**—Bruggians are connoisseurs of fine chocolate. You'll be tempted by chocolate-filled display windows all over town. While Godiva is the best big-factory/high-price/high-quality brand, there are plenty of smaller family-run places in Bruges that offer exquisite handmade chocolates. All three of the following chocolatiers are proud of their creative varieties, generous with their samples, and welcome you to assemble a 100-gram assortment of five or six chocolates.

Dumon: Perhaps Bruges' smoothest, creamiest chocolates are at Dumon (€2.20/100 grams). Madame Dumon and her children

(Stefaan, Natale, and Christophe) make their top-notch chocolate daily and sell it fresh just off the Markt (Thu-Tue 10:00-18:00 except closes Sun at 17:00, occasionally open Wed, old chocolate molds on display in basement, Eiermarkt 6, tel. 050-346-282; two other Dumon shops around town offer the same chocolate, but not the same experience). The Dumons don't provide English labels because they believe it's best to describe their chocolates in person—and they do it with an evangelical fervor. Try a small mix-and-match box to sample a few out-of-this-world flavors, and come back for more of your favorites.

The Chocolate Line: Locals and tourists alike flock to The Chocolate Line (pricey at €5/100 grams) to taste the *gastronomique* varieties concocted by Dominique Person—the mad scientist of chocolate. His unique creations mix chocolate with various, mostly savory, flavors. Even those that sound gross can be surprisingly good (be adventurous). Options include Havana cigar (marinated in rum, cognac, and Cuban tobacco leaves—so, therefore, technically illegal in the US), lemongrass, lavender, ginger (shaped like a Buddha), saffron curry, spicy chili, Moroccan mint, Pop Rocks/cola chocolate, wine vinegar, fried onions, bay leaf, sake, lime/vodka/passion fruit, wasabi, and tomatoes/olives/basil. The kitchen—busy whipping up 80 varieties—is on display in the back. Enjoy the window display, refreshed monthly (daily 9:30-18:00 except Sun-Mon opens at 10:30, between Church of Our Lady and the Markt at Simon Stevinplein 19, tel. 050-341-090).

Confiserie De Clerck: Third-generation chocolate maker Jan sells his handmade chocolates for just €1.20/100 grams, making this one of the best deals in town. Some locals claim his chocolate's just as good as at pricier places—taste it and decide for yourself. The time-warp candy shop itself is so delightfully old-school, you'll want to visit no matter what (Mon-Wed and Fri-Sat 10:00-19:00, closed Sun and Thu, Academiestraat 19, tel. 050-345-338).

Choco-Story: The Chocolate Museum—This museum is rated ▲ for chocoholics. The Chocolate Fairy leads you through 2,600 years of chocolate history—explaining why, in the ancient Mexican world of the Mayas and the Aztecs, chocolate was considered the drink of the gods, and cocoa beans were used as a means of payment. With lots of artifacts well-described in English, the museum fills you in on the production of truffles, bonbons, hollow figures,

and solid bars of chocolate. Then you'll view a delicious little video (8 minutes long, repeating continuously, alternating Flemish, French, and then English; peek into the theater to check the schedule. If you have time before the next English showing, visit the exhibits in the top room). Your finale is in the "demonstration room," where—after a 10-minute cooking demo—you get a taste (€7, €11 combo-ticket includes nearby Friet Museum, daily 10:00-17:00; where Wijnzakstraat meets Sint Jansstraat at Sint Jansplein, 3-minute walk from the Markt; tel. 050-612-237, www.choco-story.be). The Chocolate Museum is adjacent to (and offers a combo-ticket with) a lamp museum that's very skippable, unless you're a hard-core lamp enthusiast (in that case, boy, are you in luck).

Friet Museum—It's the only place in the world that enthusiastically tells the story of french fries, which, of course, aren't even French—they're Belgian (not worth €6, €11 combo-ticket includes Chocolate Museum, daily 10:00-17:00, Vlamingstraat 33, tel. 050-340-150, www.frietmuseum.be).

Windmills and Lace by the Moat—A 15-minute walk from the center to the northeast end of town (faster by bike) brings you to four windmills strung along a pleasant grassy setting on the "big moat" canal. The St. Janshuys **windmill** is open to visitors (€2; May-Aug Tue-Sun 9:30-12:30 & 13:30-17:00, closed Mon, last entry at 16:30; Sept same hours but open Sat-Sun only; closed Oct-April; go to the end of Carmersstraat and hang a right).

The **Folklore Museum,** in the same neighborhood, is cute but forgettable (€2, Tue-Sun 9:30-17:00, last entry at 16:30, closed Mon, Balstraat 43, tel. 050-448-764). To find it, ask for the Jerusalem Church. On the same street is a lace shop with a good reputation, **'t Apostelientje** (Tue 13:00-17:00, Wed-Sat 9:30-12:15 & 13:15-17:00, Sun 10:00-13:00, closed Mon, Balstraat 11, tel. 050-337-860, mobile 0495-562-420).

▲▲Biking—The Flemish word for bike is *fiets* (pronounced "feets"). And though Bruges' sights are close enough for easy walking, the town is a treat for bikers, and a bike quickly gets you into dreamy back lanes without a hint of tourism. Take a peaceful evening ride through the town's nooks and crannies and around the outer canal. Consider keeping a bike for the duration of your stay—it's the way the locals get around. Along the canal that circles the town is a park with a delightful bike lane. Rental shops have maps and ideas.

Self-Guided Bike Ride to Damme: For the best short bike trip out of Bruges, rent a bike and pedal four miles each way to the nearby town of Damme. You'll enjoy a whiff of the countryside and see a working windmill while riding along a canal to a charming (if well-discovered) small market town. Allow about two hours for the leisurely round-trip bike ride and a brief stop in Damme. The Belgium/Netherlands border is a 40-minute pedal (along the same canal) beyond Damme.

• *Head east from Bruges' Markt through Burg Square and out to the canal. (You could stop to see the Jerusalem Church and a lace shop—described earlier—on the way.) At the canal, circle to the left, riding along the former town wall and passing four windmills (one is open for viewing, described earlier). After the last windmill, named Dampoort, turn right across the second of two bridges (at the locks), then continue straight along the north/left bank of the Damme Canal (via Noorweegse Kaai/Damse Vaart-West).*

The Damme Canal (Damse Vaart): From Dampoort you'll pedal straight and level along the canal directly to Damme. There's no opportunity to cross the canal until you reach the town. The farmland to your left is a *polder*—a salt marsh that flooded each spring, until it was reclaimed by industrious local farmers. The Damme Canal, also called the Napoleon Canal, was built in 1811 by Napoleon (actually by his Spanish prisoners) in a failed attempt to reinvigorate the city as a port. Today locals fish this canal for eels and wait for the next winter freeze. Old-timers have fond memories of skating to Holland on this canal—but nowadays it's a rare event (ask locals about the winter of 2008-2009).

Schelle Windmill (Schellemolen): Just before arriving in Damme, you'll come upon a working windmill that dates from 1867. More clever than the windmills in Bruges, this one is designed so just the wood cap turns to face the wind—rather than the entire building. If it's open, climb up through the creaking, spinning, wind-powered gears to the top floor (free, April-Sept Sat-Sun 9:30-12:30 & 13:00-18:00, closed Mon-Fri and Oct-March).

In its day (13th-15th centuries), Bruges was one of the top five European ports...and little Damme was important, as well. Today all you see is land—the once-bustling former harbors silted up, causing the sea to retreat. Pause atop the bridge just beyond the windmill, with the windmill on your right and the spire of Bruges' Church of Our Lady poking up in the distance. It's easy to imagine how, at Napoleon's instructions, the canal was designed to mimic a grand Parisian boulevard—leading to the towering church back in Bruges.

• *From here, the canal continues straight to Holland. (If tempted...you're a third of the way to the border.) Instead, cross the bridge and follow Kerkstraat, which cuts through the center of town, to Damme's main square and City Hall.*

Damme: Once a thriving medieval port, and then a moated garrison town, Damme is now a tourist center—a tiny version of Bruges. It has a smaller-but-similar City Hall, a St. John's Hospital, and a big brick Church of Our Lady. You can tell by its 15th-century City Hall that, 500 years ago, Damme was rolling in herring money. Rather than being built with Belgian bricks (like other buildings around here), the City Hall was made of French limestone. Originally the ground floor was a market and fish warehouse, with government offices upstairs.

• *Continue on Kerkstraat as it leads two blocks farther to the Church of Our Lady. Along the way, you could side-trip to the left, down Pottenbakkersstraat, which takes you to a quaint little square called Haringmarkt (named for the Herring Market that made Damme rich in the 15th century). The trees you see from here mark the lines of the town's long-gone 17th-century ramparts.*

Returning to Kerkstraat, continue on to the big church.

The Church of Our Lady: This church, which rose and fell with the fortunes of Damme, dates from the 13th century. Inside are two Virgin Marys: To the right of the altar is a 1630 wooden statue of Mary, and to the left is Our Lady of the Fishermen (c. 1650, in a glass case). Over the nave stands Belgium's oldest wooden statue, St. Andrew, with his X-shaped cross.

Outside, behind the 13th-century church tower, is a three-faced, modern fiberglass sculpture by the Belgian artist Charles Delporte. Called *View of Light,* it evokes three lights: morning (grace), midday (kindness), and evening (gentleness). If you like his work, there's more at his nearby gallery.

• *To return to Bruges, continue past the church on Kerkstraat. Just before crossing the next bridge, follow a scenic dirt lane to the right that leads you back to the Damme Canal (and Damse Vaart-Zuid). Take this road back to Bruges. If you want a change of pace from the canal, about half-way back turn off to the left (at the white bridge and brick house), then immediately turn right on Polderstraat and follow the smaller canal back to the outskirts of Bruges.*

BRUGES CITY WALK

This walk, which takes you from the Markt (Market Square) to the Burg to the cluster of museums around the Church of Our Lady (the Groeninge, Gruuthuse, and Memling), shows you the best of Bruges in a day.

Orientation

Length of This Walk: Allow two hours for the walk, plus time for Bruges' two big museums (Groeninge and Memling—see chapters covering these museums).

Museum Passes: If you're planning to visit all the sights listed on this walk, save money by buying one of the city's sightseeing passes.

Bell Tower (Belfort): €8, daily 9:30-17:00, 16:15 last entry strictly enforced, on the Markt.

Basilica of the Holy Blood: Treasury-€1.50; April-mid-Oct daily 9:30-12:00 & 14:00-18:00; mid-Oct-March Thu-Tue 10:00-12:00 & 14:00-16:00, Wed 10:00-11:45 only; Burg Square, tel. 050-336-792.

City Hall's Gothic Room: €2, includes audioguide and entry to Renaissance Hall, daily 9:30-17:00, last entry 30 minutes before closing, Burg 12.

Renaissance Hall (Brugse Vrije): €2, includes audioguide and admission to City Hall's Gothic Room, daily 9:30-17:00, last entry 30 minutes before closing, entrance in corner of square at Burg 11a.

Groeninge Museum: €8, more for special exhibits, Tue-Sun 9:30-17:00, closed Mon, Dijver 12, tel. 050-448-743.

Church of Our Lady: Free peek at Michelangelo sculpture, €2 for art-filled apse, included in Gruuthuse admission; church open

Bruges City Walk

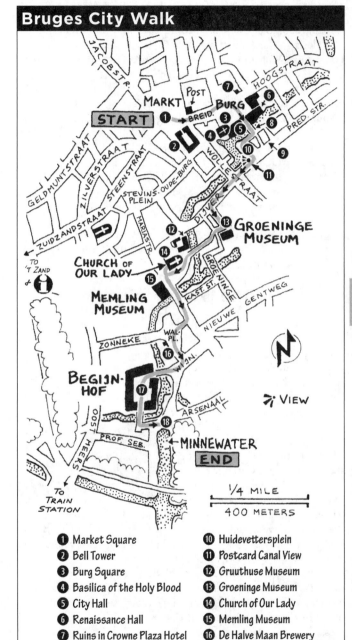

1/4 MILE

400 METERS

1. Market Square
2. Bell Tower
3. Burg Square
4. Basilica of the Holy Blood
5. City Hall
6. Renaissance Hall
7. Ruins in Crowne Plaza Hotel
8. Blinde-Ezelstraat
9. Fish Market
10. Huidevettersplein
11. Postcard Canal View
12. Gruuthuse Museum
13. Groeninge Museum
14. Church of Our Lady
15. Memling Museum
16. De Halve Maan Brewery
17. Begijnhof
18. Minnewater

Mon-Fri 9:30-17:00, Sat 9:30-16:45, Sun 13:30-17:00 only; museum and apse closed Mon, last entry 30 minutes before closing, Mariastraat.

Gruuthuse Museum: Partially open until Oct 2011, then closed through 2012; €6 when open, includes entry to apse of Church of Our Lady, Tue-Sun 9:30-17:00, closed Mon; Dijver 17, Bruges museums tel. 050-448-711.

Memling Museum: €8, includes good audioguide, Tue-Sun 9:30-17:00, closed Mon, last entry 30 minutes before closing, Mariastraat 38, Bruges museums tel. 050-448-713.

De Halve Maan Brewery Tour: €6 tour includes a beer; April-Oct daily on the hour 11:00-16:00, Sat until 17:00; 11:00 is least crowded; Nov-March Mon-Fri at 11:00 and 15:00 only, Sat-Sun on the hour 11:00-16:00; Walplein 26, tel. 050-444-223.

Begijnhof: Courtyard free and always open; Beguine's House museum costs €2, open Mon-Sat 10:00-17:00, Sun 14:30-17:00, shorter hours off-season.

The Walk Begins

Markt (Market Square)

Ringed by the post office, lots of restaurant terraces, great old gabled buildings, and the bell tower, this is the modern heart of the city. And, in Bruges' heyday as a trading city, this was also the center. The "typical" old buildings here were rebuilt in the 19th century in an exaggerated Neo-Gothic style (Bruges is often called "more Gothic than Gothic"). This pre-Martin Luther style was a political statement for this Catholic town.

A canal came right up to this square. Imagine boats moored where the post office stands today. In the 1300s, farmers shipped their cotton, wool, flax, and hemp to the port at Bruges. Before loading it onto outgoing boats, the industrious locals would spin, weave, and dye it into a finished product.

By 1400, the economy was shifting away from textiles and toward more refined goods, such as high-fashion items, tapestry, chairs, jewelry, and paper—a new invention (replacing parchment) made in Flanders with cotton that was shredded, soaked, and pressed.

The square is adorned with **flags,** including the red-white-and-blue lion flag of Bruges, the black-yellow-and-red flag of Belgium, and the blue-with-circle-of-yellow-stars flag of the

European Union.

The **statue** depicts two friends, Jan Breidel and Pieter de Coninc, clutching sword and shield and looking toward France as they lead a popular uprising against the French king in 1302. The rebels identified potential French spies by demanding they repeat two words—*schild en vriend* (shield and friend)—that only Flemish locals (or foreigners with phlegm) could pronounce. They won Flanders its freedom. Cleverly using hooks to pull knights from their horses, they scored the medieval world's first victory of foot soldiers over cavalry, and of common people over nobility. The French knights, thinking that fighting these Flemish peasants would be a cakewalk, had worn their dress uniforms. The peasants had a field day afterward scavenging all the golden spurs from the fallen soldiers after the Battle of the Golden Spurs (1302).

Geldmuntstraat, a block west of the square, has fun shops and eateries. Steenstraat is the main shopping street and is packed with people. Want a coffee? Stop by the Café-Brasserie Craenenburg on the Markt. Originally the house where Maximilian of Austria was imprisoned in 1488, it's been a café since 1905 (daily 7:30-23:00, Markt 16).

Bell Tower (Belfort)

Most of this bell tower has stood over the Markt since 1300. The octagonal lantern was added in 1486, making it 290 feet high.

The tower combines medieval crenellations, pointed Gothic arches, round Roman arches, flamboyant spires, and even a few small flying buttresses (two-thirds of the way up).

Try some Belgian-style fries from either stand at the bottom of the tower. Look for the small metal model of the tower and the Braille description of the old town. Enter the courtyard. Opposite the base of

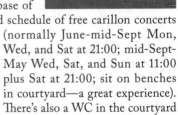

the bell tower, find the posted schedule of free carillon concerts

(normally June-mid-Sept Mon, Wed, and Sat at 21:00; mid-Sept-May Wed, Sat, and Sun at 11:00 plus Sat at 21:00; sit on benches in courtyard—a great experience). There's also a WC in the courtyard (€0.30).

Climb the tower (at €8, the price is steeper than its 366 steps). Just before you reach the top, peek into the carillon room. The 47 bells can be played mechanically with the giant barrel and movable tabs (as they are on each quarter hour), or with a manual keyboard (as they are during concerts). The carillonneur uses his fists and feet, rather than fingers. Be there on the quarter hour, when things ring. It's *wonderbaar* at the top of the hour.

Atop the tower, survey Bruges. On the horizon, you can see the towns along the North Sea coast.

• *Leaving the bell tower, turn right (east) onto Breidelstraat, and thread yourself through the lace and waffles to Burg Square.*

Burg Square

This opulent square is Bruges' historical birthplace, political center, and religious heart. Today it's the scene of outdoor concerts and local festivals.

Pan the square to see six centuries of architecture. Starting with the view of the bell tower above the gables, sweep counterclockwise 360 degrees. You'll go from Romanesque (the interior of the fancy, gray-brick **Basilica of the Holy Blood** in the corner), to the pointed Gothic arches and prickly steeples of the white sandstone **City Hall,** to the well-proportioned Renaissance windows of the **Old Recorder's**  **House** (next door, under the gilded statues), to the elaborate 17th-century Baroque of the **Provost's House** (past the park behind you). The park at the back of the square is the site of a cathedral that was demolished during the French Revolutionary period. Today, the foundation is open to the public in the **Crowne Plaza Hotel** basement (we'll visit it in a few minutes). The modern, Japanese-designed fountain plays with motifs of lace and water, but locals simply call it "the car wash."

• *Complete your spin and walk to the small, fancy, gray-and-gold building in the corner of Burg Square.*

Basilica of the Holy Blood

The gleaming gold knights and ladies on the church's gray facade remind us that this double-decker church was built (c. 1150) by a brave Crusader to house the drops of Christ's blood he'd brought back from Jerusalem.

Lower Chapel: Enter the lower chapel through the door labeled *Basiliek.* The stark and dim decor reeks of the medieval piety that drove crusading Christian Europeans to persecute Muslims. With heavy columns and round arches, the style is pure

The Legend of the Holy Blood

Several drops of Christ's blood, washed from his lifeless body by Joseph of Arimathea, were preserved in a rock-crystal vial in Jerusalem. In 1150, the patriarch of Jerusalem gave the blood to a Flemish soldier, Derrick of Alsace, as thanks for rescuing his city from the Muslims during the Second Crusade. Derrick (also called Dedric or Thierry) returned home and donated it to the city. The old, dried blood suddenly turned to liquid, a miracle repeated every Friday for the next two centuries, and verified by thousands of pilgrims from around Europe who flocked here to adore it. The blood dried up for good in 1325.

Every year on Ascension Day (June 2 in 2011, May 17 in 2012), Bruges' bankers, housewives, and waffle vendors put on old-time costumes for the parading of the vial through the city. Crusader knights re-enact the bringing of the relic, Joseph of Arimathea washes Christ's body, and ladies in medieval costume with hair tied up in horn-like hairnets come out to wave flags. Most of the remaining Bruges citizens just take the day off.

Romanesque. The annex along the right aisle displays somber statues of Christ being tortured and entombed, plus a 12th-century relief panel over a doorway showing St. Basil (a fourth-century scholarly monk) being baptized by a double-jointed priest, and a man-size dove of the Holy Spirit.
• *Go back outside and up the staircase to reach the...*

Upper Chapel: After being gutted by Napoleon's secular-humanist crusaders in 1797, the upper chapel's original Romanesque

decor was redone in a Neo-Gothic style. The nave is colorful, with a curved wooden ceiling, painted walls, and stained-glass windows of the dukes who ruled Flanders, along with their duchesses.

The painting at the main altar tells how the Holy Blood got here. Derrick of Alsace, having helped defend Jerusalem *(Hierosolyma)* and Bethlehem *(Bethlema)* from Muslim incursions in the Second Crusade, kneels (left) before the grateful Christian patriarch of Jerusalem, who rewards him with the relic. Derrick returns home (right) and kneels before Bruges' bishop to give him the vial of blood.

The relic itself—some red stuff preserved inside a clear, six-inch tube of rock crystal—is kept in the adjoining room (through the three arches). It's in the tall, silver tabernacle on the altar. (Each Friday—and increasingly on other days, too—the tabernacle's doors will be open, so you can actually see the vial of blood.) On holy days, the relic is shifted across the room and displayed on the throne under the canopy.

Treasury (next to Upper Chapel): For €1.50, you can see the impressive gold-and-silver, gem-studded, hexagonal reliquary (c.

1600, left wall) that the vial of blood is paraded around in on feast days. The vial is placed in the "casket" at the bottom of the four-foot-tall structure. On the wall, flanking the shrine, are paintings of kneeling residents who, for centuries, have tended the shrine and organized the pageantry as part of the 31-member Brotherhood of the Holy Blood. Elsewhere in the room are the Brothers' ceremonial necklaces, clothes, chalices, and so on.

In the display case by the entrance, find the lead box that protected the vial of blood from Protestant extremists (1578) and French Revolutionaries (1797) bent on destroying what, to them, was a glaring symbol of Catholic mumbo-jumbo. The broken rock-crystal tube with gold caps on either end is a replica of the vial, giving you an idea of what the actual relic looks like. Opposite the reliquary are the original cartoons (from 1541) that provided the designs for the basilica's stained glass.

• *Go back out into the square.*

City Hall (Stadhuis)

Built in about 1400, when Bruges was a thriving bastion of capitalism with a population of 35,000, this building served as a model for town halls elsewhere, including Brussels. The white sandstone facade is studded with statues of knights, nobles, and saints with prickly Gothic steeples over their heads. A colorful double band of cities' coats of arms includes those of

Bruges (Brugghe) and Dunkirk (Dunquerke). Back then, Bruges' jurisdiction included many towns in present-day France. The building is still the City Hall, and it's not unusual to see couples arriving here to get married.

Entrance Hall: The ground-level lobby leads you to a picture gallery (free, closed Mon) with scenes from Belgium's history, from the Spanish king to the arrival of Napoleon, shown meeting the mayor here at the City Hall in 1803.

• *You can pay to climb the stairs for a look at the...*

Gothic Room: Some of modern democracy's roots lie in this

ornate room, where, for centuries, the city council met to discuss the town's affairs (€2 entry includes audioguide—which explains both the upstairs and the ground floor—and entrance to the adjacent Renaissance Hall). In 1464, one of Europe's first parliaments, the Estates General of the Low Countries, convened here. The fireplace at the far end bears a proclamation from 1305, which says, "All the artisans, laborers...and citizens of Bruges are free—all of them" (provided they pay their taxes).

The elaborately carved and painted wooden ceiling (a Neo-Gothic reconstruction from the 19th century) features tracery in gold, red, and black. Five dangling arches ("pendentives") hang down the center, now adorned with modern floodlights. Notice the New Testament themes carved into the circular medallions that decorate the points where the arches meet.

The **wall murals** are late 19th-century Romantic paintings depicting episodes in the city's history. Start with the biggest painting along the left wall, and work clockwise, following the numbers found on the walls:

1. Hip, hip, hooray! Everyone cheers, flags wave, trumpets blare, and dogs bark, as Bruges' knights, dressed in gold with black Flemish lions, return triumphant after driving out French oppressors and winning Flanders' independence. The Battle of the Golden Spurs (1302) is remembered every July 11.

2. Bruges' high-water mark came perhaps at this elaborate ceremony, when Philip the Good of Burgundy (seated, in black) assembled his court here in Bruges and solemnly founded the knightly Order of the Golden Fleece (1429).

3. The Crusader knight, Derrick of Alsace, returns from the Holy Land and kneels at the entrance of St. Basil's Chapel to present the relic of Christ's Holy Blood (c. 1150).

4. A nun carries a basket of bread in this scene from St. John's Hospital.

5. A town leader stands at the podium and hands a sealed document to a German businessman, renewing the Hanseatic League's business license. Membership in this club of trading cities was a key to Bruges' prosperity.

6. As peasants cheer, a messenger of the local duke proclaims the town's right to self-government (1190).

7. The mayor visits a Bruges painting studio to shake the hand of Jan van Eyck, the great Flemish Primitive painter (1433). Jan's wife, Margareta, is there, too. In the 1400s, Bruges rivaled Florence and Venice as Europe's cultural capital. See the town in the distance, out Van Eyck's window.

8. Skip it.

9. City fathers grab a ceremonial trowel from a pillow to lay the fancy cornerstone of the City Hall (1376). Bruges' familiar towers stand in the background.

10. Skip it.

11. It's a typical market day at the Halls (the courtyard behind the bell tower). Arabs mingle with Germans in fur-lined coats and beards in a market where they sell everything from armor to lemons.

12. A bishop blesses a new canal (1404) as ships sail right by the city. This was Bruges in its heyday, before the silting of the harbor. At the far right, the two bearded men with moustaches are the brothers who painted these murals.

In the adjoining room, old paintings and maps show how little the city has changed through the centuries. A map (on the right wall) shows in exquisite detail the city as it looked in 1562. (The map is oriented with south on top.) Find the bell tower, the Church of Our Lady, and Burg Square, which back then was bounded on the north by a cathedral. Notice the canal (on the west) leading from the North Sea right to the Markt. A moat encircled the city 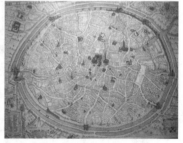 with its gates, unfinished wall, and 28 windmills (four of which survive today). The mills pumped water to the town's fountains, made paper, ground grain, and functioned as the motor of the Middle Ages. Most locals own a copy of this map that shows how their neighborhood looked 400 years ago.

• *Back on the square, leaving the City Hall, turn right and go to the corner.*

Renaissance Hall (Brugse Vrije)

Present your Gothic Room ticket to enter this elaborately decorated room with its grand Renaissance chimney carved from oak

by Bruges' Renaissance man, Lancelot Blondeel, in 1531. If you're into heraldry, the symbolism makes this room worth a five-minute stop. If you're not, you'll wonder where the rest of the museum is.

The centerpiece of the incredible carving is the Holy Roman Emperor Charles V. The hometown duke, on the far left, is related to Charles V. By making the connection to the Holy Roman Emperor clear, this carved family tree

of Bruges' nobility helped substantiate their power. Notice the well-guarded family jewels. And check out the expressive little cherubs.

• *Leaving the building, walk straight ahead and hook around the cream-colored building to your right.*

Ruins in the Crowne Plaza Hotel

One of the old town's newest buildings (1992) sits atop the ruins of the town's oldest structures. In about A.D. 900, when Viking ships regularly docked here to rape and pillage, Baldwin Iron Arm built a fort *(castrum)* to protect his Flemish people. In 950, the fort was converted into St. Donatian's Church, which became one of the city's largest.

Ask politely at the hotel's reception desk to see the archaeological site—ruins of the fort and the church—in the basement. If there's no conference in progress, they'll let you walk down the stairs and have a peek.

In the basement of the modern hotel are conference rooms lined with old stone walls and display cases of objects found in the ruins of earlier structures. On the immediate left hangs a photo of a document announcing the *Vente de Materiaux* (sale of material). When Napoleon destroyed the church in the early 1800s, its bricks were auctioned off. A local builder bought them at auction, and now the pieces of the old cathedral are embedded in other buildings throughout Bruges.

See oak pilings, carved to a point, once driven into this former peat bog to support the fort and shore up its moat. Paintings show the immensity of the church that replaced it. The curved stone walls you walk among are from the foundations of the ambulatory around the church altar.

Excavators found a town water hole—a bonanza for archaeologists—turning up the refuse of a thousand years of habitation:

pottery, animal skulls, rosary beads, dice, coins, keys, thimbles, pipes, spoons, and Delftware.

Don't miss the 14th-century painted sarcophagi—painted quickly for burial, with the crucifixion on the west end and the Virgin and Child on the east.

• *Back on Burg Square, walk south under the Goldfinger family (through the small archway) down the alleyway called...*

Blinde-Ezelstraat

Midway down on the left side (knee level, past the doorway), see an original iron hinge from the city's south gate, back when the city was ringed by a moat and closed nightly at 22:00. On the right wall, at eye level, a black patch shows you just how grimy the city had become before a 1960s cleaning. Despite the cleaning and a few fanciful reconstructions, the city today looks much as it did in centuries past.

The name "Blinde-Ezelstraat" means "Blind Donkey Street." In medieval times, the donkeys, carrying fish from the North Sea on their backs, were stopped here so that their owners could put blinders on them. Otherwise, the donkeys wouldn't cross the water between the old city and the fish market.

• *Cross the bridge over what was the 13th-century city moat. On your left are the arcades of the...*

Fish Market (Vismarkt)

The North Sea is just 12 miles away, and the fresh catch is sold here (Tue-Sat 6:00-13:00, closed Sun-Mon). Once a thriving market, today it's mostly souvenirs...and the big catch is the tourists.

• *Take an immediate right (west), entering a courtyard called...*

Huidevettersplein

This tiny, picturesque, restaurant-filled square was originally the headquarters of the town's skinners and tanners. On the facade of the Hotel Duc de Bourgogne, four old relief panels above the windows show scenes from the leather trade—once a leading Bruges industry. First, tan the hide in a bath of acid; then, with tongs, pull it out to dry; then beat it to make it soft; and, finally, scrape and clean it to make it ready for sale.

• *Continue a few steps to Rozenhoedkaai street, where you can look back to your right and get a great...*

Postcard Canal View

The bell tower reflected in a quiet canal lined with old houses—this view is the essence of Bruges. Seeing buildings rising straight from the water makes you understand why this was the Venice of the North. Can you see the bell tower's tilt? It leans about four feet. The tilt has been carefully monitored since 1740, but no change has been detected.

To your left (west) down the Dijver canal (past a flea market on weekends) looms the huge spire of the Church of Our Lady, the tallest brick spire in the Low Countries (quite possibly behind scaffolding during your visit). Between you and the church are the Europa College (a post-graduate institution for training future "Eurocrats" about the laws, economics, and politics of the European Union) and two fine museums.

• *Continue walking with the canal and the bell tower on your right. About 100 yards ahead, on the left, is the copper-colored sign that points the way to the Groeninge Museum, our next stop. If you'd like to head there now, skip ahead.*

But if you're here before October of 2011, you might want to consider a quick detour to the Gruuthuse Museum, a medieval mansion with a small exhibit. To reach it, continue past the copper sign and over the canal. Just after the gray-and-white Arentshuis, on your left, is a brick archway leading to the...

Gruuthuse Museum

This 15th-century mansion of a wealthy Bruges merchant displays period furniture, tapestries, coins, and musical instruments. Extensive renovation will have this museum in a state of disarray until it closes in October of 2011 (the earliest it'll reopen will be at the end of 2012).

If you get in, use the leaflets in each room to browse through a collection of secular objects that are both functional and beautiful. Here are some highlights:

On the left, in the first room (or **Great Hall**), the big fire-

place, oak table, and tapestries attest to the wealth of Louis Gruuthuse, who got rich providing a special herb used to spice up beer.

Tapestries like the ones you see here were a famous Flemish export product, made in local factories out of raw wool imported from England and silk brought from the Orient (via Italy). Both beautiful and useful (as insulation), they adorned many homes and palaces throughout Europe.

The Gruuthuse mansion abuts the Church of Our Lady and has a convenient little **chapel** (upstairs via the far corner of Room 16) with a window overlooking the interior of the huge church. In their private box seats above the choir, the family could attend services without leaving home. From the balcony, you can look down on two reclining gold statues in the church, marking the tombs of Charles the Bold and his daughter, Mary of Burgundy (the grandmother of powerful Charles V).

• *Leaving the Gruuthuse, head right from the archway and backtrack until you find the sign for the...*

Groeninge Museum

This sumptuous collection of paintings, which reopened in June of 2011 after a renovation, takes you from 1400 to 1945. The highlights are its Flemish Primitives, with all their glorious detail.

If you decide to visit, ✪ see the Groeninge Museum Tour chapter.

• *Leaving the Groeninge, take your first left, into a courtyard. You'll see the prickly church steeple ahead. Head up and over the picture-perfect 19th-century pedestrian bridge. From the bridge, look to the right and up at the corner of the Gruuthuse mansion, where there's a teeny-tiny window, a toll-keeper's lookout. The bridge gives you a close-up look at Our Lady's big buttresses and round apse.*

From the bridge, veer left along the hedge-lined path, and find the church entry on the right.

Church of Our Lady

This church stands as a memorial to the power and wealth of Bruges in its heyday.

A delicate ***Madonna and Child* by Michelangelo** (1504) is near the apse (to the right as you enter), somewhat overwhelmed by the ornate Baroque niche it sits in. It's said to be the only Michelangelo statue to leave Italy in his lifetime, bought in Tuscany by a wealthy Bruges businessman, who's buried beneath it.

As Michelangelo chipped away at the masterpiece of his youth, *David,* he took breaks by carving this one in 1504. Mary, slightly smaller than life-size, sits while young Jesus stands in front of her. Their expressions are mirror images—serene, but a bit melancholy, with downcast eyes, as though pondering the young child's dangerous future. Though they're lost in thought, their hands instinctively link, tenderly. The white Carrara marble is highly polished, something Michelangelo only did when he was certain he'd gotten it right.

If you like tombs and church art, pay €2 to wander through the apse (also covered by Gruuthuse Museum ticket, if museum is open). The highlight is the reclining statues marking the tombs of the last local rulers of Bruges: Mary of Burgundy, and her father, Charles the Bold. The dog and lion at their feet are symbols of fidelity and courage.

In 1482, when 25-year-old Mary of Burgundy tumbled from a horse and died, she left behind a toddler son and a husband who was heir to the Holy Roman Empire. Beside her lies her father, Charles the Bold, who also died prematurely, in war. Their twin deaths meant Bruges belonged to Austria, and would soon be swallowed up by the empire and ruled from afar by Habsburgs—who didn't understand or care about its problems. Trade routes shifted, and goods soon flowed through Antwerp, then Amsterdam, as Bruges' North Sea port silted up. After these developments, Bruges began four centuries of economic decline. The city was eventually mothballed. It was later discovered by modern-day tourists to be remarkably well-pickled, which explains its current affluence.

The wooden balcony to the left of the painted altarpiece is part of the Gruuthuse mansion next door, providing the noble family with prime seats for Mass.

Along the outside of the choir, to the left as you face the balcony, notice the row of dramatic wooden statues. (Contrast these with the meek pre-Renaissance figures in the apse's medieval stained glass.)

Excavations in 1979 turned up fascinating grave paintings on the tombs below and near the altar. Dating from the 13th century, these show Mary represented as Queen of Heaven (on a throne, carrying a crown and scepter) and Mother of God (with the baby Jesus on her lap). Since Mary is in charge of advocating with Jesus for your salvation, she's a good person to have painted on the wall of your tomb. Tombs also show lots of angels—generally patron saints of the dead person—swinging thuribles (incense burners).

The church's tower is likely to be hidden behind scaffolding during your visit, but if you're here after its structural retrofit is complete, you may be able to climb it (ask at apse entry desk).

Before leaving the church, take a moment to behold the Baroque wooden pulpit, with a roof that seems to float in mid-air.

• *Just across Mariastraat from the church entrance is the entry to the St. John's Hospital's Visitors Center, labeled* Site Oud Sint-Jan *(with a €0.50 public WC). About 20 yards farther south on Mariastraat, and to the left, is the entrance to the museum that now fills that hospital's church, the...*

Memling Museum

This medieval hospital contains some much-loved paintings by the greatest of the Flemish Primitives, Hans Memling. His *Mystical Wedding of St. Catherine* triptych deserves a close look. Catherine and her "mystical groom," the baby Jesus, are flanked by a headless John the Baptist and a pensive John the Evangelist. The chairs are there so you can study it. If you know the Book of Revelation, you'll understand St. John's wild, intricate vision. The St. Ursula Shrine, an ornate little mini-church in the same room, is filled with impressive detail.

 ☉ See the Memling Museum Tour chapter.
• *Continue south (with the museum behind you, turn right) about 150 yards on Mariastraat. Turn right on Walstraat (a small black-and-white sign points the way to Minnewater and the Begijnhof). It leads you into the pleasant square called Walplein, where you'll find the...*

De Halve Maan Brewery

If you like beer, take a tour here (Walplein 26).
• *Leaving the brewery, head right, make your first right, and just past the horse-head fountain, where the horse-and-buggy horses stop to drink, turn right and head over the pedestrian bridge. From here, the lacy cuteness of Bruges crescendos as you approach the...*

Begijnhof

*Begijnhof*s (pronounced gutturally: buh-HHHINE-hof) were built to house women of the lay order, called Beguines, who spent

their lives in piety and service without having to take the same vows a nun would. Primarily because of military fatalities, there were more women than men in the medieval Low Countries. The order of Beguines offered women (often single or widowed) a dignified place to live and work. When the order died out, many *begijnhof*s were taken over by towns for subsidized housing. Today, single religious women live in the small homes. Benedictine nuns live in a building nearby. Tour the simple museum to get a sense of Beguine life.

In the church, the rope that dangles from the ceiling is yanked by a nun to announce a sung vespers service.

• *Exiting on the other side of the brick church, hook left toward a lake.*

Minnewater

Just south of the Begijnhof is Minnewater ("Water of Love"), a peaceful, lake-filled park with canals and swans. This was once far from quaint—it was a busy harbor where small boats shuttled cargo from the big, ocean-going ships into town. From this point, the cargo was transferred again to flat-bottomed boats that went through the town's canals to their respective warehouses and to the Markt.

When locals see these swans, they recall the 15th-century mayor—famous for his long neck—who collaborated with the Austrians. The townsfolk beheaded him as a traitor. The Austrians warned them that similarly long-necked swans would inhabit the place to forever remind them of this murder. And they do.

• *You're a five-minute walk from the train station (where you can catch a bus to the Markt) or a 15-minute walk from the Markt—take your pick.*

GROENINGE MUSEUM TOUR

In the 1400s, Bruges was northern Europe's richest, most cosmopolitan, and most cultured city. New ideas, fads, and painting techniques were imported and exported with each shipload. Beautiful paintings were soon an affordable luxury, like fancy clothes or furniture. Internationally known artists set up studios in Bruges, producing portraits and altarpieces for wealthy merchants from all over Europe.

Understandably, the Groeninge Museum has one of the world's best collections of the art produced in the city and surrounding area. This early Flemish art is less appreciated and understood today than the Italian Renaissance art produced a century later. But by selecting 11 masterpieces, you'll get an introduction to this subtle, technically advanced, and beautiful style. Hey, if you can master the museum's name (HHHROON-ih-guh), you can certainly handle the art.

Orientation

Cost and Hours: €8, more for special exhibits, Tue-Sun 9:30-17:00, closed Mon.

Reorganization: The museum reopened in June of 2011 after extensive renovation. The artwork described in this tour may have moved; ask a museum staff member for help if you can't find something.

Information: Tel. 050-448-743, www.brugge.be.

Getting There: The museum is at Dijver 12, near the Gruuthuse Museum and Church of Our Lady. One big copper sign and several small *museum* signs mark the nearby area, leading you to the Groeninge's modern, glass front door.

Length of This Tour: Allow one hour.

Overview

Pick up a map as you enter and be prepared for changes from the tour outlined below. Use this chapter as background to the huge collection's highlights, then browse, seeking out the works you'd like to learn more about.

The Tour Begins

• *In Room 1, look for...*

Gerard David (c. 1455-1523)— *Judgment of Cambyses* (1498)

That's gotta hurt.

A man is stretched across a table and skinned alive in a very businesslike manner. The crowd hardly notices, and a dog just scratches himself. According to legend, the man was a judge arrested for corruption (left panel) and flayed (right panel), then his skin was draped (right panel background) over the new judge's throne.

Gerard David, Memling's successor as the city's leading artist, painted this for the City Hall. City councilors could ponder what might happen to them if they abused their offices.

By David's time, Bruges was in serious decline, with a failing economy and struggles against the powerful Austrian Habsburg family. The Primitive style also was fading. Italian art was popular, so David tried to spice up his retro-Primitive work with pseudo-Renaissance knickknacks—*putti* (baby angels, over the judgment throne), Roman-style medallions, and garlands. But he couldn't quite master the Italian specialty of 3-D perspective. We view the flayed man at an angle from slightly above, but the table he lies on is shown more from the side.

• *Head to Room 2 for...*

Jan van Eyck (c. 1390-1441)—*Virgin and Child with Canon Joris van der Paele* (1436)

Jan van Eyck was the world's first and greatest oil painter, and this is his masterpiece—three debatable but defensible assertions.

Mary, in a magnificent red gown, sits playing with her little baby, Jesus. Jesus glances up as St. George, the dragon-slaying

knight, enters the room, tips his cap, and says, "I'd like to introduce my namesake, George (Joris)." Mary glances down at the kneeling Joris, a church official dressed in white. Joris takes off his glasses and looks up from his prayer book to see a bishop in blue, St. Donatian, patron of the church he hopes to be buried in.

Canon Joris, who hired Van Eyck, is not a pretty sight. He's old and wrinkled, with a double chin, weird earlobes, and bloodshot eyes. But the portrait isn't unflattering; it just shows unvarnished reality with crystal clarity.

Van Eyck brings Mary and the saints down from heaven and into a typical (rich) Bruges home. He strips off their haloes, banishes all angels, and pulls the plug on heavenly radiance. If this is a religious painting, then where's God?

God's in the details. From the bishop's damask robe and Mary's wispy hair to the folds in Jesus' baby fat and the oriental carpet to "Adonai" (Lord) written on St. George's breastplate, the painting is as complex and beautiful as God's creation. The color scheme—red Mary, white canon, and blue-and-gold saints—are Bruges' city colors, from its coat of arms.

Mary, crowned with a jeweled "halo" and surrounded by beautiful things, makes an appearance in 1400s Bruges, where she can be adored in all her human beauty by Canon Joris...and by us, reflected in the mirror-like shield on St. George's back.

Jan van Eyck—*Portrait of Margareta van Eyck* (1439)

At 35, shortly after moving to Bruges, Jan van Eyck married 20-year-old Margareta. They had two kids, and after Jan died, Margareta took charge of his studio of assistants and kept it running until her death. This portrait (age 33), when paired with a matching self-portrait of Jan, was one of Europe's first husband-and-wife companion sets.

She sits half-turned, looking out of the frame. (Jan might have seen this

Flemish Primitives

Despite the "Primitive" label, the Low Countries of the 1400s (along with Venice and Florence) produced the most refined art in Europe. Here are some common features of Flemish Primitive art:

- **Primitive 3-D Perspective:** Expect unnaturally cramped-looking rooms; oddly slanted tables; and flat, cardboard-cutout people with stiff posture. Yes, these works are more primitive (hence the label) than those with the later Italian Renaissance perspective.

- **Realism:** Everyday bankers and clothmakers in their Sunday best are painted with clinical, warts-and-all precision. Even saints and heavenly visions are brought down to earth.

- **Details:** Like meticulous Bruges craftsmen, painters used fine-point brushes to capture almost microscopic details—flower petals, wrinkled foreheads, intricately patterned clothes, the sparkle in a ruby. The closer you get to a painting, the better it looks.

- **Oil Painted on Wood:** They were the pioneers of newfangled oil-based paint (while Italy still used egg-yolk tempera), working on wood, before canvas became popular.

- **Portraits and Altarpieces:** Wealthy merchants and clergymen paid to have themselves painted either alone or mingling with saints.

- **Symbolism:** In earlier times, everyone understood that a dog symbolized fidelity, a lily meant chastity, and a rose was love.

- **Materialism:** Rich Flanders celebrated the beauty of luxury goods—the latest Italian dresses, jewels, carpets, oak tables—and the ordinary beauty that radiates from flesh-and-blood people.

GROENINGE MUSEUM

"where-have-you-been?" expression in the window late one night.) She's dressed in a red, fur-lined coat, and we catch a glimpse of her wedding ring. Her hair is invisible—very fashionable at the time—pulled back tightly, bunched into horn-like hairnets, and draped with a headdress. Stray hairs along the perimeter were plucked to achieve the high forehead look.

This simple portrait is revolutionary—one of history's first individual portraits that wasn't of a saint, a king, a duke, or a pope, and wasn't part of a religious work. It signals the advent of humanism, celebrating the glory of ordinary people. Van Eyck proudly signed the work on the original frame, with his motto saying he painted it "*als ik kan*" *(ALC IXH KAN)*..."as good as I can."

Rogier van der Weyden (c. 1399-1464)—*St. Luke Drawing the Virgin's Portrait* (c. 1435)

Rogier van der Weyden, the other giant among the Flemish Primitives, adds the human touch to Van Eyck's rather detached precision.

As Mary prepares to nurse, baby Jesus can't contain his glee, wiggling his fingers and toes, anticipating lunch. Mary, dressed in everyday clothes, doesn't try to hide her love as she tilts her head down with a proud smile. Meanwhile, St. Luke (the patron saint of painters, who was said to have experienced this vision) looks on intently with a sketch pad in his hand, trying to catch the scene. These small gestures, movements, and facial expressions add an element of human emotion that later artists would amplify.

The painting is neatly divided by a spacious view out the window, showing a river stretching off to a spacious horizon. Van der Weyden experimented with 3-D effects like this one (though ultimately it's just window-dressing).

Rogier van der Weyden—*Duke Philip the Good* (c. 1450)

Tall, lean, and elegant, this charismatic duke transformed Bruges from a commercial powerhouse to a cultural one. In 1425, Philip

moved his court to Bruges, making it the de facto capital of a Burgundian empire stretching from Amsterdam to Switzerland.

Philip wears a big hat to hide his hair, a fashion trend he himself began. He's also wearing the gold-chain necklace of the Order of the Golden Fleece, a distinguished knightly honor he gave himself. He inaugurated the Golden Fleece in a lavish ceremony at the Bruges City Hall, complete with parades, jousting, and festive pies that contained live people hiding inside to surprise his guests.

As a lover of painting, hunting, fine clothes, and many mistresses, Philip was a role model for Italian princes, such as Lorenzo the Magnificent—the *uomo universale*, the Renaissance Man.

Hugo van der Goes (c. 1430-c. 1482)— *Death of the Virgin* (c. 1470)

The long deathwatch is over—their beloved Mary has passed on,

---

Oil Paint

Take vegetable oil pressed from linseeds (flax), blend in dry powdered pigments, whip to a paste the consistency of room-temperature butter, then brush onto a panel of whitewashed oak—you're painting in oils. First popularized in the early 1400s, oil eventually overshadowed egg-yolk-based tempera. Though tempera was great for making fine lines shaded with simple blocks of color, oil could blend colors together seamlessly.

Watch a master create a single dog's hair: He paints a dark stroke of brown, then lets it dry. Then comes a second layer painted over it, of translucent orange. The brown shows through, blending with the orange to match the color of a collie. Finally, he applies a third, transparent layer (a "glaze"), giving the collie her healthy sheen.

Many great artists were not necessarily great painters (e.g., Michelangelo). Van Eyck, Rembrandt, Hals, Velázquez, and Rubens were master painters, meticulously building objects with successive layers of paint...but they're not everyone's favorite artists.

---

and the disciples are bleary-eyed and dazed with grief, as though hit with a spiritual two-by-four. Each etched face is a study in sadness, as they all have their own way of coping—lighting a candle, fidgeting, praying, or just staring off into space. Blues and reds dominate, and there's little eye-catching ornamentation, which lets the lined faces and expressive hand gestures do the talking.

Hugo van der Goes painted this, his last major work, the same year he attempted suicide. Hugo had built a successful career in Ghent, then abruptly dropped out to join a monastery. His paintings became increasingly emotionally charged, his personality more troubled.

Above the bed floats a heavenly vision, as Jesus and the angels prepare to receive Mary's soul. Their smooth skin and serene expressions contrast with the gritty, wrinkled death pallor of those on Earth. Caught up in their own grief, the disciples can't see the silver lining.

• *Head to Room 3 for the surreal scene that's...*

Attributed to Hieronymus Bosch (c. 1450-1516)—
Last Judgment **(late 15th century)**
It's the end of the world, and Christ descends in a bubble to pass

GROENINGE MUSEUM

judgment on puny humans. Little naked people dance and cavort in a theme park of medieval symbolism, desperately trying to squeeze in their last bit of fun. Meanwhile, some wicked souls are being punished, victims either of their own stupidity or of genetically engineered demons. The good are sent to the left panel to frolic in the innocence of paradise, while the rest are damned to hell (right panel) to be tortured under a burning sky. Bosch paints the scenes with a high horizon line, making it seem that the chaos extends forever.

The bizarre work of Bosch (who, by the way, was not from Bruges) is open to many interpretations, but some see it as a warning for the turbulent times. He painted during the dawn of a new age. Secular ideas and materialism were encroaching, and the pious, serene medieval world was shattering into chaos.

• *At the entrance to Room 4 is…*

Jan Provoost (c. 1465-1529)—*Death and the Miser*

A Bruges businessman in his office strikes a deal with Death. The

grinning skeleton lays coins on the table and, in return, the man—looking unhealthy and with fear in his eyes—reaches across the divide in the panels to give Death a promissory note, then marks the transaction in his ledger book. He's trading away a few years of his life for a little more money. The worried man on the right (the artist's self-portrait) says, "Don't do it."

Jan Provoost (also known as Provost) worked for businessmen like this. He knew their offices, full of moneybags, paperwork, and books. Bruges' materialistic capitalism was at odds with Christian poverty, and society was divided over whether to praise or condemn it. Ironically, this painting's flip side is a religious work bought and paid for by…rich merchants.

GROENINGE MUSEUM

No Joke

An enthusiastic American teenager approaches the ticket seller at the Groeninge Museum:

"This is the Torture Museum, right?!"

"No," the ticket man replies, "it's art."

"Oh..." mumbles the kid, "art..."

And he walks away, not realizing that, for him, the Groeninge Museum would indeed be torture.

Petrus Christus (c. 1420-c. 1475)— *Annunciation and Nativity* (1452)

Italian art was soon all the rage. Ships from Genoa and Venice would unload Renaissance paintings, wowing the Northerners with their window-on-the-world, 3-D realism. Petrus Christus, one of Jan van Eyck's students, studied the Italian style and set out to conquer space.

The focus of Christus' *Annunciation* panel is not the winged angel announcing Jesus' coming birth, nor is it the swooning, astonished Mary—it's the empty space between them. Your eye focuses back across the floor tiles and through the open doorway to gabled houses on a quiet canal in the far distance.

In the *Nativity* panel, the three angels hovering overhead really should be bigger, and the porch over the group looks a little rickety. Compared with the work of Florence's Renaissance painters, this is quite...primitive.

• Fast-forward a few centuries (through Rooms 5-8), past paintings by no-name artists from Bruges' years of decline, to a couple of Belgium's 20th-century masters in Room 9.

Paul Delvaux (1897-1994)—*Serenity* (1970)

Perhaps there's some vague connection between Van Eyck's medieval symbols and the Surrealist images of Paul Delvaux. Delvaux gained fame for his nudes sleepwalking through moonlit, video-game landscapes.

René Magritte (1898-1967)—*The Assault* (c. 1932)

Magritte had his own private reserve of symbolic images. The cloudy sky, the female torso, windows, and a horsebell (the ball with the slit) appear in other works as well. They're arranged here side by side as if they should mean something, but they—as well as the title—only serve to short-circuit your thoughts when you try to make sense of them. Magritte paints real objects with photographic clarity, then jumbles them together in new and provocative ways.

Scenes of Bruges

Remember that Jan van Eyck, Petrus Christus, Hans Memling, Gerard David, Jan Provoost, and possibly Rogier van der Weyden (for a few years) all lived and worked in Bruges.

In addition, many other artists included scenes of the picturesque city in their art, proving that it looks today much as it did way back when. Enjoy the many painted scenes of old Bruges as a slice-of-life peek into the city and its people back in its glory days.

MEMLING MUSEUM TOUR

Memling in Sint-Jan Hospitaalmuseum

Located in the former hospital wards and church of St. John's Hospital, the Memling Museum offers you a glimpse into medieval medicine, displaying surgical instruments, documents, and visual aids as you work your way to the museum's climax: several of Hans Memling's glowing masterpieces.

Orientation

Cost: €8, includes good audioguide and free loaner folding chairs (if you'd like to sit and study the paintings).

Hours: Tue-Sun 9:30-17:00, closed Mon, last entry 30 minutes before closing.

Getting There: The museum is at Mariastraat 38, across the street from the Church of Our Lady.

Information: Bruges museums tel. 050-448-713, www.brugge.be.

Length of This Tour: Allow one hour.

Overview

Hans Memling's art was the culmination of Bruges' Flemish Primitive style. His serene, soft-focus, motionless scenes capture a medieval piety that was quickly fading. The popular style made Memling (c. 1430-1494) one of Bruges' wealthiest citizens, and his work was gobbled up by visiting Italian merchants, who took it home with them, cross-pollinating European art.

The displays on medieval medicine are all on one floor of the former church, with the Memlings in a chapel at the far end.

The Tour Begins

The Church as a Hospital

Some 500 years ago, the nave of this former church was lined with beds filled with the sick and dying. Nuns served as nurses. At the far end was the high altar, which once displayed Memling's *St. John Altarpiece* (which we'll see). Bedridden patients could gaze on this peaceful, colorful vision and gain a moment's comfort from their agonies.

As the museum displays make clear, medicine of the day was well-intentioned but very crude. In many ways, this was less a hos-pital than a hospice, helping the down-and-out make the transition from this world to the next. Religious art (displayed further along in the museum) was therapeutic, addressing the patients' mental and spiritual health. The numerous Crucifixions reminded the sufferers that Christ could feel their pain, having lived it himself.

• *Continue through the displays of religious art—past paintings that make you thankful for modern medicine. Head through the wooden doorway to the black-and-white tiled room where Memling's paintings are displayed. A large triptych (three-paneled altarpiece) dominates the space.*

St. John Altarpiece (a.k.a. *The Mystical Marriage of St. Catherine,* 1474)

Sick and dying patients lay in their beds in the hospital and looked at this colorful, three-part work, which sat atop the hospital/church's high altar. The piece was dedicated to the hospital's patron saints, John the Baptist and John the Evangelist (see the inscription along the bottom of the frame), but Memling broadened the focus to take in a vision of heaven and the end of the world.

Central Panel: Mary, with baby Jesus on her lap, sits in a canopied chair, crowned by hovering blue angels. It's an imaginary gathering of conversing saints *(Sacra Conversazione),* though nobody in this meditative group is saying a word or even exchanging meaningful eye contact.

Some Memling Trademarks

- Serene symmetry, with little motion or emotion
- Serious faces that are realistic but timeless, with blemishes airbrushed out
- Eye-catching details such as precious carpets, mirrors, and brocaded clothes
- Glowing colors, even lighting, no shadows
- Cityscape backgrounds

Mary is flanked by the two Johns—John the Baptist to the left, and John the Evangelist (in red) to the right. Everyone else

sits symmetrically around Mary. An organist angel to the left is matched by a book-holding acolyte to the right. St. Catherine (left, in white, red, and gold) balances St. Barbara, in green, who's absorbed in her book. Behind them, classical columns are also perfectly balanced left and right.

At the center of it all, baby Jesus tips the balance by leaning over to place a ring on Catherine's finger, sealing the "mystical marriage" between them.

St. Catherine of Alexandria, born rich, smart, and pagan to Roman parents, joined the outlawed Christian faith. She spoke out against pagan Rome, attracting the attention of the emperor, Maxentius, who sent 50 philosophers to talk some sense into her—but she countered every argument, even converting the emperor's own wife. Maxentius killed his wife, then asked Catherine to marry him. She refused, determined to remain true to the man she'd already "married" in a mystical vision—Christ.

Frustrated, Maxentius ordered Catherine to be stretched across a large, spiked wheel (the rather quaint-looking object at her feet), but the wheel flew apart, sparing her and killing many of her torturers. So they just cut her head off, which is why she has a sword, along with her "Catherine Wheel."

Looking through the columns, we see scenes of Bruges. Just to the right of the chair's canopy, the wooden contraption is a crane, used to hoist barrels from barges on Kraanplein.

Left Panel—The Beheading of John the Baptist: Even this gruesome scene, with blood still spurting from John's severed neck, becomes serene under Memling's gentle brush. Everyone is solemn, graceful, and emotionless—including both parts of the

decapitated John. Memling depicts Salomé (in green) receiving the head on her silver platter with a humble servant's downcast eyes, as if accepting her role in God's wonderful, if sometimes painful, plan.

In the background, left, we can look into Herod's palace, where he sits at a banquet table with his wife while Salomé dances modestly in front of him. Herod's lust is only hinted at with the naked statues—a man between two women—that adorn the palace exterior.

Right Panel—John the Evangelist's Vision of the Apocalypse: John sits on a high, rocky bluff on the island of Patmos and sees the end of the world as we know it...and he feels fine.

Overhead, in a rainbow bubble, God appears on his throne, resting his hand on a sealed book. A lamb

steps up to open the seals, unleashing the awful events at the end of time. Standing at the bottom of the rainbow, an angel in green gestures to John and says, "Write this down." John starts to dip his quill into the inkwell (his other hand holds the quill-sharpener), but he pauses, absolutely transfixed, experiencing the Apocalypse now.

He sees wars, fires, and plagues on the horizon, the Virgin in the sky rebuking a red dragon, and many other wonders. Fervent fundamentalists should bring their Bibles along, because there are many specific references brought to life in a literal way.

In the center ride the dreaded Four Horsemen, wreaking havoc on the cosmos (galloping over either islands or clouds). Horseman number four is a skeleton, followed by a human-eating monster head. Helpless mortals on the right seek shelter in the rocks, but find none.

Memling has been criticized for building a career by copying the formulas of his predecessors, but this panel is a complete original. Its theme had never been so fully expressed, and the bright, contrasting colors and vivid imagery are almost modern. In the *St. John Altarpiece*, Memling shows us the full range of his palette, from medieval grace to Renaissance symmetry, from the real to the surreal.

• *In a glass case, find the...*

St. Ursula Shrine (c. 1489)

On October 21, 1489, the mortal remains of St. Ursula were brought here to the church and placed in this gilded oak shrine, built spe-

cially for the occasion and decorated with paintings by Memling. Ursula, yet another Christian martyred by the ancient Romans, became a sensation in the Middle Ages when builders in Germany's Köln (Cologne) unearthed a huge pile of bones believed to belong to her and her 11,000 slaughtered cohorts.

The shrine, carved of wood and covered with gold, looks like a miniature Gothic church (similar to the hospital church). Memling was asked to fill in the "church's" stained-glass windows with six arch-shaped paintings describing Ursula's well-known legend.

• *Stand with your back to the wall, facing the shrine. "Read" the shrine's story from left to right, circling counterclockwise, but begin with the...*

Left Panel: Ursula—in white and blue—arrives by boat at the city of Köln and enters through the city gate. She's on a pilgrimage to Rome, accompanied by 11,000 (female) virgins. That night (look in the two windows of the house in the background, right), an angel appears and tells her this trip will mean her death, but she is undaunted.

Center Panel: Continuing up the Rhine, they arrive in Basel. (Memling knew the Rhine, having grown up near it.) Memling condenses the 11,000 virgins to a more manageable 11, making each one pure enough for a thousand. From Basel they set out on foot (in the background, right) over the snowy Alps.

Right Panel: They arrive in Rome—formally portrayed by a round Renaissance tower decorated with *putti* (little angels)— where Ursula falls to her knees before the pope at the church steps. Kneeling behind Ursula is her fiancé, Etherus, the pagan prince of England. She has agreed to marry him only if he becomes a Christian and refrains from the marriage bed long enough for her to make this three-year pilgrimage as a virgin (making, I guess, number 11,001). Inside the church, on the right side, he is baptized a Christian.

Opposite Side—Left Panel: They head back home. They're leaving Basel, boarding ships to go north on the Rhine. The pope was so inspired by these virgins that he joined them. These "crowd" scenes are hardly realistic—more like a collage of individual poses and faces. And Memling tells the story with extremely minimal acting. Perhaps his inspiration was the pomp and ceremony of

Bruges parades, which were introduced by the Burgundian dukes. He would have seen *tableaux vivants,* where Brugeois would pose in costume like human statues to enact an event from the Bible or from city history. (Today's "living Christmas crèches" carry on this medieval art form.)

Middle Panel: Back in Köln, a surprise awaits them—the city has been taken over by vicious Huns. They grab Etherus and stab him. He dies in Ursula's arms.

Right Panel: The Hun king (in red with turban and beard)

woos Ursula, placing his hand over his heart, but she says, "No way." So a Hun soldier draws his arrow and prepares to shoot her dead. Even here, at the climax of the story, there are no histrionics. Even the dog just sits down, crosses his paws, and watches. The whole shrine cycle is as posed, motionless, and colorful as the *tableaux vivants* that may have inaugurated the shrine here in this church in 1489.

In the background, behind Ursula, a Bruges couple looks on sympathetically. This may be Memling himself (in red coat with fur lining) and his wife, Anna, who bore their three children. Behind them, Memling renders an accurate city skyline of Köln, including a side view of the Köln Cathedral (missing its still-unfinished tall spires).

• *In the small adjoining room, find more Memlings.*

Diptych of Martin van Nieuwenhove (1489)

Three-dimensional effects—borrowed from the Italian Renaissance style—enliven this traditional two-panel altarpiece. Both Mary and Child and the 23-year-old Martin, though in different panels, inhabit the same space within the painting.

Stand right in front of Mary, facing her directly. If you line up the paintings' horizons (seen in the distance, out the room's windows), you'll see that both panels depict the same room— with two windows at the back and two along the right wall.

Want proof? In the convex mirror on the back wall (just to the left of Mary), the scene is reflected back at us, showing Mary and Martin from behind, silhouetted in the

two "windows" of the picture frames. Apparently, Mary makes house calls, appearing right in the living room of the young donor Martin, the wealthy, unique-looking heir to his father's business.
• *Before leaving this area, find, to your right, a...*

Portrait of a Young Woman (1480)

Memling's bread and butter was portraits created for families of wealthy merchants (especially visiting Italians and Portuguese). This portrait takes us right back to that time.

The young woman looks out of the frame as if she were look-ing out a window. Her hands rest on the "sill," with the fingertips sticking over. The frame is original, but the banner and Van Eyck-like lettering are not.

Her clothes look somewhat sim-ple, but they were high-class in their day. A dark damask dress is brightened by a red sash and a detachable white collar. She's pulled her hair into a tight bun at the back, pinned there with a fez-like cap and draped with a trans-parent veil. She's shaved her hairline and plucked her brows to get that clean, high-forehead look. Her ensemble is animated by a well-placed necklace of small stones.

Memling accentuates her fashionably pale complexion and gives her a pensive, sober expression, portraying her like a medieval saint. Still, she keeps her personality, with distinct features like her broad nose, neck tendons, and realistic hands. She peers out from her subtly painted veil, which sweeps down over the side of her face. What's she thinking? (My guess: "It's time for a waffle.")

MEMLING MUSEUM

BRUGES SLEEPING, EATING, NIGHTLIFE & CONNECTIONS

Bruges is the most inviting town in Belgium for an overnight. This chapter describes the town's top accommodations, eateries, and nightlife options, as well as train connections to other cities.

Sleeping in Bruges

Bruges is a great place to sleep, with Gothic spires out your window, no traffic noise, and the cheerily out-of-tune carillon heralding each new day at 8:00 sharp. (Thankfully, the bell tower is silent from 22:00 to 8:00.) Most Bruges accommodations are located between the train station and the old center, with the most distant (and best) being a few blocks to the north and east of the Markt (Market Square).

B&Bs offer the best value. All are on quiet streets and (with a few exceptions) keep the same prices throughout the year.

Bruges is most crowded Friday and Saturday evenings from Easter through October—July and August weekends are the worst. Many hotels charge a bit more on Friday and Saturday, and won't let you stay just one night if it's a Saturday.

Hotels

$$$ Hotel Heritage offers 24 rooms, with chandeliers that seem hung especially for you, in a solid and completely modernized old building with luxurious public spaces. Tastefully decorated and offering all the amenities, it's one of those places that does everything just right yet still feels warm and inviting—if you can afford it (Db-€170, superior Db-€218, deluxe Db-€270, extra bed-€60, wonderful buffet breakfast-€21/person, continental breakfast-€11/person, air-con, elevator, free Internet access and Wi-Fi, sauna, tanning bed, fitness room, bike rental, free 2-hour guided city tour,

Sleep Code

(€1 = about $1.40, country code: 32)
S = Single, **D** = Double/Twin, **T** = Triple, **Q** = Quad, **b** = bathroom,
s = shower only. Everyone speaks English. Unless otherwise
noted, breakfast is included and credit cards are accepted.

To help you easily sort through these listings, I've divided
the rooms into three categories, based on the price for a
standard double room with bath:

$$$ Higher Priced—Most rooms €125 or more.
$$ Moderately Priced—Most rooms between €80-125.
$ Lower Priced—Most rooms €80 or less.

Prices can change without notice; verify the hotel's
current rates online or by email. For other updates, see www
.ricksteves.com/update.

parking-€22/day, Niklaas Desparsstraat 11, a block north of the
Markt, tel. 050-444-444, fax 050-444-440, www.hotel-heritage
.com, info@hotel-heritage.com). It's run by cheery and hardworking Johan and Isabelle Creytens.

$$$ Hotel Adornes is small and classy—a great value situ-
ated in the most charming part of town. This 17th-century canal-
side house has 20 rooms with full modern bathrooms, free parking
(reserve in advance), free loaner bikes, and a cellar lounge with
games and videos (small Db-€120, larger Db-€140-150, Tb-€175,
Qb-€180, elevator, free Wi-Fi in lobby, some street noise, near
Carmersstraat at St. Annarei 26, tel. 050-341-336, fax 050-342-
085, www.adornes.be, info@adornes.be). Nathalie runs the family
business.

$$ Hotel Patritius, family-run and centrally located, is a
grand, circa-1830 Neoclassical mansion with hardwood oak floors
in its 16 stately, high-ceilinged rooms. It features a plush lounge,
a chandeliered breakfast room, and a courtyard garden. This
is the best value in its price range (Db-€100-130, Tb-€140-155,
Qb-€165-180, cheaper in off-season, rates depend on room size and
demand—check site for best price, extra bed-€25, air-con, elevator,
pay Internet access, free Wi-Fi on ground floor, coin-op laundry,
parking-€8, garage parking-€14, Riddersstraat 11, tel. 050-338-
454, fax 050-339-634, www.hotelpatritius.be, info@hotelpatritius
.be, Garrett and Elvi Spaey).

$$ Hotel Egmond is a creaky mansion located in the middle
of the quietly idyllic Minnewater. Its eight 18th-century rooms are
plain, with small modern baths shoehorned in, and the guests-only
garden is just waiting for a tea party. This hotel is ideal for romantics

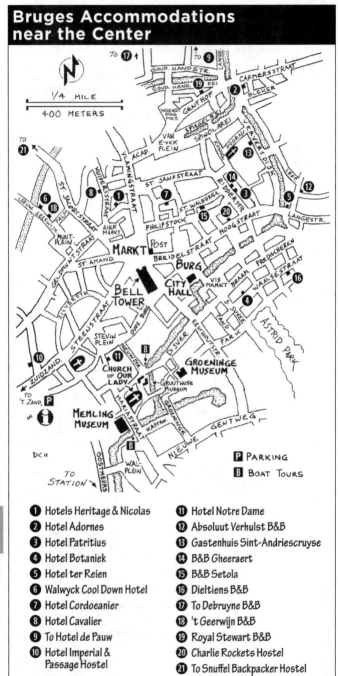

Bruges Accommodations near the Center

SLEEPING IN BRUGES

❶ Hotels Heritage & Nicolas
❷ Hotel Adornes
❸ Hotel Patritius
❹ Hotel Botaniek
❺ Hotel ter Reien
❻ Walwyck Cool Down Hotel
❼ Hotel Cordoeanier
❽ Hotel Cavalier
❾ To Hotel de Pauw
❿ Hotel Imperial & Passage Hostel

⓫ Hotel Notre Dame
⓬ Absoluut Verhulst B&B
⓭ Gastenhuis Sint-Andriescruyse
⓮ B&B Gheeraert
⓯ B&B Setola
⓰ Dieltiens B&B
⓱ To Debruyne B&B
⓲ 't Geerwijn B&B
⓳ Royal Stewart B&B
⓴ Charlie Rockets Hostel
㉑ To Snuffel Backpacker Hostel

who want a countryside setting—where you sleep surrounded by a park, not a city (Sb-€95, small twin Db-€105, larger Db-€115, Tb-€150, cheaper in winter, free Wi-Fi, parking-€10, Minnewater 15, tel. 050-341-445, fax 050-342-940, www.egmond.be, info @egmond.be, Steven).

$$ Hotel Botaniek, quietly located a block from Astrid Park, is a lovely pint-sized hotel with a comfy lounge, renting nine rooms—some of them quite big (Db-€95 weekday special for my readers, €99 Fri-Sat; Tb-€130 on weekdays, €140 Fri-Sat; Qb-€145, €149 Fri-Sat; less for longer and off-season stays, free museum-discount card, elevator, Waalsestraat 23, tel. 050-341-424, fax 050-345-939, www.botaniek.be, info@botaniek.be, Yasmine).

$$ Hotel ter Reien is big and basic, with 26 rooms overlooking a canal in the town center (Db-€80-110, Tb-€110-130, Qb-€140-160, rates vary widely with demand—check their website for best prices; cheapest rates for weekdays, stays of at least 3 nights, rooms without canal views; extra bed-€24-29, 5 percent Rick Steves discount if you book directly and show this book at check-in, pay Internet access and Wi-Fi, Langestraat 1, tel. 050-349-100, fax 050-340-048, www.hotelterreien.be, info@hotelter reien.be, owned by Diederik and Stephanie Pille-Maes).

$$ Walwyck Cool Down Hotel—a bit of modern comfort, chic design, and English verbiage in a medieval shell—is a nicely located hotel with 18 spacious rooms (small Db-€90, standard Db-€100, "superior" Db-€120, Tb-€135, family room-€155, "superior" family room-€180, Internet access, free Wi-Fi, Leeuwstraat 8, tel. 050-616-360, fax 050-616-560, www.walwyck .com, rooms@walwyck.com).

$$ Hotel Cordoeanier, a charming family-run hotel, rents 22 simple, fresh, hardwood-floor rooms on a quiet street two blocks off the Markt. It's one of the best deals in town (Sb-€70-95, Db-€75-100, twin Db-€85-100, Tb-€95-110, Qb-€125, Quint/b-€145, cheaper with cash if you show this book, breakfast buffet served in their pleasant Café Rose Red, no elevator, pay Internet access, free Wi-Fi, patio, Cordoeanierstraat 16-18, tel. 050-339-051, fax 050-346-111, www.cordoeanier.be, info@cordoeanier.be, Kris).

$ Hotel Cavalier, with more stairs than character, rents eight decent rooms and serves a hearty buffet breakfast in a once-royal setting (Sb-€55, Db-€70, Tb-€85, Qb-€100, 2 lofty en-suite "backpackers' doubles" on fourth floor-€45-50, book direct and mention this book for special Rick Steves price, pay Wi-Fi, Kuipersstraat 25, tel. 050-330-207, fax 050-347-199, www.hotelcavalier.be, info @hotelcavalier.be, run by friendly Viviane De Clerck).

$ Hotel de Pauw is tall, skinny, flower-bedecked, and family-run, with eight straightforward rooms on a quiet street next to a church (Sb-€65-75, Db-€70-85, no elevator, free and easy street parking, Sint Gilliskerkhof 8, tel. 050-337-118, fax 050-345-140, www.hoteldepauw.be, info@hoteldepauw.be, Philippe and Hilde).

$ Hotel 't Keizershof is a dollhouse of a hotel that lives by its motto, "Spend a night...not a fortune." (Its other motto: "When you're asleep, we look just like those big fancy hotels.") It's simple and tidy, with seven small, cheery, old-time rooms split between two floors, with a shower and toilet on each (S-€25, D-€44, T-€66, Q-€80, cash only, free and easy parking, laundry service-€7.50, Oostmeers 126, a block in front of station, tel. 050-338-728, www.hotelkeizershof.be, info@hotel keizershof.be). The hotel is run by Stefaan and Hilde, with decor by their children, Lorie and Fien; it's situated in a pleasant area near the train station and Minnewater, a 15 minute-walk from the Markt.

$ Hotel Nicolas feels like an old-time boarding house that missed Bruges' affluence bandwagon. Its 14 big, plain rooms are a good value, and the location is ideal—on a quiet street a block off the Markt (Sb-€55, Db-€63, Tb-€75, elevator, pay Wi-Fi, TV on request, closed in Jan, Niklaas Desparsstraat 9, tel. 050-335-502, fax 050-343-544, www.hotelnicolas.be, hotel.nicolas@telenet.be, Yi-Ling and Thomas).

$ Hotel Imperial is an old-school hotel with seven old-school rooms. It's simple and well-run in a charming building on a handy, quiet street (Db-€70-90, cash only, no elevator, pay Wi-Fi, Dweersstraat 24, tel. 050-339-014, www.hotelimperial.be, info @hotelimperial.be, Paul Bernolet and Hilde).

$ Hotel Notre Dame is a humble and blocky little budget option, renting 12 worn rooms in the busy thick of things (Db-€70-75, free Internet access and Wi-Fi, Mariastraat 3, tel. 050-333-193, fax 050-337-608, www.hotelnotredame.be, info@hotelnotre dame.be).

Bed-and-Breakfasts

These B&Bs, run by people who enjoy their work, offer a better value than hotels. Most families rent out their entire top floor—generally three rooms and a small sitting area. And most are mod and stylish—they're just in medieval shells. Each is central, with lots of stairs and €70 doubles you'd pay €100 for in a hotel. Most places charge €10 extra for one-night stays. It's possible to find parking on the street in the evening (pay 9:00-19:00, 2-hour maximum for metered parking during the day, free overnight).

$$ Absoluut Verhulst is a great, modern-feeling B&B with three rooms in a 400-year-old house, run by friendly Frieda and Benno (Db-€95; huge and lofty suite-€130 for 2, €160 for 3, €180 for 4; €10 more for one-night stays, cash only, non-smoking, free

Wi-Fi, 5-minute walk east of the Markt at Verbrand Nieuwland 1, tel. 050-334-515, www.b-bverhulst.com, b-b.verhulst@pandora.be).

$$ Gastenhuis Sint-Andriescruyse offers warmly decorated rooms with high ceilings in a spacious, cheerfully red canalside house a short walk from the Old Town action. Owners Luc and Christiane treat guests like long-lost family (S-€75, D/Db-€100, T-€125, Q-€150, family room for up to 5 comes with board games, cash only, free soft drinks, free Internet access, free pick-up at station, Verversdijk 15A, tel. 050-789-168, mobile 0477-973-933, www.gastenhuisst-andriescruyse.be, luc.cluoet@telenet.be).

$$ B&B Gheeraert is a Neoclassical mansion where Inne rents three huge, bright, comfy rooms (Sb-€85, Db-€95, Tb-€115, two-night minimum stay required, cash only, personal check required for first-night's deposit, strictly non-smoking, fridges in rooms, free Internet access and Wi-Fi, Riddersstraat 9, 5-minute walk east of the Markt, tel. 050-335-627, fax 050-345-201, www .bb-bruges.be, bb-bruges@skynet.be).

$ B&B Setola, run by Lut and Bruno Setola, offers three expansive rooms and a spacious breakfast/living room on the top floor of their house. Wooden ceiling beams give the modern rooms a touch of Old World flair, and the family room has a fun loft (Sb-€60, Db-€70, €20 per extra person, €10 more for one-night stays, free Wi-Fi, 5-minute walk from the Markt, Sint Walburgastraat 12, tel. 050-334-977, fax 050-332-551, www.bedandbreakfast -bruges.com, setola@bedandbreakfast-bruges.com).

$ Koen and Annemie Dieltiens are a friendly couple who enjoy getting to know their guests while sharing a wealth of information on Bruges. You'll eat a hearty breakfast around a big table in their comfortable house (Sb-€60, Db-€70, Tb-€90, €10 more for one-night stays, cash only, free Internet access and Wi-Fi, Waalsestraat 40, three blocks southeast of Burg Square, tel. 050-334-294, www.bedandbreakfastbruges.be, dieltiens@bedand breakfastbruges.be).

$ Debruyne B&B, run by Marie-Rose and her architect husband, Ronny, offers three rooms with artsy, modern decor (check out the elephant-size white doors—Ronny's design) and genuine warmth (Sb-€60, Db-€65, Tb-€85, €10 more for one-night stays, cash only, Internet access, free Wi-Fi, 7-minute walk north of the Markt, 2 blocks from the little church at Lange Raamstraat 18, tel. 050-347-606, www.bedandbreakfastbruges.com, mietjedebruyne @yahoo.co.uk).

$ 't Geerwijn B&B, run by Chris de Loof, offers homey rooms in the old center. Check out the fun, lofty A-frame room upstairs (Ds/Db-€70-80 depending on season, Tb-€85, cash only, pleasant breakfast room and royal lounge, free Wi-Fi, Geerwijn-straat 14, tel. 050-340-544, fax 050-343-721, www.geerwijn.be, info@geerwijn.be). Chris also rents an apartment that sleeps five.

$ Royal Stewart B&B, run by Scottish Maggie and her husband, Gilbert, has three thoughtfully decorated rooms in a quiet, almost cloistered 17th-century house that was inhabited by nuns until 1953 (S-€48, D/Db-€65, Tb-€85, cash only, pleasant breakfast room, Genthof 25-27, 5-minute walk from the Markt, tel. 050-337-918, fax 050-337-918, www.royalstewart.be, r.stewart @pandora.be).

$ Waterside B&B two fresh, Zen-like rooms, one floor above a peaceful canal south of the town center (D-€75, €5 more on Sat, continental breakfast, free Wi-Fi, 15-minute walk from Burg Square at Kazernevest 88, tel. & fax 050-616-686, mobile 0476-744-525, www.waterside.be, waterside@telenet.be, run by Mieke of recommended Pink Bear Bike Tours).

$ B&B AM/PM sports three ultra-modern rooms in a residential neighborhood just west of the old town (Db-€70, Tb-€90, €10 more for one-night stay, cash only, free Internet access—mornings only, free Wi-Fi, 5-minute walk from 't Zand at Singel 10, mobile 0485-071-003, www.bruges-bedandbreakfast.com, info @bruges-bedandbreakfast.com, artsy young couple Tiny and Kevin). From the train station, head left down busy Buiten Begijnevest to the roundabout. Stay to the left, take the pedestrian underpass, then follow the busy road (now on your left). Just before the next bridge, turn right onto the footpath called Buiten Boeverievest, then turn left onto Singel; the B&B is at #10.

Hostels

Bruges has several good hostels offering beds for around €15 in two- to eight-bed rooms. Breakfast is about €3 extra. The American-style **$ Charlie Rockets** hostel (and bar), a backpacker dive, is the liveliest and most central. The ground floor feels like a 19th-century sports bar, with a foosball-and-movie-posters party ambience. Upstairs is an industrial-strength pile of hostel dorms (90 beds, €18/bed with sheets, €20/bed with sheets and breakfast, 4-6 beds/room, D-€50 includes breakfast, lockers, pay Internet access, Hoogstraat 19, tel. 050-330-660, www.charlierockets.com). Other small and loose places are the minimal, funky, and central **$ Passage** (€15/bed with sheets, 4-7 beds/room, D-€50, Db-€65, Dweerstraat 26, tel. 050-340-232, www.passagebruges.com, info @passagebruges.com) and **$ Snuffel Backpacker Hostel,** which is less central and pretty grungy, but friendly and laid-back (60 beds, €15-19/bed includes sheets and breakfast, 4-14 beds/room, Ezelstraat 47, tel. 050-333-133, www.snuffel.be).

SLEEPING IN BRUGES

Eating in Bruges

Bruges' specialties include mussels cooked a variety of ways (one order can feed two), fish dishes, grilled meats, and french fries. The town's two indigenous beers are the prize-winning Brugse Zot (Bruges Fool), a golden ale, and Straffe Hendrik, a potent, bitter triple ale.

You'll find plenty of affordable, touristy restaurants on floodlit squares and along dreamy canals. Bruges feeds 3.5 million tourists a year, and most are seduced by a high-profile location. These can be great experiences for the magical setting and views, but the quality of food and service will likely be low. I wouldn't blame you for eating at one of these places, but I won't recommend any. I prefer the candle-cool bistros that flicker on back streets.

Restaurants

Rock Fort is a chic spot with a modern, fresh coziness and a high-powered respect for good food. Two young chefs, Peter Laloo and Hermes Vanliefde, give their French cuisine a creative, gourmet twist. At the bar they serve a separate tapas menu. Reservations are required for dinner and recommended for lunch. This place is a winner (€6-12 tapas, great pastas and salads, €15 Mon-Fri lunch special, beautifully presented €19-34 dinner plates, €40 five-tapas special, fancy €50 fixed-price four-course meal, open Mon-Fri 12:00-14:30 & 18:30-23:00, closed Sat-Sun, Langestraat 15, tel. 050-334-113).

Bistro de Bekoring, cute, candlelit, and Gothic, fills two almshouses and a delightful terrace with people thankful for good food. Rotund and friendly Chef Roland and his wife, Gerda, love to tempt the hungry—as the name of their bistro implies. They serve traditional Flemish food (especially eel and beer-soaked stew) from a small menu to people who like holding hands while they dine. Reservations are smart (€15 weekday lunch, €30 fixed-price dinners, €42 with wine, Wed-Sat 11:45-13:45 & 18:30-21:00, closed Sun evening and Mon-Tue; out past the Begijnhof at Arsenaalstraat 53, tel. 050-344-157).

Bistro in den Wittenkop, very Flemish, is a stylishly small, laid-back, old-time place specializing in the local favorites. It's a classy spot to enjoy hand-cut fries, which go particularly well with Straffe Hendrik beer (€37-40 three-course meal, €20-25 plates, Tue-Sat 18:00-21:30, closed Sun-Mon, reserve ahead, terrace in

EATING IN BRUGES

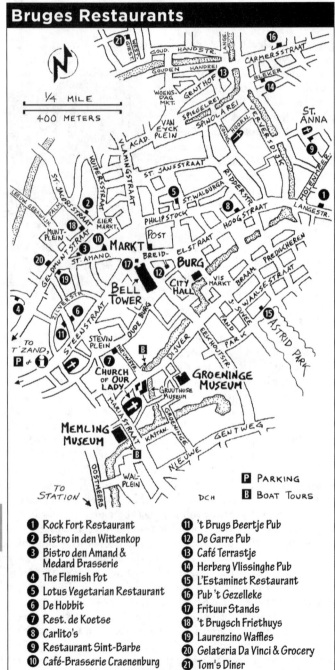

Bruges Restaurants

1/4 MILE
400 METERS

MARKT

BURG

BELL
TOWER

CITY
HALL

CHURCH
OF OUR
LADY

GROENINGE
MUSEUM

GRUUTHUSE
MUSEUM

MEMLING
MUSEUM

TO
T'ZAND,

TO
STATION

ST.
ANNA

ASTRID
PARK

P PARKING

B BOAT TOURS

DCH

1 Rock Fort Restaurant
2 Bistro in den Wittenkop
3 Bistro den Amand & Medard Brasserie
4 The Flemish Pot
5 Lotus Vegetarian Restaurant
6 De Hobbit
7 Rest. de Koetse
8 Carlito's
9 Restaurant Sint-Barbe
10 Café-Brasserie Craenenburg

11 't Brugs Beertje Pub
12 De Garre Pub
13 Café Terrastje
14 Herberg Vlissinghe Pub
15 L'Estaminet Restaurant
16 Pub 't Gezelleke
17 Frituur Stands
18 't Brugsch Friethuys
19 Laurenzino Waffles
20 Gelateria Da Vinci & Grocery
21 Tom's Diner

back in summer, Sint Jakobsstraat 14, tel. 050-332-059).

Bistro den Amand, with a plain interior and a few outdoor tables, exudes unpretentious quality the moment you step in. In this mussels-free zone, Chef An is enthusiastic about vegetables, as her busy wok and fun salads prove. The creative dishes—some with a hint of Asian influence—are a welcome departure from Bruges' mostly predictable traditional restaurants. It's on a busy pedestrian lane a half-block off the Markt (€33-35 three-course meal, €20 plates; Mon-Tue and Thu-Sat 12:00-14:00 & 18:00-21:00, closed Wed and Sun; Sint-Amandstraat 4, tel. 050-340-122, An Vissers and Arnout Beyaert). Reservations are smart for dinner.

The Flemish Pot (a.k.a. The Little Pancake House) is a hard-working eatery serving up traditional peasant-style meals. They crank out pancakes (savory and sweet) and homemade *wafels* for lunch. Then, at 18:00, enthusiastic chefs Mario and Rik stow their waffle irons and pull out a traditional menu of vintage Flemish specialties served in little iron pots and skillets. Seating is tight and cluttered. You'll enjoy huge portions, refills from the hovering "fries angel," and a good selection of local beers (€26-30 three-course meals, €16-24 plates, Wed-Sun 12:00-22:00, closed Mon-Tue, reservations smart, family-friendly, just off Geldmuntstraat at Helmstraat 3, tel. 050-340-086).

Lotus Vegetarian Restaurant serves serious lunch plates (€10 *plat du jour* offered daily), salads, and homemade chocolate cake in a pleasantly small, bustling, and upscale setting. To keep carnivorous companions happy, they also serve several very good, organic meat dishes (Mon-Fri from 11:45, last orders at 14:00, closed Sat-Sun, cash only, just north of Burg Square at Wapenmakersstraat 5, tel. 050-331-078).

De Hobbit, featuring an entertaining menu, is always busy with happy eaters. For a swinging deal, try the all-you-can-eat spareribs with bread and salad for €18.50. It's nothing fancy, just good, basic food served in a fun, crowded, traditional grill house (daily 18:00-23:00, Fri-Sat until 23:30, family-friendly, Kemelstraat 8-10, reservations smart, tel. 050-335-520).

Tom's Diner is a trendy, cozy little candlelit bistro in a quiet, cobbled residential area a 10-minute walk from the center. Young chef Tom gives traditional dishes a delightful modern twist. If you want to flee the tourists and experience a popular neighborhood joint, this is it—the locals love it (€15-20 plates, Wed-Mon 18:00-24:00, closed Tue, north of the Markt near Sint-Gilliskerk at West-Gistelhof 23, tel. 050-333-382).

Restaurant de Koetse is a good spot for central, good-quality, local-style food. The feeling is traditional, a bit formal (stuffy even), and dressy, yet accessible. The cuisine is Belgian and French, with an emphasis on grilled meat, seafood, and mussels (€30

EATING IN BRUGES

three-course meals, €20-30 plates include vegetables and a salad, Fri-Wed 12:00-14:30 & 18:00-22:00, closed Thu, non-smoking section, Oude Burg 31, tel. 050-337-680, Piet).

Carlito's is a good choice for basic Italian fare. Their informal space, with whitewashed walls and tea-light candles, is two blocks from Burg Square (€8-13 pizzas and pastas, daily 12:00-14:00 & 18:00-22:30, patio seating in back, Hoogstraat 21, tel. 050-490-075).

Restaurant Sint-Barbe, on the eastern edge of town, serves classy Flemish dishes made from local ingredients in a fresh, modern space on two floors. Their €12 soup-and-main lunch is a great deal (€14-25 main courses, Thu-Mon 11:30-14:30 & 18:00-22:00, closed Tue-Wed, food served until 21:00, St. Annaplein 29, tel. 050-330-999, Evi).

Restaurants on the Markt: Most tourists seem to be eating on the Markt with the bell tower high overhead and horse carriages clip-clopping by. The square is ringed by tourist traps with aggressive waiters expert at getting you to consume more than you intended. Still, if you order smartly, you can have a memorable meal or drink here on one of the finest squares in Europe at a reasonable price. Consider **Café-Brasserie Craenenburg,** with a straightforward menu, where you can get pasta and beer for €15 and spend all the time you want ogling the magic of Bruges (daily 7:30-23:00, Markt 16, tel. 050-333-402).

Cheap Eats: **Medard Brasserie,** just a block off the Markt, serves the cheapest hot meal in town—hearty meat spaghetti (big plate-€3, huge plate-€5.50, sit inside or out, Fri-Wed 11:00-20:30 except opens on Sun at 12:30, closed Thu, Sint Amandstraat 18, tel. 050-348-684).

Bars Offering Light Meals, Beer, and Ambience

My best budget-eating tip for Bruges: Stop into one of the city's bars for a simple meal and a couple of world-class beers with great Bruges ambience. The last three pubs listed are in the wonderfully *gezellig* (cozy) quarter, northeast of the Markt.

The **'t Brugs Beertje** is young and convivial. Although any pub or restaurant carries the basic beers, you'll find a selection here of more than 300 types, including brews to suit any season. They serve light meals, including pâté, spaghetti, toasted sandwiches, and a traditional cheese plate. You're welcome to sit at the bar and talk with the staff (5 cheeses, bread, and salad for €11; Thu-Tue 16:00-24:00, closed Wed, Kemelstraat 5, tel. 050-339-616, run by fun-loving manager Daisy).

De Garre is another good place to gain an appreciation of the Belgian beer culture. Rather than a noisy pub scene, it has a dressy, sit-down-and-focus-on-your-friend-and-the-fine-beer vibe. It's mature and cozy with tables, light meals (cold cuts, pâtés, and toasted sandwiches), and a selection of 150 beers (daily 12:00-24:00, additional seating up tiny staircase, off Breidelstraat between Burg and Markt, on tiny Garre alley, tel. 050-341-029).

Café Terrastje is a cozy pub serving light meals. Experience the grown-up ambience inside, or relax on the front terrace overlooking the canal and heart of the *gezellig* district (€6-8 sandwiches, €10-18 dishes; food served Fri-Mon 12:00-21:00, open until 23:30; Tue 12:00-18:00; closed Wed-Thu; corner of Genthof and Langerei, tel. 050-330-919, Ian and Patricia).

Herberg Vlissinghe is the oldest pub in town (1515). Bruno keeps things simple and laid-back, serving simple plates (lasagna, grilled cheese sandwiches, and famous €8 angel-hair spaghetti) and great beer in the best old-time tavern atmosphere in town. This must have been the Dutch Masters' rec room. The garden outside comes with a *boules* court—free for guests to watch or play (Wed-Sat 11:00-24:00, Sun 11:00-19:00, closed Mon-Tue, Blekersstraat 2, tel. 050-343-737).

L'Estaminet is a youthful, jazz-filled eatery, similar to one of Amsterdam's brown cafés. Don't be intimidated by its lack of tourists. Local students flock here for the Tolkien-chic ambience, hearty €9 spaghetti, and big dinner salads. This is Belgium—it serves more beer than wine. For outdoor dining under an all-weather canopy, enjoy the relaxed patio facing peaceful Astrid Park (Fri-Wed 11:30-24:00, Thu 16:00-24:00, Park 5, tel. 050-330-916).

Pub 't Gezelleke lacks the mystique of the Vlissinghe, but it's a true neighborhood pub offering quality fare and a good chance to drink with locals. Its name is an appropriate play on the word for *cozy* and the name of a great local poet (Mon-Fri 11:00-24:00, closed Sat-Sun, Carmersstraat 15, tel. 050-338-381, Zena).

Fries, Fast Food, and Picnics

Local french fries *(frites)* are a treat. Proud and traditional *frituurs* serve tubs of fries and various local-style shish kebabs. Belgians dip their *frites* in mayonnaise, but ketchup is there for the Yankees (along with spicier sauces). For a quick, cheap, hot, and scenic snack, hit a *frituur* and sit on the steps or benches overlooking the Markt (convenience benches are about 50 yards past the post office).

Markt Frituurs: Twin take-away fry carts are on the Markt at the base of the bell tower (daily 10:00-24:00). Skip the ketchup and have a sauce adventure. I find the cart on the left more user-friendly.

EATING IN BRUGES

't **Brugsch Friethuys,** a block off the Markt, is handy for fries you can sit down and enjoy. Its forte is greasy, fast, deep-fried Flemish fast food. The €11 "menu 1" comes with three traditional gut bombs: shrimp, *frikandel* minced-meat sausage, and "gypsy stick" sausage (daily 11:00-late, at the corner of Geldmuntstraat and Sint Jakobstraat).

Delhaize-Proxy Supermarket is ideal for picnics. Its push-button produce pricer lets you buy as little as one mushroom (Mon-Sat 9:00-19:00, closed Sun, 3 blocks off the Markt on Geldmuntstraat). For midnight snacks, you'll find Indian-run corner grocery stores scattered around town.

Belgian Waffles and Ice Cream

You'll see waffles sold at restaurants and take-away stands. **Laurenzino** is particularly good, and a favorite with Bruges' teens when they get the waffle munchies. Their classic waffle with chocolate costs €2.50 (daily in summer 10:00-22:00, until 23:00 Fri-Sat; winter 10:00-20:00, until 22:00 Fri-Sat; across from Gelateria Da Vinci at Noordzandstraat 1, tel. 050-333-213).

Gelateria Da Vinci, the local favorite for homemade ice cream, has creative flavors and a lively atmosphere. As you approach, you'll see a line of happy lickers. Before ordering, ask to sample the Ferrero Rocher (chocolate, nuts, and crunchy cookie) and plain yogurt (daily 10:00-22:00, until 24:00 April-Sept and in good-weather off-season, Geldmuntstraat 34, run by Sylvia from Austria).

Nightlife in Bruges

Herberg Vlissinghe and **De Garre,** are great places to just nurse a beer and enjoy new friends.

Charlie Rockets is an American-style bar—lively and central—with foosball games, darts, and five pool tables (€9/hour) in the inviting back room. It also runs a youth hostel upstairs and therefore is filled with a young, international crowd (a block off the Markt at Hoogstraat 19). It's open nightly until 3:00 in the morning with nonstop rock 'n' roll.

Nighttime Bike Ride: Great as these pubs are, my favorite way to spend a late-summer evening in Bruges is in the twilight on a rental bike, savoring the cobbled wonders of its back streets, far from the touristic commotion.

Evening Carillon Concerts: The tiny courtyard behind the bell tower has a few benches where people can enjoy the free carillon concerts (generally Mon, Wed, and Sat at 21:00 in the summer; schedule posted on courtyard wall).

Bruges Connections

From Bruges by Train to: Brussels (2/hour, usually at :31 and :58, 1 hour, €12.90), **Brussels Airport** (2/hour, 1.5 hours, transfer at Brussels Nord), **Ghent** (4/hour, 30 minutes), **Antwerp** (2/hour, 1.5 hours, half the trains change in Ghent), **Ypres/Ieper** (hourly, 2 hours, change in Kortrijk), **Ostende** (3/hour, 15 minutes), **Delft** (hourly, 3 hours, change in Ghent, Antwerp, and Rotterdam), **The Hague** (hourly, 3 hours, change in Antwerp), **Köln** (8/day, 3.25 hours, change to fast Thalys train at Brussels Midi), **Paris** (roughly hourly via Brussels, 2.5 hours on fast Thalys trains—it's best to book by 20:00 the day before), **Amsterdam** (hourly, 3.25-3.75 hours, transfer at Ghent and Antwerp Central or Brussels Midi; transfer can be tight—be alert and check with conductor; some trips via Thalys train, which requires supplement), **Amsterdam's Schiphol Airport** (hourly, 3.5 hours, change in Ghent and/or Antwerp; less frequent connections via Brussels with Thalys save 30 minutes), **Haarlem** (hourly, 3.5 hours, 2-3 changes—avoid Thalys if traveling with a railpass). Train info: tel. 050/302-424.

Trains from London: Bruges is an ideal "Welcome to Europe" stop after London. Take the Eurostar train from London to Brussels (10/day, 2.5 hours), then transfer, backtracking to Bruges (2/hour, 1 hour, entire trip just a few dollars more with Eurostar ticket).

FLANDERS FIELDS

These World War I battlefields, about 40 miles southwest of Bruges, remain infamous in military history. In Flanders Fields, the second decade of the 20th century saw the invention of modern warfare: Machine guns, trenches, poison gas, and a war of attrition. The most intense fighting occurred in the area called the Ypres Salient, a nondescript but hilly—and therefore terrifically strategic—bulge of land just east of the medieval trading town of Ypres (which the Flemish call "Ieper"). Over a period of three and a half years, it was here that hundreds of thousands of soldiers from fifty nations and five continents drew their last breath. Fields and forests were turned first to trenches and battlefields, and then to desolate wastelands with mud several feet deep, entirely devoid of life.

Poppies are the first flowers to bloom in a desolate battlefield once the dust (and mustard gas) clears. And today, this far-western corner of Belgium is blooming once more, having adopted that flower as its symbol. It represents sacrifice and renewal.

Today visitors can't drive through this part of Flanders without passing countless artillery craters, monuments and memorials, stones marking this advance or that conquest, and war cemeteries standing stoically between the cow-speckled pastures. Local farmers pull live shells and ammunition from the earth when they till their fields each spring and fall. (It's so commonplace, most don't even bother to call the bomb squad... they just throw it on a pile with the rest of the rusty ordnance.) Every local has his own garage collection of rusty "Great War" debris

he fished out of a field. Human remains are also regularly disinterred here, with every effort made to identify the fallen soldier and notify any surviving family.

If you're interested in this chapter of history, you can visit several Flanders Fields sites in a one-day side-trip from Bruges (best by car or guided tour). The most important and accessible sites are the pleasant and completely rebuilt market town of Ypres, with its impressive In Flanders Fields Museum (closed mid-Nov of 2011 until June of 2012); the town of Passchendaele (a.k.a. "Passiondale"), with a nearby, more humble, but still interesting museum; and Tyne Cot Cemetery, where thousands of enlisted men from the British Commonwealth are buried and honored. Because most of the fighting here involved British Commonwealth troops, the vast majority of visitors are Brits, Canadians, Australians, and New Zealanders, for whom the stories of Flanders Fields are etched, like names on gravestones, into their national consciousness. You'll notice on maps that many places have English names—often anglicized approximations of the Flemish names (Passiondale for Passchendaele), or more blunt new names for existing locales (Mount Sorrow, Hellfire Corner).

The years 2014 through 2018 will be a banner time in this area, as the centennial of various battles and other events are commemorated.

Between the sites, you'll drive through idyllic Belgian countryside, streaked with cornfields, dotted with pudgy cows, and punctuated by the occasional artillery crater—now overgrown with grass or trees, or serving as a handy little pond. On your Flanders Fields journey, be sure to take time to slow down and smell the cabbage.

Planning Your Time

By Tour: If you really want to delve into Flanders Fields, your best bet is to take a **tour.** These come with a rolling history lecture, and take you to off-the-beaten-path sites you'd likely not find on your own. Several companies based in Ypres run tours of the area; if you're coming from Bruges, it's more convenient to take either Nathan's minibus tours or the Quasimodo big-bus tours.

By Car: Drivers can easily link the three main sites in a day. Be aware that road signs use the Flemish "Ieper," not "Ypres." Shop around locally for a good guidebook to point you to additional

In Flanders Fields

In Flanders fields the poppies blow
Between the crosses, row on row,
That mark our place; and in the sky
The larks, still bravely singing, fly
Scarce heard amid the guns below.

We are the Dead. Short days ago
We lived, felt dawn, saw sunset glow,
Loved and were loved, and now we lie,
In Flanders fields.

Take up our quarrel with the foe:
To you from failing hands we throw
The torch; be yours to hold it high.
If ye break faith with us who die
We shall not sleep, though poppies grow
In Flanders fields.

John McCrae

options. The local tourist board publishes a free guidebooklet called *The Flanders Fields Country & The Great War*, which is a good starting place.

Here's a one-day plan for seeing the sites listed in this chapter. There's much more to see; if you're a WWI battlefield buff, invest in a good local guidebook and map to hunt down the many sites.

From Bruges, head south on the A17 expressway. If you want to make a beeline to Ypres, take this all the way to A19, which you'll take east and follow *Ieper Centrum* signs. For a slower, much more scenic route that takes you to more sites, exit the A17 expressway at R32 and circle around the northern edge of Roeselare, then head west on N36, then south on N313. This takes you to Langemark and the German cemetery there. Then take Zonnebaekestraat southeast to the village of Zonnebaeke and the Passchendaele Museum. From there follow the Menin Road (N37) right on into Ypres, crossing under the Menin Gate as you enter town. After touring Ypres' excellent In Flanders Fields Museum, you can explore more countryside sites, or head directly back to Bruges (fastest route between Ypres and Bruges: A19 expressway east to the A17 interchange near Kortrijk, then zip north on A17).

By Public Transportation: Non-drivers will find it time-consuming to get from Bruges to Ypres (2 hours one-way with a transfer in Kortrijk; note that Ypres is "Ieper" on timetables). Once at Ypres, it's very difficult to see the scattered sites using

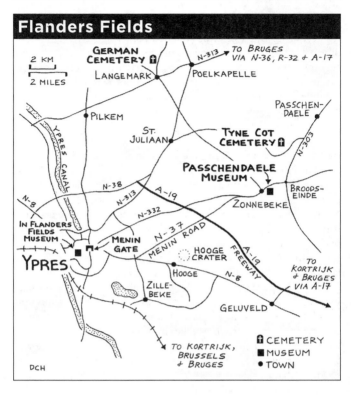

Flanders Fields

2 KM
2 MILES

GERMAN CEMETERY 🏳
LANGEMARK
N-313 → TO BRUGES VIA N-36, R-32 & A-17
POELKAPELLE
PILKEM
PASSCHEN-DAELE
ST. JULIAAN
TYNE COT CEMETERY 🏳
N-303
PASSCHENDAELE MUSEUM
N-38
A-19
N-313
ZONNEBEKE
BROODS-EINDE
N-8
N-332
N-37
IN FLANDERS FIELDS MUSEUM →
MENIN GATE
MENIN ROAD
HOOGE CRATER
A-19 FREEWAY
TO KORTRIJK & BRUGES VIA A-17
YPRES
HOOGE
N-8
ZILLE-BEKE
GELUVELD
TO KORTRIJK, BRUSSELS & BRUGES
🏳 CEMETERY
■ MUSEUM
● TOWN
DCH

public transit. Taking a tour (from Ypres or Bruges) or renting a car is a must.

Background

Flanders Fields and the Ypres Salient

Because American forces played a relatively minor role in the fighting at Flanders Fields, its history is obscure to many visitors from the US. If visiting the sites, it helps to get up to speed by doing a little homework to make it all more meaningful. This section will give you a good start.

From 1830, Belgium was established as an independent and neutral state—an essential buffer zone to protect European peace, surrounded as it was by four big powers: France, Prussia, the Netherlands, and Britain. After defeating France and unifying in 1870, Germany was on the rise—an upstart powerhouse hungry for overseas colonies to fuel its growing economy. Germany amassed an intimidating army, and the rest of Europe worriedly watched flickering newsreel footage of wave after wave of German soldiers, goose-stepping past the camera in perfect sync, followed by gleaming, state-of-the-art cannons. Some of Europe's nations scrambled to ally with their neighbors against potential German encroachment; others allied with Germany. Because many alliances were secret, and often conflicting, no one knew for sure exactly where anyone else stood. As H. G. Welles said, "Every intelligent person in the world knew that disaster was impending and knew no way to avoid it."

On June 28, 1914, while on a visit to Sarajevo, the heir to the Austro-Hungarian throne, Archduke Franz Ferdinand, and his wife were assassinated by a teenage terrorist working for Bosnian Serb separatists. The Austrians held Serbia responsible and declared war. Germany joined Austria, and Russia (allied with France) backed Serbia. Through an intricate web of alliances—which ironically had been created to prevent war—soon all of Europe was drawn in the conflict. On August 4, 1914, Germany sent some 800,000 troops across the border into neutral Belgium en route to France. By August 20, they had already taken Brussels, and four days later they were in western Flanders. The Germans expected to blow through the country quickly. Their ultimate goal: Paris to the south and, to the north, the French ports of Dunkerque and Calais. If they could control those, Germany would command the English Channel.

However, the small but determined Belgian army—less than a quarter the size of the German army—pushed back hard, as they waited for British reinforcements to come from across the Channel. In the **Battle of the IJzer River,** the Belgians opened a sea gate at a pivotal moment to flood a low-lying plain just before a German advance. This diverted the German effort slightly to the south, around the town of Ypres.

Ypres (Ieper in Flemish)—an important market center in the Middle Ages (similar to Bruges)—was just an ordinary town. But its location, surrounding terrain, and modern weaponry turned it into a perpetual battlefield. This conflict saw the advent of the machine gun—a new invention that, before the war, had been called "the peacekeeper," because it was assumed that no sane commander would ever send his boys into its fire. The extremely flat terrain of Flanders Fields, combined with these newly emerging battlefield techniques, made even the slightest gain in elevation strategically important. From any ridge, machine guns and artillery could be used to mow down enemy troops—advancing armies would be sitting ducks. (The names of some of the land features here—such as "Hill 60," as in 60 meters above sea level—indicate how the surrounding flatness emphasized even the most modest gain in elevation.) Consequently, the low-lying ridges just east of Ypres—which came to be known as the **Ypres Salient** (the French term for "bulge")—saw some of the fiercest, most devastating fighting of World War I.

The **First Battle of Ypres** began on October 20, 1914, when German troops attempted to invade the town. It became a priority of the Allies—Belgians, French, and British Commonwealth troops—to hold the Germans at bay. Both sides sustained huge losses, but the German troops—mostly inexperienced young conscripts who had underestimated the opposition—were devastated; to this day, Germans call the battle *Kindermord*, "Massacre of the Innocents." For a while, at least, the Allies succeeded in preventing Germany from pushing through. It was the last mobile combat of a conflict that would come to be known for its grueling trench warfare.

Both sides regrouped and prepared for a harsh winter. They dug trenches. Nobody planned it—it was simply human nature for soldiers ducking machine-gun bullets to burrow down. Separated by as little as 50 yards, enemy armies were close enough to offer each other a *Gesundheit!* after each sneeze. It was during this time that the famous "Christmas Truce" took place, in which the German soldiers erected little candlelit *Tanenbaum*s beside their trenches and even approached the English trenches with gifts, kind words, and a pick-up soccer game.

In the spring of 1915, the Germans tried again in the **Second Battle of Ypres.** During this battle, the Germans used poison gas for the first time on a large scale, catching the Allies off-guard. Chlorine gas (a.k.a. bertholite) reacts with moisture in the lungs to form hydrochloric acid—choking soldiers from the inside out. It was also one of the first times flamethrowers were used in battle. Despite these gruesome innovations, Germany was still unable to take the town. By May of 1915, the opposing forces were deadlocked near the town of Passchendaele, seven miles east of Ypres; for two years, little progress was made in either direction.

Although the Western Front appeared to be "all quiet," each side fortified its positions. The Germans in particular established an elaborate network of five successive trenches, connected to and supplied by one another with perpendicular "switches." They built stout fortresses with flat tops, designed to protect troops from British artillery while allowing them to quickly emerge to man nearby machine-gun nests. These flat-topped German fortresses—which you'll still see everywhere—were dubbed "pillboxes." The British opted for underground wooden tunnels called "dugouts," and reserved concrete bunkers for more specialized use, as command posts and shelters for the wounded. (Their rounded-top bunkers proved to be a more effective deterrent to artillery blasts than the Germans' flat-top design—leading the Germans to adopt the round British style in World War II.)

In the summer of 1917, the Allies attempted their own offensive against the newly strengthened German threat, the **Third Battle of Ypres** (a.k.a. the Battle of Passchendaele). After a sustained two-week artillery bombardment of German positions, some four million projectiles turned the countryside into a desolate wasteland. One solider said that "the earth had been churned and rechurned"; another termed it "as featureless as the Sahara."

Then British infantry took to the battlefield...going "over the top" (giving us that phrase), rather than staying in the trenches. They faced barbed wire, machine-gun fire, dangerously exposed high ground, and liquid mud. The utter devastation of the shelling, combined with historic rainfall (the most in the history of Flanders), turned the Ypres Salient into a sea of mud. The same flatness that made the high ground here so strategic turned the low ground into quicksand in heavy rain. Fields became flooded with stagnant water. Troops' boots and tank treads could barely move, causing the British to gain only two of the four miles they so desperately needed to conquer. This battle was also the first time the Germans used the notorious mustard gas, which causes exposed skin to blister agonizingly on contact.

As the summer of 1917 turned to fall, and the heavy rains continued to deluge the area, British soldiers made more and more inroads, bunker by bunker. Their goal was the destroyed village of **Passchendaele,** perched on a modest ridge with a strategic view over the flat lands below. The village's name literally meant "passing the valley," but the Brits dubbed it "Passiondale"...the valley of suffering. Menin Road, which connected Ypres to Passchendaele (now road N37), was the focus of much warfare—especially the notorious intersection dubbed "Hellfire Corner."

But British forces never succeeded in taking Passchendaele, and it became clear that this would be a **war of attrition.** Each side had lost about a quarter of a million men. And, as both sides poured troops and resources into the fighting, neither could actually break through; they simply wanted to be the last man standing.

Two pivotal events took place over the winter of 1917-1918: The United States entered the war on the side of the Allies; and Germany agreed to a separate peace with Russia, allowing it to steer more resources to the Ypres Salient. In spring of 1918, the **Fourth Battle of Ypres** (a.k.a. the Battle of the Lys) saw German forces trying to push through to the town of Ypres before US troops could arrive. They were emboldened by the collapse of Russia in the Bolshevik Revolution, which freed up more German troops and resources to direct at this front. Always innovative on the battlefield, the Germans introduced an elite squad of storm

Dulce et Decorum Est

Bent double, like old beggars under sacks,
Knock-kneed, coughing like hags, we cursed
     through sludge,
Till on the haunting flares we turned our backs
And towards our distant rest began to trudge.
Men marched asleep. Many had lost their boots
But limped on, blood-shod. All went lame; all
     blind;
Drunk with fatigue; deaf even to the hoots
Of tired, outstripped Five-Nines that dropped
     behind.

Gas! Gas! Quick, boys!—An ecstasy of fumbling,
Fitting the clumsy helmets just in time;
But someone still was yelling out and stumbling,
And flound'ring like a man in fire or lime...
Dim, through the misty panes and thick green
     light,
As under a green sea, I saw him drowning.

In all my dreams, before my helpless sight,
He plunges at me, guttering, choking, drowning.

If in some smothering dreams you too could
     pace
Behind the wagon that we flung him in,
And watch the white eyes writhing in his face,
His hanging face, like a devil's sick of sin;
If you could hear, at every jolt, the blood
Come gargling from the froth-corrupted lungs,
Obscene as cancer, bitter as the cud
Of vile, incurable sores on innocent tongues, —
My friend, you would not tell with such high zest
To children ardent for some desperate glory,
The old Lie: *Dulce et decorum est*
Pro patria mori.

Wilfred Owen

troopers (*Stosstruppen*, literally "shock troops")—lightly armed but well-trained and highly mobile special units tasked with breaking through enemy lines.

But by late April, the German advance stalled for lack of supplies; meanwhile, American troops had come to the rescue. By summer it was evident that Germany was losing the war of attrition, and in September and October of 1918, in the **Fifth Battle of Ypres,** Allied forces made huge gains. Less than a month later,

Armistice Day (Nov 11, 1918) brought an end to the war to end all wars...until the next war.

World War I claimed the lives of an estimated nine million people; about a million were killed, wounded, or declared missing in action here in the Ypres Salient. By war's end, the British Commonwealth forces had suffered 720,000 casualties, including (officially) 185,000 dead. In the century since, Flanders Fields has recovered, and has become a compelling tourist attraction for the descendants of the victims and survivors of the fighting here. As you tour the place, keep in mind that everything you see—every building, every tree—dates from after 1918.

Sites in Flanders Fields

Ypres (Ieper)

About 40 miles southwest of Bruges is the town most English-speakers call Ypres (EE-preh, though some pronounce it "Wipers"); its official Flemish name is Ieper (YEE-per). By the end of the war, Ypres was so devastated that Winston Churchill advocated keeping it in ruins as a monument to the travesty of warfare. But locals did rebuild, resurrecting its charming main market square (Grote Markt), watched over by the grand and impressive Cloth Hall (which houses the In  Flanders Fields Museum). Today's Ypres is a downright pleasant market town, with a steady stream of mostly British tourists interested in the WWI sites. The **TI,** downstairs in the Cloth Hall, has information on tours (below the museum; April-mid-Nov Mon-Sat 9:00-18:00, Sun 10:00-18:00; mid-Nov-March Mon-Sat 9:00-17:00, Sun 10:00-17:00; tel. 057-239-220, www.ieper.be). Saturday morning is **market** day.

Getting There: If you're based in Bruges without a car, take a tour. Less than an hour away, Ypres is easy for drivers (see route tips under "Planning Your Time," earlier). There's parking right on the main market square, next to the giant Cloth Hall that houses the museum (€0.50/hour, 3-hour limit).

▲▲**In Flanders Fields Museum**—This excellent museum provides a moving look at the battles fought near Ypres. The focus is not on the strategy and the commanders, but on the ordinary people who fought and died here. The evocative descriptions personalize the miserable day-to-day existence in the trenches, and interactive computer displays trace the wartime lives of individual soldiers and citizens. Actual artifacts, engaging descriptions, and thoughtful presentations all bring the war-torn places to life.

The museum began an extensive renovation in 2011 (open during renovation until mid-Nov 2011, when it will close until June of 2012). When the museum reopens, it will expand its focus to the entire Belgian front, rather than just the Ypres Salient. They're planning a renewed focus on specific locations where wartime events took place (tying the museum's exhibits to the actual sites in the surrounding countryside) and a look at the century of remembrances that have passed since the war's end.

As a part of the renovation, they plan to open the Cloth Hall's **belfry** to visitors (200 steps to the top, likely €2 extra), offering a panoramic view of the surrounding countryside, which was so prized and so costly in human lives a century ago.

Cost and Hours: €8; April-mid-Nov daily 10:00-18:00; mid-Nov-March Tue-Sun 10:00-17:00, closed Mon and for three weeks in Jan; last entry one hour before closing; closed mid-Nov 2011 to June 2012; in Ypres' huge Cloth Hall at Grote Markt 34, tel. 057-239-220, www.inflandersfields.be.

▲**Menin Gate**—This impressive Victorian archway is an easy two-block walk from the museum (past the end of Grote Markt). Built

into the old town wall of Ypres, it's etched with the names of British Commonwealth victims of the fighting here. It marks the Menin Road, where many Brits, Canadians, Aussies, and Kiwis left this town for the grueling battlefields and trenches, never to return. The gate is formally a mausoleum for "the Missing," 54,896 troops who likely perished at Flanders Fields but whose remains were never found. To honor the hundreds of thousands of British subjects who gave their lives, every night under the arch at 20:00, a Belgian bugle corps plays the **"Last Post"** to honor the dead.

Other Sites

Most of the following sites are on or near the Menin Road between Ypres and Passchendaele (to the northeast), where the most famous battles took place. The German Cemetery is a bit to the north (but still within a few miles).

▲**Passchendaele Museum**—Although not as extensive or well-presented as the In Flanders Fields Museum, this good exhibit supplements it nicely, with a focus on the strategy and battles of the fighting here. Presented chronologically on the top floor of a chalet-like mansion, it details each advance and retreat from the first German boot on Belgian soil to Armistice Day. You'll see displays of uniforms, medical instruments, and objects illustrating day-to-day life at the front. One exhibit explains—and lets you sniff—the four basic types of poison gas used here. You'll exit through a simulation of the wooden underground "dugout" tunnels used by British forces as their headquarters, after the ground level was so scorched by artillery that nothing was left up above (€5, Feb-Nov daily 10:00-18:00, closed Dec-Jan, Ieperstraat 5, in Zonnebeke about 5 miles east of Ypres and 2 miles west of Passchendaele, tel. 051-770-441, www.passchendaele.be).

▲Tyne Cot Cemetery—This evocative site is the largest cemetery honoring soldiers of the British Commonwealth. It's the final resting place of 11,956 British, Canadian, Australian, New

Zealander, South African, and other British Commonwealth soldiers. Named for a blockhouse on this site that was taken by British forces, who nicknamed it "Tyne Cottage" after the river in North England, the cemetery grounds also hold three German pillbox bunkers. Between those are seemingly endless rows of white headstones, marked with the deceased soldier's name and the emblem from his unit (many of these are regional, such as the maple leaf of Canada). Many graves are marked simply "A soldier of the Great War, known to God." In the center of the cemetery, near the tallest cross (marking the location of Tyne Cottage), notice the higgledy-piggledy arrangement of graves. During the war, when this cottage was a makeshift medic station, this area became an impromptu burial ground. (In contrast, any cemetery that's neat and symmetrical—like the surrounding headstones—dates from after the war.) Running along the top of the cemetery is a wall inscribed with the names of 34,857 "officers and men to whom the fortune of war denied the known and honoured burial given to their comrades in death." Inside the visitors center, you'll see a few artifacts and exhibits about the fighting here (cemetery and visitors center free, open daily 10:00-18:00, closed Dec-Jan, just northeast of Zonnebeke, off of N37 toward Passchendaele, about 6.5 miles east of Ypres, www.cwgc.org).

Hooge Crater—This giant flooded crater, about three miles east of Ypres, was created when British forces detonated a vast store of artillery that destroyed the château they had been using as a headquarters. This desperate act was only partly successful, as the strategic high ground around the château (now a crater) switched hands repeatedly throughout the war. Today the Hooge Crater area has a large British Commonwealth **cemetery**, the **Hooge**

Crater Museum (a touristy exhibit with historic information about the fighting here, €4.50, Tue-Sun 10:00-18:00, closed Mon, www .hoogecrater.com), and—hiding out in the woods just down the road—a hotel/restaurant called **Kasteelhof 't Hooghe,** where you can pay €1 to stroll around the adjacent crater-pond and see some old bunkers and trenches (www.hotelkasteelhofthooghe.be).

German Military Cemetery (Deutscher Soldatenfriedhof) at Langemark—A relatively rare site dedicated to the invaders

of this region, this is the final resting place of 44,324 Central Powers soldiers (along with two Brits who were originally mis-identified). Compared with the gleaming British Commonwealth cemeteries nearby, it's dull and drab. That's because the Treaty of Versailles (which concluded World War I) forbade German WWI cemeteries from using white stones; instead, it uses basalt and even oak. As you wander the cemetery, you'll notice that many of these "German" troops have Slavic names, as they were imported here to fight from the far-eastern corners of the multiethnic Austro-Hungarian Empire. In the center is a mass grave with 25,000 soldiers (free, always open, on the northern outskirts of Langemark, about five miles north/northeast of Ypres).

Other Cemeteries, Memorials, and Craters—The sites listed above are just the beginning. You can't drive a mile or two without passing a monument or a memorial. Tranquil forests suddenly open into clearings with eerily rippled contours—overgrown trenches, pockmarks, and craters. Several nondescript ponds and lakes in the area are actually huge, flooded artillery craters. Joining a tour helps you find some of the more out-of-the-way remnants of the war, but if you're exploring on your own, be sure to get a good guidebook on the region (several are available at local bookstores and tourist offices—find one that suits your needs). If you have a special interest—for example, a nationality or a specific battle an ancestor participated in—just ask around, and you'll find it's easy to seek out related sites.

BRUSSELS
Bruxelles

ORIENTATION TO BRUSSELS

Six hundred years ago, Brussels was just a nice place to stop and buy a waffle on the way to Bruges. With no strategic importance, it was allowed to grow as a free trading town. Today it's a city of 1.8 million, the capital of Belgium, the headquarters of NATO, and the seat of the European Union.

The Bruxelloise are cultured and genteel—even a bit snobby compared to their more earthy Flemish cousins. And yet you may notice an impish sparkle and *joie de vivre,* as evidenced by their love of comic strips (giant comic-strip panels are painted on buildings all over town) and their civic symbol: a statue of a little boy peeing.

Many of the people you'll encounter here, however, aren't Bruxelloise, or even Belgian. As the unofficial capital of Europe, Brussels is multicultural, hosting politicians and businesspeople (not to mention immigrants) from around the globe, and featuring a world of ethnic restaurants.

Brussels enjoyed a Golden Age of peace and prosperity (1400-1550) while England and France were duking it out in the Hundred Years' War. It was then that many of the fine structures that distinguish the city today were built. In the late 1800s, Brussels had another growth spurt, fueled by industrialization, wealth taken from the Belgian Congo, and the exhilaration of the country's recent independence (1830). City expansion peaked at the end of the 19th century, when the "Builder King" Leopold II erected grand monuments and palaces.

Brussels speaks French. Bone up on *bonjour* and *s'il vous plaît* (see the French Survival Phrases in the appendix). Although it's entirely contained within the Flemish-speaking region of Flanders, 65 percent of Bruxelloise speak French as their first language, and only 5 percent speak Flemish. The remaining third are non-natives who speak their own languages (English is the common default). Traditionally, locals spoke a French-Flemish hybrid dialect...but, like French-Flemish unity, that's dying away. Language aside, the whole feel of the town is urban French, not rural Flemish.

Tourists zipping between Amsterdam and Bruges or Paris by train usually miss Brussels, but its rich, chocolaty mix of food and culture pleasantly surprises those who stop.

Planning Your Time

For a city of its size and prominence, Brussels is low on great sights, but high on ambience. On a quick trip, a day and a night are enough for a good first taste (but if you have more time, Brussels has enjoyable ways to fill it). Even better, if you're in a hurry, Brussels can be done as a day trip by train from Bruges, Ghent, or Antwerp (frequent trains, less than an hour from any of these) or a stopover on the Amsterdam-Paris or Amsterdam-Bruges ride (hourly trains). The main reason to visit Brussels—the Grand Place—takes only a few minutes to see. With very limited time, skip the indoor sights and just enjoy a coffee or a beer on the square.

Brussels in Three to Five Hours

Brussels makes a great stopover between trains. First toss your bag in a locker at Central Station and confirm your departure time and station (if you're catching a fast international train, factor in any necessary transit time to the Midi/Zuid/South Station). Then walk about five minutes into town and do this Brussels blitz:

Head directly for the Grand Place and take my Grand Place Walk. To streamline, skip the *Manneken-Pis* until later, and end the walk at the Bourse (stock-exchange building), where you can catch bus #95 to Place Royale/Koningsplein. Enjoy a handful of masterpieces at the Royal Museums of Fine Arts (twin museums—ancient and modern—covered by the same ticket) or the Magritte Museum (devoted entirely to this Belgian pioneer of Modernism). If you're rushing to get back to your train, make a beeline to the station; if you have another hour or two to kill, do my Upper Town Walk, which ends back at the *Manneken-Pis* and the Grand Place. Buy a box of chocolates and a bottle of Belgian beer, and pop the top as your train pulls out of the station. Ahhh!

Brussels in a Day or More

A full day (with one or two overnights) is about right to get a more complete taste of Brussels. With a second day, you can slow things down and really delve into the city. A side-trip to Bruges, Antwerp, or Ghent (each a short train-ride away) is more satisfying than a third day in Brussels.

Get your bearings in the morning with my Grand Place Walk, then tour the Royal Museums of Fine Arts of Belgium and the Magritte Museum (enjoyable to art-lovers and novices alike), and do the Upper Town Walk. With additional time, choose from a good selection of other sights. Very near the Royal Museums, historians enjoy the excellent story of Belgium at the BELvue Museum, and even the tone-deaf can appreciate the Musical Instruments Museum. In the Lower Town, aficionados of the funny pages head for the Belgian Comic Strip Center (a 15-minute walk from the Grand Place). And political-science majors visit the EU Parliament complex for a lesson in Euro-civics. In the evening, consider exploring the fun and colorful streets around Place St-Géry and Ste. Catherine, where you'll find plenty of good dinner options. With more time or a special interest, head out to the museums at the Park of the Cinquantenaire, visit the kitschy former fairgrounds at the giant Atomium, or venture to the adjacent town of Tervuren to tour the Royal Museum of the Belgian Congo and relax in a big park.

Brussels Overview

Central Brussels is surrounded by a ring of roads (which replaced the old city wall) called the Pentagon. (Romantics think it looks more like a heart.) All hotels and nearly all the sights I mention are within this ring. The epicenter holds the main square (the Grand Place), the TI, and Central Station (all within three blocks of one another).

What isn't so apparent from maps is that Brussels is a city divided by altitude. A ridgeline that runs north-south splits the town into the Upper Town (east half, elevation 200 feet) and Lower Town (west, at sea level), with Central Station in between. The Upper Town, traditionally the home of nobility and the rich, has big marble palaces, broad boulevards, and the major museums.

The Lower Town, with the Grand Place (grahn plahs; in Flemish: Grote Markt, HHHROH-teh markt), narrow streets, old buildings, modern shops, colorful eateries, and the famous *Manneken-Pis* peeing-boy statue, has more character. Running along the western edge of the touristic center is a bustling boulevard (Boulevard Anspach/Anspachlaan) that runs over the city's forgotten river. Just beyond that—past a block or two of high-rise ugliness—is the lively market square called Place St-Géry/Sint-Goriksplein, and a charming village-within-a-city huddled around the old fish market: the Ste. Catherine neighborhood, home to several recommended hotels and restaurants.

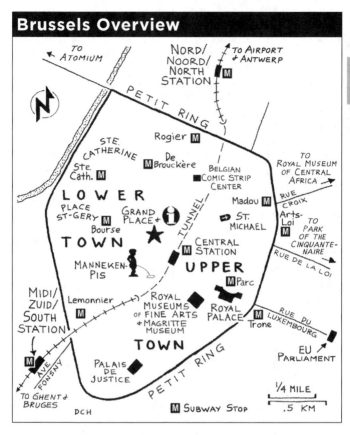

Brussels Overview

TO ATOMIUM

NORD/ NOORD/ NORTH STATION

TO AIRPORT & ANTWERP

PETIT RING

Rogier

STE. CATHERINE

Ste. Cath.

De Brouckère

BELGIAN COMIC STRIP CENTER

TO ROYAL MUSEUM OF CENTRAL AFRICA

RUE CROIX

Madou

Arts-Loi

TO PARK OF THE CINQUANTE-NAIRE

L O W E R

PLACE ST-GERY

GRAND PLACE

Bourse

ST. MICHAEL

RUE DE LA LOI

T O W N

MANNEKEN-PIS

CENTRAL STATION

U P P E R

Parc

MIDI/ ZUID/ SOUTH STATION

Lemonnier

ROYAL MUSEUMS of FINE ARTS & MAGRITTE MUSEUM

ROYAL PALACE

RUE DU LUXEMBOURG

Trone

T O W N

EU PARLIAMENT

TO GHENT & BRUGES

AVE. FONSNY

PALAIS DE JUSTICE

PETIT RING

¼ MILE

.5 KM

DCH

Subway Stop

Outside the pentagon-shaped center, sprawling suburbs and vast green zones contain more tourist attractions. To the east are the European Parliament and, beyond that, the Park of the Cinquantenaire (Royal Museum of the Army and Military History, Autoworld, and a lesser art museum). And far to the north is the 1958 World's Fair site, with the Atomium and Mini-Europe.

Because the city is officially bilingual, most of Brussels' street signs and maps are in both French and Flemish; I've tried to follow suit in this text, but due to space constraints, on my maps I've generally only given the French name. Because the languages are so different (French is a Romance language, Flemish is Germanic), many places have two names that barely resemble each other (for example, Marché-aux-Herbes/Grasmarkt, or Place Royale/Koningsplein). This can make navigating the city confusing. Use one of the good local maps (such as the TI's free map), which list both languages, so you'll know both street names to look for.

Tourist Information

Brussels has two competing TIs (indicative of Belgium's latent French-Flemish tension). The TI at Rue du Marché-aux-Herbes/Grasmarkt 63 covers **Brussels and Flanders,** with a good room-recommendation service (July-Aug daily 9:00-19:00; April-June and Sept Mon-Sat 9:00-18:00, Sun 10:00-17:00; Oct-March Mon-Sat 9:00-17:00, Sun 10:00-16:00; three blocks downhill from Central Station, tel. 02-504-0390, www.visitflanders.com, fun Europe store nearby). They offer free Wi-Fi and one Internet terminal where you can get online free for up to 15 minutes (and print a few pages—handy for checking in for a flight and printing boarding passes).

The other TI, which focuses on just the **city of Brussels** (no outlying towns), is inside the Town Hall on the Grand Place (Mon-Sat 9:00-18:00; Sun 9:00-18:00 April-Nov, 10:00-14:00 Dec, and closed Sun Jan-March; tel. 02-513-8940, www.brussels international.be).

Both TIs have countless fliers. Day-trippers should pick up a free city map and a public transit map. The €4 *Brussels Guide & Map* booklet is worthwhile if you want a better map (map also sold separately for €0.50), a more complete explanation of the city's many museums, and a series of neighborhood walks (including ones focusing on Art Nouveau, comic strips, and shopping). For current listings of concerts and other entertainment options, look for the free weekly magazines *Agenda* (in English, French, and Flemish) and *Brussels Unlimited* (only in English).

Sightseeing Deals: The **Brussels Card,** sold at the TIs, provides unlimited public transportation and free entrance to nearly all the major museums (€24/24 hours, €34/48 hours, €40/72 hours, also sold at museums, public transportation offices, and some hotels, www.brusselscard.be). If you're in town for less than a day, it's unlikely this pass will pay for itself; but with more time here, busy sightseers will get their money's worth. The TIs also offer a deal called **Must of Brussels**—you pay €18 for 10 vouchers that you can mix and match for discounted entries into top sights. Though complicated to figure out, it could save you a few euros (www.mustofbrussels.com).

Alternative Tourist Information: The excellent, welcoming **USE-IT** information office, which is geared toward youthful backpackers, offers free Internet access and Wi-Fi, free coffee and tea, and in-the-know advice about Brussels and other Belgian destinations, including Bruges, Antwerp, and Ghent (Mon-Sat 10:00-13:00 & 14:00-18:00, closed Sun, Rue de la Fourche/Greepstraat 50, www.use-it.be). They also publish free user-friendly maps of Brussels and several other Belgian cities; all of their maps are packed with homegrown insight.

Arrival in Brussels

By Train

Brussels has three different stations: Centraal/Central, Nord/
Noord/North, and Midi/Zuid/South. Although none is officially
the "main" train station, Central Station (a short walk from the
Grand Place) is by far the easiest for arriving sightseers, whereas
Midi/Zuid/South Station is the only one served by high-speed
trains (with the fastest connections to Paris, Amsterdam, and
Germany). If you're arriving on one of these fast trains, you'll enter
the city through Midi/Zuid/South Station; all other trains stop
at all three stations. No matter how you arrive, your goal is eventually to reach Central Station (pay close attention and ask your
conductor for help to ensure you get off at the right stop).

Nord/Noord/North Station

Any train that goes through North Station (surrounded by a seedy
red light district, far from any significant sightseeing) will also
stop at the other two. Don't bother getting off at North Station—
disembark at Central Station instead.

Midi/Zuid/South Station

About a mile and a half southwest of the city center, this station's
various names mystify tourists (especially since *midi* is French for
"middle," not "south"). But as Brussels' lone station for speedy,
long-distance trains, it's considered the city's primary international hub. Fortunately, the station is a lot more user-friendly than
its name.

South Station serves the fastest high-speed connections:
Eurostar (to/from London); Thalys (to/from Amsterdam, Paris,
Köln in Germany, and a few other destinations—such as Marseille,
France, in the summer and the French Alps in the winter); TGV
(to/from Paris' Charles de Gaulle Airport—but not central Paris,
as Thalys has a monopoly there, and then on to destinations in
southern France); and ICE (to/from Frankfurt). These special fast
trains stop only at South Station, not at the other two Brussels
stations. All other trains—including slower trains to many of these
same destinations, and trains to anywhere in Belgium—stop at all
three stations. Unless your train only stops here, get off at Central
Station instead (explained later).

South Station's tracks are connected by a long, gloomy, gray-
steel concourse with ample computer screens showing upcoming
trains. High-speed trains use tracks 1-6 (1-2 for Eurostar and
3-6 for the others). The station has plenty of luggage lockers
(€3-4, between tracks 6 and 7), as well as three separate Travel
Centre ticket offices (for domestic, international, and interna-
tional/immediate departures). The area around South Station

is a rough-and-tumble immigrant neighborhood (marked by its towering Ferris wheel).

Getting from Midi/Zuid/South Station to Central Station: If you must disembark at South Station, your first step on arrival will be to make your way to Central Station. It's fast and easy by train, but also possible by taxi.

Trains zip under the city, connecting all three stations every few minutes or so. The €1.70 fare between the stations is covered by any train ticket into or out of Brussels (or an activated railpass). Scan the computer departure screens for trains leaving in the next few minutes. While these boards usually don't list Central Station as a destination, trains headed for any of the following places will stop there: the Airport, Alost/Aalst, Antwerpen, Leuven, Liège, Namur, and many others. If you see a train going to any of these places in the next few minutes, just head to that track. (But note that trains headed in the opposite direction—including those to Ghent and Bruges—do *not* stop at Central Station.)

Alternatively, you can take a **taxi** from South Station into the city center. It should cost you no more than €10; however, cabbies from this station are notorious for taking a roundabout route to overcharge arriving tourists. If you do opt for a taxi, insist on the meter, follow the route on a map, and if the total fare seems too high, enlist the help of your hotel receptionist.

Centraal/Central Station

This station, nearest to the sights and my recommended hotels, has handy services: a small grocery store, fast food, waiting rooms, and luggage lockers (€3-4, between tracks 3 and 4). Walking from Central Station to the Grand Place takes about five minutes: Exit the station from the top floor (to the left of the ticket windows), where you'll see Le Meridien Hôtel across the square. Pass through the arch of Le Meridien Hôtel, turn right, and walk one block downhill on l'Infante Isabelle street to a small square with a fountain (officially "Herb Market"—Rue du Marché-aux-Herbes/ Grasmarkt—but nicknamed "Agora"). For the Grand Place, turn left at the far end of the little square. Or, to head directly to the TI, exit the small square at the far end and continue straight for one block, then look left.

Competitive hop-on, hop-off tourist buses depart from just in front of Central Station (you'll meet ticket hustlers as you leave). You could hop on one of these buses upon arrival to orient yourself from the top deck (see "Tours in Brussels," later).

By Plane

Brussels is served by two airports. Most flights use the primary

Brussels Airport, a.k.a. Zaventem; no-frills carriers use the Brussels South Charleroi Airport.

Helpful Hints

Theft Alert: Brussels is a huge, international, multiethnic city—the type of place that attracts diplomats, tourists...and thieves. As you would in any big city, keep your wits about you and wear a money belt. And though the tourist zone—the area within the pentagon-shaped ring road—is basically safe at any hour of day or night, muggings do occur in some rough-and-tumble areas farther afield. (Near the Midi/Zuid/South Station is a mostly Muslim immigrant neighborhood; near the North Station is a red-light district. Locals joke that as you walk from one end of town to the other, you go from seeing women entirely covered to women entirely uncovered.) If you're venturing beyond the city center, get local advice about safety—and, if you're outside of this area after midnight, when the Métro shuts down, consider taking a taxi back to your hotel.

Sightseeing Schedules: Brussels' most important museums are closed on Monday. Of course, the city's single best sight—the Grand Place—is always open. You can also enjoy a bus tour any day of the week, or visit the more far-flung sights (which *are* open on Monday), such as the Atomium/Mini-Europe and the European Parliament. Most importantly, this is a city to browse and wander.

Internet Access: The **USE-IT** information office (listed earlier) has four free Internet terminals and free Wi-Fi; the **Brussels and Flanders TI** on Rue du Marché-aux-Herbes/Grasmarkt has one Internet terminal and offers 15 minutes free (plus unlimited free Wi-Fi). There's also an **Internet café** in a dreary urban area between the Grand Place and Ste. Catherine (€1.50/hour, also cheap calls and printing, calling cabins downstairs, computer terminals upstairs, daily 9:30-23:15, 18 Rue Marché aux Poulets/Kiekenmarkt).

Laundry: Coin-op launderettes aren't too hard to find. There's one near the Grand Place at Rue du Midi/Zuidstraat 65 (daily 7:00-21:00, change machine) and another in Ste. Catherine, at Rue Flandres/Vlaamsesteenweg 51 (daily 7:00-22:00, no change machine).

Travel Bookstore: Anticyclone des Açores has a wide selection of maps and travel books, including many in English (Mon-Sat 11:00-18:00, closed Sun, Rue Fossé aux Loups/Wolvengracht 34, tel. 02-217-5246).

Getting Around Brussels

Most of central Brussels' sights can be reached on foot. But public transport is handy for connecting the train stations, climbing to the Upper Town (bus #95 from the Bourse), or visiting sights outside the central core. To reach these outlying sights, such as the European Parliament, take the Métro or jump on a hop-on, hop-off tour bus from Central Station (described under "Tours in Brussels," next page; check tour bus route map to make sure it covers the sights you want to see).

By Métro, Bus, Tram, and Train: A single €1.70 ticket is good for one hour on all public transportation—Métro, buses, trams, and even trains shuttling between Brussels' three train stations. Validate your ticket when you enter, feeding it into one of the breadbox-size orange machines. Notice the time when you first stamp it (you have an hour), and stamp your ticket again if you transfer lines. Transit info: tel. 02-515-2000, www.mivb.be.

A five-ride card costs €7.30 (€1.46/ride), and a 10-ride card is €12.50. An all-day pass is €4.50—cheaper than three single tickets—and on Sat-Sun and holidays, this pass covers two people. A 72-hour ticket costs €9.50. (Skip the Mobib, a prepaid card for public transit that's practical only for locals.)

Buy individual tickets at newsstands, in Métro stations (vending machines accept credit cards or coins), or (for €0.30 extra) from the bus driver. Get multiride cards and passes from the Brussels and Flanders TI or at Métro stations. The excellent, free *Métro Tram Bus Plan* is available at either TI or any Métro station.

Like the streets, Brussels' transit stops are labeled in both French and Flemish (unless the spelling is the same in both languages); I've followed suit in this book.

Brussels' Métro has four lines: Line 1 runs west-east (from Gare de l'Ouest/Weststation to Stockel/Stokkel); the circular line 2 starts and ends at Simonis; line 5 runs west-east from Erasme/ Erasmus to Herrmann-Debroux; and line 6 starts at Roi Baudouin/ Koning Boudewijn in the northwest, then ties into the circular line at Simonis. A series of tram lines run north-south through the city center, connecting the Métro lines and the North, Central, and Midi/Zuid/South train stations; two of these are considered part of the Métro (lines 3 and 4). Buses go where the Métro and trams don't (buses marked *Noctis* travel at night, after other transit stops running).

Near the Grand Place are two transportation hubs: Central Station and the Bourse. If you're staying at a hotel northwest of the Grand Place, you've got good access to the Métro system via the Ste. Catherine/Sint-Katelijne and De Brouckère stops.

By Taxi: Drivers in big-city Brussels are happy to take you for a ride; find out the approximate cost to your destination before you head out. Cabbies charge a €2.40 drop fee, as well as €1.50 per additional kilometer. After 22:00, they hit you with a €2 surcharge. You'll pay about €10 to ride from the center to the European Parliament. Convenient taxi stands are at the Bourse (near the Grand Place), at the "Agora" square near the Grand Place (Rue du Marché-aux-Herbes/Grasmarkt), and at Place du Grand Sablon (in the Upper Town). To call a cab, try **Taxi Bleu** (tel. 02-268-0000) or **Autolux** (tel. 02-512-3123).

By Bike: The city of Brussels subsidizes a network of cheap bikes designed to be borrowed for short rides within the city. The program, called **Villo,** has rental stations around town. After you register at the automated kiosk with your credit card (€1.50/day, €7/week), you can borrow bikes at will for short durations, then drop them off at any other station (free for up to 30 minutes, €0.50/30-60 minutes, €1/1-1.5 hours, €2/1.5-2 hours, www.villo .be). Stations with an automated kiosk also show you which nearby stations have bikes available, and how many. But bike stands at higher altitudes (in the Upper Town) are often empty, whereas they're full—surprise, surprise—at lower altitudes (in the Lower Town).

Tours in Brussels

Hop-On, Hop-Off Bus Tours—Various companies offer nearly identical introductory city tours. The 1.5-hour loop and recorded narration give you a once-over-lightly of the city from the top deck (open on sunny days) of a double-decker bus. You can hop on and off for 24 hours with one ticket, but schedules are sparse (figure €18-20 for each company, about 2/hour, times listed on each flier; all companies run roughly April-Oct daily 10:00-16:00, Sat until 17:00; Nov-March daily 10:00-15:00, Sat until 16:00). Except for the trip out to the European Parliament and Cinquantenaire Park (which hosts the military and auto museums), I'd just stay on to enjoy the views and the minimal commentary. The fiercely competitive companies often have hustlers at Central Station trying to get you on board (offering "student" discounts to customers of all ages). The handiest starting points are Central Station and the Bourse. The companies are **City Tours** (tel. 02-513-7744, www .brussels-city-tours.com), **CitySightseeing/Open Tours** (tel. 02-466-1111, www.citysightseeingbrussel.be), and **Golden Tours** (mobile 0486-053-981, www.goldentours.be).

Bus Tours—City Tours also offers a typical three-hour guided (in up to five languages) bus tour, providing you an easy way to get the grand perspective on Brussels. You start with a walk around the Grand Place, then jump on a tour bus (€27, year-round daily at 10:00 and 14:00, they'll pick you up at your hotel or depart from their office a block off Grand Place at Rue du Marché-aux-Herbes 82; you can buy tickets there, at TI, or in your hotel; tel. 02-513-7744, www.brussels-city-tours.com). You'll get off the bus at the Atomium for a quick photo stop.

Private Guide—Claude and Dominique Janssens are a father-and-son team who lead tours both in Brussels and to other Belgian cities, including Bruges, Ghent, and Antwerp (€110/3 hours, €230/full day plus €25 for lunch, Claude's mobile 0485-025-423, Dominique's mobile 0486-451-155, www.discover-b.be, claude@discover-b.be).

SIGHTS IN BRUSSELS

The Grand Place may be Brussels' top sight, but the city offers a variety of museums, big and small, to fill your time here. I've divided the sights between the Lower Town, the Upper Town, and the outskirts.

In the Lower Town

On the Grand Place

Brussels' Grand Place—as well as some of the sights fronting it, including the Town Hall, City Museum, and chocolate shops—are described in more detail in the ✪ Grand Place Walk chapter.

▲▲▲**Grand Place**—Brussels' main square, aptly called the Grand Place (grahn plahs; in Flemish: Grote Markt, HHHROH-teh markt), is the heart of the old town and Brussels' greatest sight. Any time of day, it's worth swinging by to see what's going on. Concerts, flower markets, sound-and-light shows, endless people-watching—it entertains (as do the streets around it). The museums on the square are well-advertised but dull.

Town Hall (Hôtel de Ville)—With the Grand Place's tallest spire, this is the square's centerpiece, but its interior is no big deal. Admission is only possible with a 45-minute English tour, which also covers city history and the building's tapestries and architecture (€3, Tue-Wed at 15:15, Sun at 10:45 and 12:15 except no Sun tours Oct-March). Only 25 people are allowed per tour; assure a spot by buying tickets from the guide exactly 40 minutes before the tour starts (in the courtyard behind the spire).

▲**City Museum (Musée de la Ville de Bruxelles)**—Inside the King's House (Maison du Roi) building, across the Grand Place from the Town Hall, is the one museum on the square that's

Brussels

Legend:

|||| Stairs

Ⓜ Subway Stop

Ⓑ Tour Bus Departure Points (2)

➡ 5 Min. Walk - Central Station to Grand Place

200 YARDS

200 METERS

DCH

actually worth visiting. The museum's top floor has a roomful of goofy costumes the *Manneken* statue has pissed through (and an engrossing video of tourists' reactions to the statue), the middle floor features maps and models of old Brussels, and the bottom floor has some old artwork.

Cost and Hours: €3, borrow English descriptions in each room, Tue-Sun 10:00-17:00, closed Mon, Grand Place, tel. 02-279-4350. For local history, the best choice is not this museum, but the BELvue Museum.

▲**Chocolate Shops on the Grand Place**—For many, the best thing about the Grand Place is the chocolate sold at the five venerable chocolate shops: Godiva, Neuhaus, Galler, Leonidas, and Corné Port-Royal (shops generally open Mon-Sat 9:00-22:00, Sun 10:00-22:00). Each has inviting displays and sells mixes of 100 grams (your choice of 6-8 pieces) or individual pieces for about €1.60. It takes a lot of sampling to judge. See the "choco-crawl" described in the Grand Place Walk chapter.

Brewery Museum—This little bar-like place has one room of old brewing paraphernalia and one room of new, plus a beer video in English. It's pretty lame...but a good excuse for a beer (€6 includes an unnamed local beer, daily 10:00-17:00, Dec-March Sat-Sun opens at 12:00, Grand Place 10, tel. 02-511-4987).

Museum of Cocoa and Chocolate—This touristy exhibit, to the right of Town Hall, is a delightful concept and tries hard, but it's overpriced at €5.50 for three floors of meager displays, a ho-hum video, a look at a "chocolate master" at work (live demos 2/hour), and a choco-sample (Tue-Sun 10:00-16:30, until 17:00 July-Aug, closed Mon, Rue de la Tête d'Or 9, tel. 02-514-2048, www.mucc.be).

Near the Grand Place

▲▲*Manneken-Pis*—Brussels is a great city with a cheesy mascot: a statue of a little boy urinating (apparently symbolizing the city's irreverence and love of the good life). Read up on his story at any postcard stand. He's three short blocks off the Grand Place, but, for exact directions, take my Grand Place Walk; look for small, white *Manneken-Pis* signs; or just ask a local, *"Où est le Manneken-Pis?"* (oo ay luh man-ay-kehn peese). The little squirt may be wearing some clever outfit, as costumes are sent to Brussels from around the world. Cases full of these are on display in the City Museum (described earlier).

For more details, ✪ see the Grand Place Walk chapter.

Costume and Lace Museum—This is worthwhile only to those few who have devoted their lives to the making or wearing of lace (€3, Mon-Tue and Thu-Fri 10:00-12:30 & 13:30-17:00, Sat-Sun

SIGHTS IN BRUSSELS

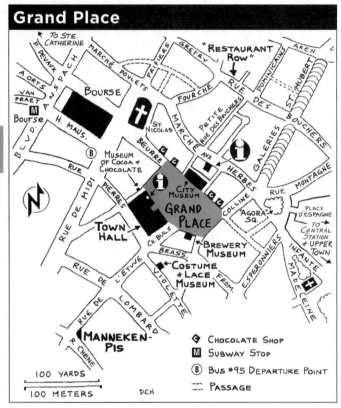

Grand Place

TO STE. CATHERINE

"RESTAURANT ROW"

BOURSE

Bourse Ⓜ

MUSEUM OF COCOA & CHOCOLATE

CITY MUSEUM

GRAND PLACE

TOWN HALL

BREWERY MUSEUM

COSTUME & LACE MUSEUM

MANNEKEN-PIS

100 YARDS

100 METERS

DCH

⬧ CHOCOLATE SHOP
Ⓜ SUBWAY STOP
Ⓑ BUS #95 DEPARTURE POINT
... PASSAGE

14:00-17:00, closed Wed, Rue de la Violette 12, a block off the Grand Place, tel. 02-213-4450).

West of the Grand Place

These two fun-to-explore neighborhoods, just across the busy Boulevard Anspach from the Bourse, offer some of Brussels' most appealing restaurants (far less touristy than those near the Grand Place). Ste. Catherine is also a fine place to sleep. If you're look-ing for a bustling nighttime neighborhood full of inviting eateries and bars, you'll enjoy strolling these two areas and the five-minute walk between them.

Ste. Catherine and the Old Fish Market (Vieux Marché aux Poissons/Vismet)—Two blocks northwest of the Bourse is the ragtag Church of Ste. Catherine, which marks an inviting "village in the city" area with great eating options. The church itself is falling apart—during its construction, the architect got the commission for the Place of Justice in the Upper Town, and rushed to complete this church so he could begin the more lucrative new job as quickly as possible. In front of the church stretches the long, skinny former fish market, lined with a range of upscale fish restaurants. Alongside the church is Place Ste. Catherine/ Sint-Katelijneplein, with more restaurants, bars, and the city's best cheap-and-fast lunch options (including a charming little cheese shop and a pair of seafood bars).

Place St-Géry/Sint-Goriksplein—This square was actually once an island, and the market hall in the middle of the square evokes a time when goods—which were offloaded a few blocks away, at the old fish market (see above)—were brought here for sale. Today the hall houses a café and special exhibits. On Sunday mornings, the surrounding square is filled with a comics market. Across from the southwest corner of the hall, at #23 (next to the *Au Lion d'Or* information board), duck through the little gateway to find a relaxing courtyard. You might see businesspeople dozing on their lunch break here, in this oasis in the heart of the city. At the far end of the courtyard you'll see a small stretch of the river that used to be Brussels' trading lifeline, but was long ago covered over and forgotten.

North of Central Station

▲**St. Michael's Cathedral**—One of Europe's classic Gothic churches, built between roughly 1200 and 1500, Brussels' cathedral is made from white stone and topped by twin towers. For nearly 1,000 years, it's been the most important church in this largely Catholic country. (Whereas the Netherlands went in a Protestant direction in the 1500s, Belgium remains 80 percent Catholic—although only about 20 percent attend Mass.)

The white-themed nave is bare but impressive, with a few nice stained-glass windows and a marvelous carved pulpit of Adam and Eve supporting the preacher. On top, St. Michael stabs Satan in serpent form.

This church is where royal weddings and funerals take place. Photographs (to the right of the entrance) show the funeral of the popular King Baudouin, who died in 1993. He was succeeded by his younger brother, Albert II (whose face is on Belgium's euro coins). Albert will be succeeded by his son, Prince Philippe. Traditionally, the ruler was always a male, but in 1992 the constitution was changed to allow the oldest child of either gender—boy or girl—to take the throne. In 1999, Prince Philippe and his bride, Mathilde—after a civil ceremony at the Town Hall—paraded up

Brussels at a Glance

▲▲▲**Grand Place** Main square and spirited heart of the Lower Town, surrounded by mediocre museums and delectable chocolate shops. **Hours:** Always open. See page 105.

▲▲▲**Royal Museums of Fine Arts of Belgium** Museums displaying ancient art (14th-18th centuries) and modern art (19th-20th centuries). **Hours:** Tue-Sun 10:00-17:00, closed Mon. See page 114.

▲▲*Manneken-Pis* World-famous statue of a leaky little boy. **Hours:** Always peeing. See page 107.

▲▲**Magritte Museum** Biographical collection of works by the prominent Belgian Surrealist painter René Magritte. **Hours:** Tue-Sun 10:00-17:00, Wed until 20:00, closed Mon. See page 116.

▲▲**BELvue Museum** Interesting Belgian history museum with a focus on the popular royal family. **Hours:** Tue-Fri 10:00-17:00, Sat-Sun 10:00-18:00, closed Mon. See page 117.

▲**City Museum** Costumes worn by the *Manneken-Pis* statue and models of Brussels' history. **Hours:** Tue-Sun 10:00-17:00, closed Mon. See page 105.

▲**Chocolate on Grand Place** Choco-crawl through Godiva, Neuhaus, Galler, Leonidas, and Corné Port-Royal. **Hours:** Generally Mon-Sat 9:00-22:00, Sun 10:00-22:00. See page 107.

▲**St. Michael's Cathedral** White-stone Gothic church where Belgian royals are married and buried. **Hours:** Mon-Fri 7:00-18:00, Sat-Sun 8:30-18:00, until 19:00 in summer. See page 109.

▲**Belgian Comic Strip Center** Homage to hometown heroes including the Smurfs, Tintin, and Lucky Luke. **Hours:** Tue-Sun 10:00-18:00, closed Mon. See page 112.

▲**Musical Instruments Museum** Exhibits with more than 1,500 instruments, complete with audio. **Hours:** Tue-Fri 9:30-16:45, Sat-Sun 10:00-16:45, closed Mon. See page 116.

▲**European Parliament** Soaring home of Europe's governing body. **Hours:** Mon-Thu 9:00-17:15, Fri 9:00-13:00, closed Sat-Sun; audioguide tours Mon-Thu at 10:00 and 15:00, additional tours

July-Aug—last departure at 16:00, Fri at 10:00 only. See page 119.

▲**Royal Army and Military History Museum** Vast collection of weaponry and uniforms. **Hours:** Tue-Sun 9:00-16:45, closed Mon. See page 123.

▲**Autoworld** Hundreds of historic vehicles, including Mr. Benz's 1886 motorized tricycle. **Hours:** Daily April-Sept 10:00-18:00, Oct-March 10:00-17:00. See page 123.

▲**Royal Museum of Central Africa** Excellent but far-flung exhibit about the former Belgian Congo, featuring ethnology, artifacts, and wildlife. **Hours:** Tue-Fri 10:00-17:00, Sat-Sun 10:00-18:00, closed Mon. See page 125.

Town Hall Focal point of the Grand Place, with arresting spire but boring interior. **Hours:** Tours depart Tue-Wed at 15:15, Sun at 10:45 and 12:15, no Sun tours Oct-March. See page 105.

Costume and Lace Museum World-famous Brussels lace, as well as outfits, embroideries, and accessories from the 17th-20th centuries. **Hours:** Mon-Tue and Thu-Fri 10:00-12:30 & 13:30-17:00, Sat-Sun 14:00-17:00, closed Wed. See page 107.

Ste. Catherine Neighborhood and Place St-Géry Pleasant areas with fun eateries west of the Grand Place. **Hours:** Always buzzing. See page 108.

Royal Belgian Institute of Natural Sciences Europe's largest dinosaur gallery. **Hours:** Tue-Fri 9:30-17:00, Sat-Sun 10:00-18:00, closed Mon. See page 122.

Royal Museum of Art and History Eclectic but unexciting art museum. **Hours:** Tue-Fri 9:30-17:00, Sat-Sun 10:00-17:00, closed Mon. See page 124.

Atomium Giant homage to the atomic age with fun exhibit and panorama deck. **Hours:** Daily 10:00-18:00, later in summer. See page 124.

Mini-Europe Models of 350 famous European landmarks. **Hours:** Easter-Sept daily 9:30-18:00, July-Aug until 20:00; Oct-Dec 10:00-18:00; closed Jan-Easter. See page 125.

Shopping in Brussels

The obvious temptations—available absolutely everywhere—are **chocolate** and **lace.** (For tips on specific shops for each one, see the Grand Place Walk chapter.) Other popular Brussels souvenirs include EU gear (flags, T-shirts, etc., with the gold circle of stars on a blue background) and miniature reproductions of the *Manneken-Pis.*

To get beyond the touristy city center, consider browsing along some of the following streets:

Rue Neuve/Nieuwstraat, a few blocks north of the Grand Place, is where you'll find big department stores and other international shops. The giant **City2** complex on this street is the downtown's primary modern shopping mall.

Antoine Dansaert street, directly across the boulevard from the Bourse, is lined with boutiques and galleries.

The somewhat seedy **Marolles neighborhood** is well-known for its secondhand shops. Rue Blaes/Blaesstraat and Rue Haute/Hoogstraat, which run southwest from near the old Tour d'Angle (described in the Upper Town Walk chapter) to the Midi/Zuid/South Train Station, are lined with several characteristic stores. There's a lively flea market each morning (7:00-14:00, best on weekends) on Place du Jeu de Balle/Vossenplein, just off of Rue Blaes/Blaesstraat.

here for a two-hour Catholic ceremony with all the trimmings. Their daughter Elisabeth, born in 2001, is in line to become Belgium's queen.

Before leaving, pause on the outer porch to enjoy the great view of the Town Hall spire with its gold statue of St. Michael.

Cost and Hours: Free, but small fees to visit the underwhelming crypt and treasury, Mon-Fri 7:00-18:00, Sat-Sun 8:30-18:00, until 19:00 in summer.

▲Belgian Comic Strip Center (Centre Belge de la Bande Dessinée)—Belgians are as proud of their comics as they are of their beer, lace, and chocolates. Something about the comic medium resonates with the wry and artistic-yet-unpretentious Belgian sensibility. Belgium has produced some of the world's most popular comic characters, including the Smurfs, Tintin, and Lucky Luke. You'll find these, and many less famous local comics, at the Comic Strip Center.

Even if you don't have time or interest to visit the museum's collection, pop in to the lobby to

see the groundbreaking Art Nouveau building (a former department store designed in 1903 by Belgian architect Victor Horta), browse through comics in the bookshop, and snap a photo with a three-foot-tall Smurf. That's enough for many people. Kids might find the museum, like, totally boring, but those who appreciate art in general will enjoy this sometimes humorous, sometimes probing, often beautiful medium. The displays are mostly in French and Flemish, but there is some English. The free, essential English guidebooklet describes the comics-making process (comparing it to the filmmaking process) and has short bios of famous cartoonists.

The collection changes often, but no matter what's on you'll see how comics are made and watch early animated films. The heart of the collection is the golden age of comics in the 1950s and 60s. You'll likely see a sprawling exhibit on Tintin, the intrepid young reporter with the button eyes and wavy shock of hair, launched in 1929 by Hergé and much loved by older Europeans (see sidebar on next page). Brussels' own Peyo (a.k.a. Pierre Culliford, 1928-1992) invented the Smurfs—the little blue forest creatures that stand "three apples high." First popular across much Europe, especially in Belgium (where they're known as Les Schtroumpfs), the Smurfs became well-known to a generation of Americans after they starred in Hanna-Barbera's 1980s televised cartoons. The cowboy Lucky Luke (by Morris, a.k.a. Maurice De Bevere, 1923-2001) exemplifies Belgians' fascination for exotic locales, especially America's Wild West.

The top floor's temporary exhibits are often dedicated to "serious" comics, where more adult themes and high-quality drawing aspire to turn kids' stuff into that "Ninth Art." These works can be grimly realistic, openly erotic or graphic, or darker in tone, often featuring flawed antiheroes. The museum's bookstore is nearly as interesting, giving you the chance to page through reproductions of classic comics.

Cost and Hours: €7.50, Tue-Sun 10:00-18:00, closed Mon, 10-minute walk from the Grand Place to Rue des Sables 20, tel. 02-219-1980, www.comicscenter.net.

Getting There: From Central Station, walk north along the big boulevard, then turn left down the stairs at the giant comic character.

Nearby: The related **Marc Sleen Museum,** across the street, is dedicated to one Belgian cartoonist in particular. Sleen's big-nosed, caricatured drawings are recognizable even to many Americans, and is oh-so-typically Belgian. His *Adventures of Nero and Co.,* which he churned out in two strips a day for a staggering 55 years, holds the record for the longest-running comic by a single artist. Still, the collection is worth a visit only to his fans (€1 extra

Tintin 101

Although relatively unknown in the United States, the Belgian comic character Tintin is beloved to several generations of Europeans who have grown up reading of his adventures.

In 1929, a French-speaking Brussels comics artist named Georges Rémi (1907-1983) created a dedicated young reporter with a shock of blond hair who's constantly getting into and out of misadventures. The artist reversed his initials to create the pseudonym Hergé (the French pronunciation for "R.G."). A precise artist, Hergé used a simple, uncluttered style called *ligne claire* ("clear line").

Combining fantasy, mystery, and sci-fi, with a dash of humor, the Tintin stories quickly found an appreciative audience. *The Adventures of Tintin* spanned 47 years and 24 books (selling some 200 million copies—and counting—in 50 languages). Tintin's popularity continues even today, as nostalgic parents buy the comics they grew up on for their own kids.

Tintin (pronounced a nasal "tan-tan" in French) is the smart, upbeat, inquisitive, noble, brave-but-not-foolhardy young man whose adventures propel the plot. His newspaper sends him on assignments all over the world. **Snowy** (Milou in French), Tintin's loyal fox terrier, is his constant canine companion—and often saves the day. The grizzled, grouchy, heavy-drinking **Captain Haddock** is as cynical as Tintin is optimistic, with a penchant

with Comic Strip Center entry, or €2.50 alone, Tue-Sun 11:00-18:00, closed Mon, tel. 02-219-1980, www.marc-sleen.be).

In the Upper Town

Brussels' grandiose Upper Town, with its huge palace, is described in the ✪ Upper Town Walk chapter. Along that walk, you'll pass the following sights.

▲▲▲**Royal Museums of Fine Arts of Belgium (Musées Royaux des Beaux-Arts de Belgique)**—This sprawling complex is worth visiting for its twin museums that show off the country's best all-around art collection (as well as the Magritte Museum—described next—which is in the same complex). The **Museum of Ancient Art** and the **Museum of Modern Art** are covered by the same ticket (enter through the main foyer for both). The Museum of Ancient Art—featuring Flemish and Belgian art of the 14th-18th centuries—is packed with a dazzling collec-

for colorful curses ("Blistering barnacles!"). **Professor Calculus** (a.k.a. Professeur Tournesol) is as brilliant as he is absentminded and hard of hearing, and comic relief is provided by the bumbling, nearly identical detectives called **Thomson and Thompson** (Dupont et Dupond).

Throughout his swashbuckling adventures, Tintin travels far and wide to many exotic destinations. Hergé has been acclaimed for his meticulous research—he studied up on the actual places he portrayed, and tried to avoid basing his stories on assumptions or stereotypes (though by today's standards, some of the comics still betray an ugly Eurocentrism—one of the earliest, *Tintin in the Congo*, Hergé himself later acknowledged was regretfully racist).

And though the supporting characters are dynamic and colorful, Tintin himself has a rather bland personality. His expressions are usually indistinct (Hergé wanted the young reader to project his or her own emotions onto Tintin's blank-canvas face). While presumably a teenager, Tintin's age is unclear—at times we imagine him to be a young boy, while others he's seen drinking a beer, piloting a plane, or living in his own apartment (we never meet his family, if he has one). All of this is intentional: Hergé's style subconsciously encourages each reader to put him- or herself in Tintin's everyman shoes.

While Tintin has found success in the United States elusive, things might be changing. Stephen Spielberg's film *The Adventures of Tintin: Secret of the Unicorn*—created in partnership with *Lord of the Rings* filmmaker Peter Jackson, and using the motion-capture animation technique made famous by those films and *Avatar*—is scheduled for release in 2011.

tion of masterpieces by Van der Weyden, Brueghel, Bosch, and Rubens. The Museum of Modern Art gives visitors an easy-to-enjoy walk through the art of the 19th and 20th centuries, from Neoclassical to Surrealism. Highlights here include works by Seurat, Gauguin, and Delvaux.

Cost and Hours: €8, €13 combo-ticket with Magritte Museum, free first Wed of month after 13:00; open Tue-Sun 10:00-17:00, closed Mon, last entry 30 minutes before closing; audioguide-€4, tour booklet-€2.50, pricey cafeteria with salad bar, Rue de la Régence 3, recorded info tel. 02-508-3211, www.fine-arts -museum.be.

○ See the Royal Museums of Fine Arts and Magritte Museum Tour chapter.

▲▲Magritte Museum (Musée Magritte)—This exhibit, examining Surrealist painter René Magritte, is in the same museum complex as the Royal Museums of Fine Arts (above), and contains more than 150 works housed on three floors of a Neoclassical building. Although you won't see many of Magritte's most famous pieces, this lovingly presented museum offers an unusually intimate look at the life and work of one of Belgium's top artists.

Cost and Hours: €8, €13 combo-ticket with Royal Museums of Fine Arts, free first Wed of month after 13:00; open Tue-Sun 10:00-17:00, Wed until 20:00, closed Mon, last entry 30 minutes before closing; tel. 02-508-3333, www.musee-magritte-museum .be. Your ticket comes with an assigned entry time. It's possible to buy tickets in advance (and reserve an entry time) on the Magritte Museum's website, avoiding possible wait time at the museum.

○ See the Royal Museums of Fine Arts and Magritte Museum Tour chapter.

▲Musical Instruments Museum (Musée des Instruments de Musique)—One of Europe's best music museums (nicknamed "MIM") is housed in one of Brussels' most impressive Art Nouveau buildings, the beautifully renovated Old England department store. Part of the Royal Museum of Art and History, this museum has more than 1,500 instruments—from Egyptian harps, to medieval lutes, to groundbreaking harpsichords, to the Brussels-built saxophone. Inside you'll be given a pair of headphones and set free to wander several levels: folk instruments from around the world on the ground floor, a history of Western musical instruments on the first, and an entire floor devoted to strings  and pianos on the second. As you approach an instrument, you hear it playing on your headphones (which actually work...most of the time). On the fifth floor is an exhibit about the history of the building and Brussels Art Nouveau in general. The museum is skimpy on English information—except for a laminated sheet in each section that simply identifies instruments—but the music you'll hear is an international language.

Cost and Hours: €5, Tue-Fri 9:30-16:45, Sat-Sun 10:00-16:45, closed Mon, last entry 45 minutes before closing, Rue Montagne de la Cour 2, just downhill and toward the Grand Place from the Royal Museums of Fine Arts, tel. 02-545-0130, www.mim.be.

Cuisine Art and Views: The sixth floor has a restaurant, a terrace, and a great view of Brussels (€10-15 *plats du jour,* same hours as museum but also open until 23:00 Thu-Sat, pick up free access pass at museum entrance). The corner alcoves on each level (accessible as you tour the museum) have even better views.

▲▲**BELvue Museum**—In a remarkable feat of museum magic, this sight achieves the impossible: It makes Belgian history fas-

cinating. The exhibit—which fills two palatial floors with lots of real historical artifacts—illustrates the short sweep of this nation's story, from its 1830 inception to today. To make the most of your visit, follow along with the wonderful and extensive flier translating all of the descriptions. Skip the €2.50 audioguide, which simply repeats the information on the flier.

With rooms that proceed in chronological order, the museum explains Belgium's push for independence from the Netherlands, the roots of the ongoing friction between its Francophone-dominated ruling class and its generally Flemish peasant class, and how Belgium cleverly managed to assert itself as a fledgling nation in a changing world (for example, its new royalty agreed to not wear crowns or sit on a throne, in deference to its parliament).

The exhibit doesn't shy away from the controversial, such as the appalling story of the Belgian Congo, which King Leopold II acquired as his personal property in 1885 and proceeded to exploit mercilessly until a storm of public anger forced him to turn it over to the Belgian government in 1908. Leopold's wealth was poured into city development—including the stately Neoclassical buildings of the Upper Town, as well as some slinky Art Nouveau masterpieces—making the 1890s a belle époque for Belgium. But it was also a time of extreme social stratification, when only French aristocrats (about 2 percent of the population) had the power to elect the government. (One poster provocatively compares the disenfranchised Flemish to the oppressed Congolese.) The Belgian workers' movement, based in the socialist hotbed of Ghent, achieved universal male suffrage in 1893.

After outlining the devastation of the World Wars, the exhibit examines postwar Belgium's recovery, its successful implementation of one of Europe's most socialistic governments, and its gradual emergence as the capital of Europe. The conclusion explains how even today, the Flemish-Francophone conflict festers, while reforms implemented since 1970 aspire to prevent Belgium from splitting completely in half.

Outside in the hallway, biographical sketches and intimate family photos provide you a chance to get to know the (generally) much-loved royal family. Since these imported German monarchs arrived in 1830, each of the six "Kings of the Belgians" (as they're officially known) has had his own style and claim to fame—or infamy: visionary Leopold I; "Builder King" and Congo exploiter Leopold II; appreciated World War I leader Albert I (who won many fans for the monarchy); controversial World War II-era Leopold III (who abdicated in disgrace); well-respected Baudouin (r. 1950-1993); and his equally popular brother, current King Albert II.

Cost and Hours: €5, €8 combo-ticket includes Coudenberg Palace, Tue-Fri 10:00-17:00, Sat-Sun 10:00-18:00, closed Mon, to the right of the palace at place des Palais 7, tel. 070-220-492, www .belvue.be.

Cuisine Art: Healthy lunches are served in the cool "Green Kitchen" café in the lobby of this former princess' palace (€10-15 plates, same hours as museum).

Coudenberg Palace—The BELvue Museum stands atop the barren archaeological remains of a 12th-century Brussels palace. Though well-lit and well-described, these long, vaulted cellars require too much imagination to make them meaningful. A small museum explains artifacts from the palace. The best thing is the free orientation video you see before descending. If you do tour the palace ruins, do so after you're finished at the BELvue Museum, because you'll exit the Coudenberg downhill, near the Musical Instruments Museum.

Cost and Hours: €5, €8 combo-ticket includes BELvue Museum; €2.50 audioguide does not cover BELvue Museum, yet must be (inconveniently) returned to BELvue entrance; same hours as BELvue Museum.

Outer Brussels

East of Downtown

Several interesting sights lie just east of the city center: First, the European Parliament (just beyond the Pentagon ring road); beyond that, the museums at the Park of the Cinquantenaire. Because these are in the same direction and connected by a quick bus ride (explained next), they're easy to visit in one fell swoop.

Connecting the Sights: Handy public-transportation connections make it easy to see both the European Parliament and the Park of the Cinquantenaire. The Métro zips you from the center out to the Park of the Cinquantenaire in minutes (Métro stop: Merode). From the park, catch bus #27 (bus stop: Gaulois/Galliërs, direction: Gare du Midi/Zuidstation, 4-5/hour Mon-Fri, 2-3/hour Sat-Sun) to the Luxembourg stop (for the European Parliament) and on to the Royale/Koning stop (for the Royal Palace and great nearby museums). It's cheap and easy, plus you'll feel quite clever doing it.

▲European Parliament

Europe's governing body welcomes visitors with an information center and audioguide tours. This sprawling complex of glass

skyscrapers is a cacophony of black-suited politicians speaking 23 different Euro-languages. It's exciting just to be here—a fly on the wall of a place that aspires to chart the future of Europe "with respect for all political thinking... consolidating democracy in the spirit of peace and solidarity." The 785 parliament members, representing 27 countries and more than 500 million citizens, shape Europe with an €130 billion budget.

Getting There: The European Parliament is next to Place du Luxembourg. From the Bourse in downtown Brussels, take bus #95; from the museums at the Park of the Cinquantenaire or the Royal Palace, take bus #27. Place du Luxembourg is also a seven-minute walk from the Trône/Troon Métro stop (straight ahead up Luxembourg street). To find the Info Point (described next) from Place du Luxembourg, go behind the old train station and beneath the semicircular glass walkway, and look for the *Info* sign.

Visitors Center: The **Info Point** is a welcoming place, with 28 flags (one for each member country, plus the EU's circle of gold stars on a blue field), videos promoting the concept and beauties of the European Union, and racks of entertaining freebies—including maps outlining the member states, the free *Troubled Waters* comic book that explains how the parliament works, and bins of miniature *My Fundamental Rights in the EU* booklets—everything in 23 different languages, of course (free entry, Mon-Thu 9:00-17:15, Fri 9:00-13:00, closed Sat-Sun, www.europarl.europa.eu). An adjacent bigger-and-even-better visitors center, planned for September 2011, may be open in time for your visit.

Audioguide Tours: The only way to get inside the European Parliament itself is to join a free 30-minute audioguide tour. These leave from the visitors entrance, down the stairs and across the street from the Info Point (around the left side of the round, glassy building; Mon-Thu at 10:00 and 15:00, additional tours in July-Aug—last one usually departs at 16:00; Fri only at 10:00; busiest on Mon, no visitors under 14 years old). It's smart and easy to call ahead to confirm the schedule and reserve a space (tel. 02-284-2111). If you're just showing up, try to arrive about 30 minutes early to secure a place on busy days. *Note:* On the two days each month that parliament is in session, visitors are allowed to watch the proceedings, but no tours are offered.

The European Union

Brussels is the capital of one of the biggest, most powerful, and most idealistic states in the world (and, arguably, in history): The European Union (EU). In just one genera-tion, more than two dozen European countries have gone from being bitter rivals to compatriots. This union of such a diverse collection of separate nations—with different languages, cultures, and soccer teams—is almost unprecedented. And it all started in the rubble of a devastating war.

World War II left 40 million dead and a continent in ruins, and it convinced Europeans that they had to work together to maintain peace. Poised between competing superpowers (the US and the USSR), they also needed to cooperate economically to survive in an increasingly globalized economy. Just after the war ended, visionary "Eurocrats" began the task of convincing reluctant European nations to relinquish elements of their sovereignty and merge into a united body.

The transition happened very gradually, in fits and starts. It began in 1948, when Belgium, the Netherlands, and Luxembourg—jointly called "BeNeLux"—established a free-trade zone. That evolved into an ever-broadening alliance of states (the European Coal and Steel Union, then the European Economic Community, or "Common Market"). In 1992, with the Treaty of Maastricht, the 12 member countries of the Common Market made a leap of faith: They created a "European Union" that would eventually allow for free movement of capital, goods, services, and labor.

In 2002, most EU members adopted a single currency (the euro), and for all practical purposes, economic unity was a reality. Ten additional member states joined in 2004 and two more in 2007, bringing the total to 27—encompassing the British Isles, nearly all of Western Europe, and much of Eastern Europe and Scandinavia. Almost all EU members have joined the open-borders Schengen Agreement, making passport checkpoints

When you check in, you'll be given an audioguide and sent through a security checkpoint. Head up the stairs and wait for your tour to begin in the atrium, with exhibits and a gift shop. At the appointed time, your escort leads you to various viewpoints in the complex where you'll be instructed to listen to the related audioguide commentary.

The slow-paced audioguide—with helpful video illustrations—dryly takes you through the history of the EU, as well as its

obsolete. This makes the EU the world's seventh-largest "country" (1.7 million square miles), with the third-largest population (more than 500 million people), and an economy that beats the US's as the world's biggest ($16 trillion GDP).

The EU is governed from Brussels (though some EU institutions meet in Strasbourg, Frankfurt, Luxembourg, and other cities). While it has a parliament, the EU is primarily led by the European Commission (with commissioners appointed by individual member governments and approved by its parliament) and the Council of Ministers. Daily business is conducted by an army of bureaucrats and policy wonks.

Unlike America's federation of 50 states, Europe's member states retain the right to opt out of some EU policies. Britain, for example, belongs to the EU but chose not to adopt the euro as its currency. While the Lisbon Treaty (enacted in 2009) streamlines EU responses to conflicts and issues, there's no unified foreign or economic policy among the member countries. The EU also lacks a powerful chief executive—the president of the European Council, appointed for a two-and-a-half-year term, is much weaker than the US president, as EU laws require consensus on taxes, foreign policy, defense, and social programs.

The EU is currently financing an ambitious 21st-century infrastructure of roads, high-speed trains, high-tech industries, and communication networks. The goal is to create a competitive, sustainable, environmentally friendly economy that improves the quality of life for all Europeans.

Still, many "Euroskeptics" remain unconvinced that the EU is a good thing. Some chafe at the highly regulated business environment and high taxes. They complain about the bureaucracy and worry that their national cultures will be swallowed up and Euro-fied. The wealthier member countries (mostly in the north) are reluctant to bail out their economically unsound compatriots (mostly in the south) in order to prop up the euro, while the troubled countries resent the cuts demanded by the richer ones.

Despite the problems facing them, Europeans don't want to go back to the days of division and strife. Most recognize that a strong, unified Europe is necessary to keep the peace and compete in a global economy.

current structure and procedures. You'll learn how early visionary utopians (like Churchill, who in 1946 called for a "United States of Europe" to avoid future wars) led the way as Europe gradually evolved into the European Union (1992).

From the balcony overlooking the building's lobby, you can see the giant *Confluence* sculpture with moving metal-wire pieces—representing people coming together for a common purpose. The audioguide tells you all about the building itself: In line with EU idealism, it's functional, transparent, and very "green."

The grand finale is the vast "hemicycle," where the members of the European Parliament sit. Here you'll listen to a political-science lesson about the all-Europe system of governance. Parliamentarians representing 160 different national political parties, organized into seven different voting blocs based on political ideals (rather than nationality), hash out pan-European issues in this hall. It's the largest multilingual operation on the planet. Yet somehow things get done; recent pieces of legislation include a crackdown on mobile-phone roaming fees within EU member states and a cap on carbon dioxide emissions.

Near the European Parliament
Royal Belgian Institute of Natural Sciences (Institut Royal des Sciences Naturelles de Belgique)—Dinosaur enthusiasts come to this museum, practically next door to the European Parliament, for the world's largest collection of iguanodon skeletons (€7, Tue-Fri 9:30-17:00, Sat-Sun 10:00-18:00, closed Mon, last entry 30 minutes before closing, Rue Vautier 29; bus #95 from the Bourse to Luxembourg, plus a 10-minute walk; or bus #34 from the Porte de Namur/Naamsepoort or Trône/Troon Métro stops to Museum; tel. 02-627-4211, www.naturalsciences.be).

Park of the Cinquantenaire
(Parc du Cinquantenaire)
Standing proudly in a big park in eastern Brussels is a trio of sprawling museums housed in cavernous halls: the Royal Army and Military History Museum, Autoworld, and the Royal Museum

of Art and History. These decent attractions thrill specialists but bore most others. The complex itself is interesting to see and has a grandiose history: The ambitious 19th-century Belgian King Leopold II wanted Brussels to rival Paris. In 1880 he celebrated the 50th anniversary *(cinquantenaire)* of Belgian independence by building a huge monumental arch flanked by massive exhibition halls, which today house the museums.

Getting There: The Merode Métro stop is 200 yards from the museums (exit the Métro station following signs to *Yser/IJzer,* then cross the street toward the big arch). All of these are also within steps of the Gaulois/Galliërs stop for bus #27 (with handy connections to the European Parliament, then the Royal Palace and Upper Town).

▲**Royal Army and Military History Museum (Musée Royal de l'Armée et d'Histoire Militaire)**—Wander through this enor-

mous collection of weaponry, uniforms, tanks, warplanes, and endless exhibits about military history, focusing on the 19th and 20th centuries. The museum—which is gradually getting a much-needed makeover—is filled with real, tangible history. This impressively complete museum made me want to
watch my favorite war movies all over again. It's a nirvana for fans of military history and aviation, but skippable for those who think a "panzer" is a pretty flower. Current renovation work might mean that some sections are closed during your visit, and staff cuts may temporarily close some sections midday.

Exploring the whole place is exhausting, so be selective and use the floor plan and directional signs to navigate. Each item is labeled in French and Flemish, but some good English descriptions are available; to get the most out of your visit, pay €3 for the essential audioguide (available 9:00-11:30 & 13:00-16:30).

From the entrance, to the right is a hall with historic exhibits, then a large and very good section on World War I, with the best collection of WWI weaponry anywhere. Don't miss the primitive WWI tanks—able to break through the stalemated "Western Front," but so clumsy that they couldn't do anything in enemy territory. The grand finale of this wing is the vast (and I mean vast) hall filled with warplanes. To the left from the entrance are impressively displayed armor and weapons, and a huge hall with information on modern conflict (including World War II) and temporary exhibits. Upstairs is a rooftop terrace with "Napoleonic" views over the park complex and the Brussels skyline (open in summer only, find the elevator at the front of the armory section).

Cost and Hours: Free, Tue-Sun 9:00-16:45, closed Mon, Parc du Cinquantenaire 3, tel. 02-737-7811, www.klm-mra.be. Most of the museum (except for the aviation section) closes from 12:00 to 13:00.

▲**Autoworld**—Starting with Mr. Benz's motorized tricycle of 1886, stroll through a giant hall filled with 400 historic cars, each one labeled and briefly explained in four languages. Car buffs can ogle circa-1905 models from Peugeot, Renault, Oldsmobile, Cadillac, and Rolls-Royce. It's well-described in English (€6, daily April-Sept 10:00-18:00, Oct-March 10:00-17:00, in Palais Mondial, Parc du Cinquantenaire 11, tel. 02-736-4165, www.autoworld.be).

Royal Museum of Art and History—This varied, decent (but not spectacular) collection features both European and non-European items from prehistoric times to the present. As you wander the almost-empty halls, you'll see fine tapestries, exquisite altarpieces, an impressive Islamic collection, gorgeous Art Nouveau and Art Deco, and a "museum of the heart" (featuring various creative depictions of everyone's favorite organ, donated by a local heart doctor). The collection is arranged somewhat haphazardly; pick up the brochure at the entry to figure out which items you'd like to find, then follow the signposts. While it's sometimes called the "Belgian Louvre," that's an overstatement; this place pales in comparison to the excellent Royal Museums of Fine Art in the Upper Town.

Cost and Hours: €5, includes audioguide that covers only some of the museum, limited English information posted, Tue-Fri 9:30-17:00, Sat-Sun 10:00-17:00, closed Mon, hiding behind Autoworld at Jubelpark 10, Parc du Cinquantenaire, tel. 02-741-7211.

North of Downtown: The 1958 World's Fair Grounds

These sights are next to each other about four miles north of the Grand Place at Bruparck, a complex of tacky-but-fun attractions at the old 1958 World's Fair grounds.

Getting There: It's easy but fairly time-consuming to reach from the center. Ride the Métro to Heysel/Heizel and walk about five minutes toward the can't-miss-it Atomium. You'll come to a little pavilion with a walkway going over the train tracks; to reach Mini-Europe, take this walkway and enter "The Village," a corny food circus (with a giant cineplex and a water park) done up like a European village. Entering this area, turn left and head down the stairs to reach the Mini-Europe entrance. If you're only going to the Atomium, simply go straight through the pavilion and head for the big silver balls.

Atomium—This giant, silvery iron molecule, with escalators and stairs connecting the various "atoms" and a view from the top sphere, was the über-optimistic symbol of the 1958 World's Fair. It's Brussels' answer to Paris' Eiffel Tower, Seattle's Space Needle,

and St. Louis' Gateway Arch. Recently reopened after an extensive renovation, the Atomium celebrates its kitschy past with fun space-age videos and displays. Your ticket includes an elevator ride to the panorama deck, with views over the fairgrounds and Mini-Europe (which looks *really* mini from up here)—but, disappointingly, you can't actually see the landmarks of downtown Brussels. Then meander on endless escalators and stairs through five of the nine balls on your way back down. The good €2 audioguide explains the building and the 1958 World Expo, including sound clips from people who actually attended the festivities. If you don't like heights or tight spaces, tell your friends you'll wave to them...from the ground.

Cost and Hours: €11, €22.50 combo-ticket with Mini-Europe, daily 10:00-18:00, later in summer, last entry 30 minutes before closing, overpriced restaurant inside, tel. 02-475-4777, www.atomium.be.

Mini-Europe—This kid-pleasing sight, sharing a park with the Atomium, has 1:25-scale models of 350 famous European landmarks, such as Big Ben, the Eiffel Tower, and Venice's canals. The "Spirit of Europe" section is an interactive educational exhibit about the European Union (€13, €22.50 combo-ticket with Atomium, Easter-Sept daily 9:30-18:00, July-Aug until 20:00, Oct-Dec 10:00-18:00, closed Jan-Easter, last entry one hour before closing, tel. 02-474-1313, www.minieurope.com).

In Tervuren, East of Brussels

▲Royal Museum of Central Africa (Musée Royal de l'Afrique Centrale)—Remember the Belgian Congo? About an hour by public transit from downtown Brussels, this worthwhile museum covers the Congo and much more of Africa, including ethnography, sculpture, jewelry, colonial history, flora, and fauna. It's a great place to learn about both the history of Belgian adventure in the Congo (when it was the king's private plantation) and the region's natural wonders. Unfortunately, there's barely a word of English. The museum, housed in an immense palace, is surrounded by a vast, well-kept park. A trip out here puts you in a lush, wooded oasis a world away from the big, noisy city.

Cost and Hours: €4, more for special exhibits, audioguide-€2, Tue-Fri 10:00-17:00, Sat-Sun 10:00-18:00, closed Mon, Leuvensesteenweg 13 in the town of Tervuren, tel. 02-769-5211, www.africamuseum.be.

Getting There: Take Métro line 1 (direction: Stockel/ Stokkel) to Montgomery, and then catch tram #44 and ride it about 20 minutes to its final stop, Tervuren. From there, walk 300 yards through the park to the palace. On summer weekend after- noons, a charming old-time trolley connects Tervuren to the Tram Museum at Brussels' Woluwe Park; on Sundays, it goes all the way to the Park of the Cinquantenaire (€8 one-way, April-Oct Sat-Sun only).

GRAND PLACE WALK

This walk takes in Brussels' delightful old center, starting at its spectacular main square. After exploring the Grand Place, we'll loop a couple blocks north, see the Bourse, and then end south of the Grand Place at the *Manneken-Pis*.

Orientation

Length of This Walk: Allow two hours.
Brewery Museum: €6, daily 10:00-17:00 except Dec-March opens Sat-Sun at 12:00, Grand Place 10, tel. 02-511-4987.
City Museum: €3, Tue-Sun 10:00-17:00, closed Mon, Grand Place, tel. 02-279-4350.
Chocolate Shops: Generally Mon-Sat 9:00-22:00, Sun 10:00-22:00, along the north side of the Grand Place.

The Walk Begins

The Grand Place

This colorful cobblestone square is the heart—historically and geographically—of heart-shaped Brussels. As the town's market square for 1,000 years, this was where farmers and merchants sold their wares in open-air stalls, enticing travelers from the main east-west highway across Belgium, which ran a block north of the square. Today, shops and cafés sell chocolates, *gaufres* (waffles), beer, mussels, fries, *dentelles* (lace), and flowers.

Brussels was born about 1,000 years ago around a now-long-gone castle built by Germans to fight off the French (long before either of those countries actually existed as nations). The villagers supplied the needs of the soldiers, and a city grew up on the banks of the Senne (not Seine) River, which today is completely bricked

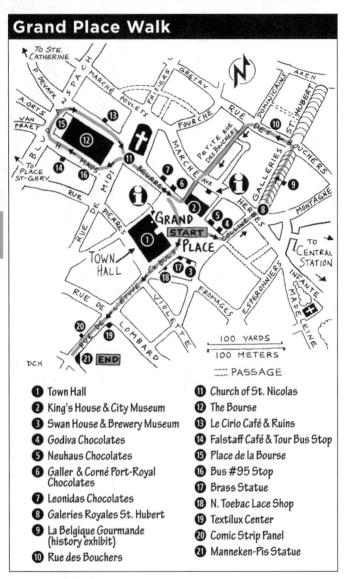

Grand Place Walk

GRAND PLACE WALK

1. Town Hall
2. King's House & City Museum
3. Swan House & Brewery Museum
4. Godiva Chocolates
5. Neuhaus Chocolates
6. Galler & Corné Port-Royal Chocolates
7. Leonidas Chocolates
8. Galeries Royales St. Hubert
9. La Belgique Gourmande (history exhibit)
10. Rue des Bouchers
11. Church of St. Nicolas
12. The Bourse
13. Le Cirio Café & Ruins
14. Falstaff Café & Tour Bus Stop
15. Place de la Bourse
16. Bus #95 Stop
17. Brass Statue
18. N. Toebac Lace Shop
19. Textilux Center
20. Comic Strip Panel
21. Manneken-Pis Statue

over. The river crossed the main road from Köln to Bruges.

Pan the square to get oriented. Face the Town Hall, with your back to the King's House. You're facing roughly southwest. The TI is one block behind you, and "restaurant row" is another block beyond that. To your right, a block away, catch a glimpse of the Bourse building (with buses, taxis, and cafés). The Upper Town is to your left, rising up the hill beyond the Central Station. Over your left shoulder a few blocks away is St. Michael's Cathedral. And most important? The *Manneken-Pis* is three blocks ahead, down the street that runs along the left side of the Town Hall.

The **Town Hall** (Hôtel de Ville) dominates the square with its 300-foot-tall tower, topped by a golden statue of St. Michael slaying a devil (skippable interior). This was where the city council met to rule this free trading town. Brussels

proudly maintained its self-governing independence while dukes, kings, and clergymen ruled much of Europe. These days, the Town Hall hosts weddings—Crown Prince Philippe got married here in 1999. (The Belgian government demands that all marriages first be performed in simple civil ceremonies.)

Opposite the Town Hall is the impressive, gray **King's House** (Maison du Roi), used by the Habsburg kings not as a house, but as an administrative center. Rebuilt in the 1890s, it's a stately and prickly Neo-Gothic building. Inside is the mildly interesting City Museum (described later).

The fancy smaller buildings giving the square its uniquely grand medieval character are former **guild halls** (now mostly shops and restaurants), their impressive gabled roofs topped with

statues. Once the home offices for the town's different professions (brewers, bakers, and *Manneken-Pis*-corkscrew-makers), they all date from shortly after 1695—the year French king Louis XIV's troops surrounded the city, sighted their cannons on the Town Hall spire, and managed to level everything around it (4,000 wooden buildings) without ever hitting the spire itself. As a matter of pride, these Brussels businessmen rebuilt their offices better than ever, completing everything within seven years. They're in stone, taller, and with ornamented gables and classical statues.

The **Swan House** (#9, just to the left of the Town Hall) once housed a bar where Karl Marx and Friedrich Engels met in February of 1848 to write their *Communist Manifesto*. Later that year, when the treatise sparked socialist revolution around Europe,

Brussels exiled them. Today, the once-proletarian bar is one of the city's most expensive restaurants. Next door (#10) was and still is the brewers' guild, now housing the **Brewery Museum.**

Each rooftop **statue** comes with its own uninteresting legend, but the Bruxelloise have an earthier explanation: "What's that smell?" say the statues on the roof of the Swan House. "Someone farted." "Yeah," says the golden man riding a horse atop the Brewery Museum next door, "it was that guy over there," and he points north across the square to another statue. "It wasn't me," says that statue, "it was him—way over there." Follow his gaze to the middle of the northwest side of the square, where the statue of a saint with a shepherd's staff hangs his head in shame.

GRAND PLACE WALK

Imagine this already glorious square filled with a **carpet of flowers.** Every other year (next on the weekend of August 15, 2012; www.flowercarpet.be), florists create a colorful 19,000-square-foot pattern of tightly packed begonias—that's about three-quarters of a million individual flowers. Begun in 1971 by a begonia salesman as a way to promote his wares, this gorgeous display has become a biannual Brussels fixture that makes this grand space even grander.

• *Inside the King's House (Maison du Roi)—across the Grand Place from the Town Hall—is the only museum of any importance on the square, the...*

City Museum

This museum has three stories of exhibits: The top floor displays a chronological history of the city and an enjoyable room full

of costumes dampened by the *Manneken-Pis* statue; the middle floor has a 20-minute film on city history and maps and models of 13th- and 17th-century Brussels; and the ground floor features tapestries and paintings. Borrow the English descriptions in each room.

Most visitors aim straight for the *Manneken-Pis* outfits, **upstairs.** It's a longstanding tradition for the statue to be outfitted in clothing—the little guy goes through several costume changes each week. Many of the costumes you'll see here were donated by other countries—you'll see everything from a Civil War Union soldier to an El Salvadorian farmer, from a Polish hussar to a Japanese samurai, from an Indian maharajah to a Spanish bullfighter, from a Russian cosmonaut to a Fiji islander... and much more. Once up here, sit down and enjoy the video showing visitors' reactions to the ridiculous little statue.

On the **middle floor,** be sure to find the model of the city in the 13th century. (To follow the directions in this description, uphill is east.) The largest structure is St. Michael's Cathedral (northeast). The Upper Town hasn't a hint of its monumental future. The Grand Place's embryonic beginning is roughly in the center of town, amid a cluster of houses.

The city was a port town—see the crane unloading barges—since it was at this point that the shallow Senne became navigable. Grain from the area was processed in the watermills, then shipped downstream to Antwerp and on to the North Sea.

By the 1200s, Brussels—though tiny by today's standards—was an important commercial center, and St. Michael's was the region's religious hub. Still, most of the area inside the 2.5-mile-long city wall was farmland, dotted with a few churches, towers, markets, and convents (such as the Carmelite convent hugging the south wall).

The model in the far end of the room shows the city a couple centuries later—much bigger, but still within the same wall. By this time, the Upper and Lower Towns are clearly defined. In the Upper Town, the huge palace of the dukes of Burgundy marks the site of today's Royal Palace.

On the **ground floor** you'll see the original statues that once adorned the Town Hall. The limestone is no match for the corrosive acidic air, so they were brought inside for protection. Also on this floor are a few old paintings, fine carved altarpieces, tapestries, sculpture, and porcelain.

Tasty Treats on the Grand Place

Cafés: Mussels in Brussels, Belgian-style french fries, yeasty local beers, waffles...if all you do here is plop down at a café on the square, try some of these specialties, and watch the world go by—hey, that's a great afternoon in Brussels.

The outdoor cafés are casual and come with fair prices (a good Belgian beer costs €3.50—with no cover or service charge). Have a seat, and a waiter will serve you. The half-dozen or so cafés are all roughly equal in price and quality for simple drinks and foods—check the posted menus.

Choco-Crawl: The best chocolate shops all lie along the north (uphill) side of the square, starting with Godiva at the high end (higher in both altitude and price). The cost goes down slightly as

A Brief History of Chocolate

In 1519, Montezuma served Cortés a cup of hot cocoa *(xocoatl)* made from cocoa beans, which were native to the New World.

It ignited a food fad in Europe—by 1700, elegant "chocolate houses" in Europe's capitals served hot chocolate (with milk and sugar added) to wealthy aristocrats. By the 1850s, the process of making chocolate candies for eating was developed, and Brussels, with a long tradition of quality handmade luxuries, was at the forefront.

Cocoa beans are husked, fermented, and roasted, then ground into chocolate paste. (Chocolate straight from the bean is very bitter.) The vegetable fat is pressed out to make cocoa butter. Cocoa butter and chocolate paste are mixed together and sweetened with sugar to make chocolates. In 1876, a Swiss man named Henry Nestlé added concentrated milk, creating milk chocolate—a lighter, sweeter variation, with less pure chocolate.

you descend to the other shops. Each shop has a mouth-watering display case of 20 or so chocolates and sells mixes of 100 grams—your choice of 6-8 pieces—for about €5, or individual pieces for about €1.60. Americans use the word "chocolates" indiscriminately to describe the different varieties you'd find in a box of chocolates, but the Belgians call them either "truffles" (soft, crumbly chocolate shells filled with buttercream) or "pralines" (made of a hard chocolate shell with a wide range of fillings—uniquely Belgian and totally different from the sugar-and-nuts French praline). Chocolate shops are generally open Monday to Saturday from 9:00 to 22:00 and Sunday from 10:00 to 22:00.

Godiva, with the top reputation internationally, is synonymous with fine Belgian chocolate. Now owned by a Turkish company, Godiva still has its management and the original factory (built in 1926) in Belgium. This store, at Grand Place 22, was Godiva's first (est. 1937). The almond and honey goes way beyond almond roca.

Neuhaus, a few doors down at #27, has been encouraging local chocoholics since 1857. Their main store is in the Galeries St. Hubert (described later). Neuhaus publishes a good little pamphlet explaining its products. The "caprice" (toffee with vanilla crème) tastes like Easter. Neuhaus claims to be the inventor of the praline.

Galler, just off the square at Rue au Beurre 44, is homier and less famous because it doesn't export. Still family-run (and the royal favorite), it proudly serves less sugary chocolate—dark. The new top-end choice, 85 percent pure chocolate, is called simply "Black 85"—and worth a sample if you like chocolate without the sweetness. Galler's products are well-described in English.

Leonidas, four doors down at Rue au Beurre 34, is where cost-conscious Bruxelloise get their fix, sacrificing 10 percent in quality to nearly triple their take (machine-made, only €1.60/100 grams). White chocolate is their specialty.

Corné Port-Royal outlets are sprouting up everywhere. It seems like the new kid on the block, but only the name is new—they've been making chocolates for 75 years.

If all the chocolate has made you thirsty, wash it down with **250 Beers,** next to Leonidas.

• *Exit the Grand Place next to Godiva (from the northeast, or uphill, corner of the square), and go north one block on Rue de la Colline (passing a popular Tintin shop at #13 and a Europe shop across the street) to Rue du Marché-aux-Herbes/Grasmarkt, which was once the main east-west highway through Belgium. The little park-like square just to your right—a modest gathering place with market stalls—is nicknamed "Agora" (after the marketplaces of ancient Greece).*

Looking to the right, notice that it's all uphill from here to the Upper Town, another four blocks (and 200-foot elevation gain) beyond. Straight ahead, you enter the arcaded shopping mall called...

Galeries Royales St. Hubert

Built in 1847, Europe's oldest still-operating shopping mall served as the glass-covered model that inspired many other shopping galleries in Paris, London, and beyond. It celebrated the town's new  modern attitude (having recently gained its independence from the Netherlands). Built in an age of expansion and industrialization, the mall demonstrated efficient modern living, with elegant apartments upstairs above trendy shops, theaters, and cafés. Originally, you had to pay to get in to see its fancy shops, and that elite sensibility survives today. Even today, people live in the upstairs apartments.

Looking down the arcade, you'll notice that it bends halfway down, designed to lure shoppers farther. Its iron-and-glass look is still popular, but the decorative columns, cameos, and pastel colors evoke a more elegant time. It's Neo-Renaissance, like a pastel Florentine palace.

There's no Gap (yet), no Foot Locker, no Karmelkorn. Instead, you'll find hat, cane, and, umbrella stores that sell...hats, canes, and umbrellas—that's it, all made on the premises. **Philippe** (halfway down the first section, on the left), carries shoes made especially for the curves of your feet, handcrafted by a family that's been doing it for generations. Since 1857, **Neuhaus** (near the end of the first section, on the right) has sold chocolates from here at its flagship store, where many Brussels natives buy their pralines. Across from Neuhaus, the **Taverne du Passage** restaurant serves the same local specialties that singer Jacques Brel used to come here for: *croquettes de crevettes* (shrimp croquettes), *tête de veau* (calf's head), *anguilles au vert* (eels with herb sauce), and *fondue au fromage* (cheese fondue; €10-20 meals, daily 12:00-24:00).

Inside **La Belgique Gourmande** chocolate shop (on the right, at #17) is a strange and sprawling exhibit about the history of Brussels. You enter through the back of the chocolate shop and descend into a huge underground exhibit that cleverly and artistically gives you the sweep of the city with fine English descriptions (€6, daily 10:00-17:00, tel. 02-512-5745).

• *Midway down the mall, where the two sections bend, turn left and exit the mall onto...*

Rue des Bouchers

Yikes! During meal times, this street is absolutely crawling with tourists browsing through wall-to-wall, midlevel-quality restaurants. Brussels is known worldwide for its food, serving all kinds of cuisine, but specializing in seafood (particularly mussels). You'll have plenty to choose from along this table-clogged "restaurant row." To get an idea of prices, compare their posted *menùs*—the fixed-price, several-course meal offered by most restaurants. But don't count on getting a good value—better restaurants are just a few steps away.

Many diners here are day-trippers. Colin from London, Marie from Paris, Martje from Holland, and Dietrich from Frankfurt could easily all "do lunch" together in Brussels—just three hours away.

The first intersection, with Petite Rue des Bouchers, is the heart of the restaurant quarter, which sprawls for several blocks around. The street names reveal what sorts of shops used to stand here—butchers *(bouchers)*, herbs, chickens, and cheese.

• *At this intersection, turn left onto Petite Rue des Bouchers and walk straight back to the Grand Place. (You'll see the Town Hall tower ahead.) At the Grand Place, turn right (west) on Rue du Beurre. Comparison-*

shop a little more at the Galler and Leonidas chocolate stores and pass by the little "Is it raining?" fountain. At the intersection with Rue du Midi is the...

Church of St. Nicolas

Since the 12th century, there's been a church here. Inside, along the left aisle, see rough stones in some of the arches from the early church. Outside, notice the barnacle-like shops, such as De Witte Jewelers, built right into the church. The church was rebuilt 300 years ago with money provided by the town's jewelers. As thanks, they were given these shops with apartments upstairs. Close to God, this was prime real estate. And jewelers are still here.

• *Just beyond the church, you run into the back entrance of a big Neoclassical building.*

The Bourse (Stock Exchange) and Art Nouveau Cafés

The stock exchange was built in the 1870s in the Historicist style—a mix-and-match, Neo-everything architectural movement. The **ruins** under glass on the right side of the Bourse are from a 13th-century convent; there's a small museum inside.

Several **historic cafés** huddle around the Bourse. To the right (next to the covered ruins) is the woody **Le Cirio,** with its delightful circa-1900 interior. Around the left side of the Bourse is the **Falstaff Café,** which is worth a peek inside. Some Brussels cafés, like the Falstaff, are still decorated in the early 20th-century style called Art Nouveau. Ironwork columns twist and bend like flower stems, and lots of Tiffany-style stained glass and mirrors make them light and spacious. Slender, elegant, willowy Gibson Girls decorate the wallpaper, while waiters in bowties glide by.

• *Circle around to the front of the Bourse, toward the busy Boulevard Anspach. Note that the street in front of the Falstaff Café is a convenient place to catch a hop-on, hop-off bus tour.*

Place de la Bourse and Boulevard Anspach

Brussels is the political nerve center of Europe (only Washington, DC, has more lobbyists), and the city sees several hundred dem-

onstrations a year. When the local team wins a soccer match or some political group wants to make a statement, this is where people flock to wave flags and honk horns.

It's also where the old town meets the new. To the right along Boulevard Anspach are two shopping malls and several first-run movie theaters. Rue Neuve, which parallels Anspach, is a bustling pedestrian-only shopping street.

Boulevard Anspach covers the still-flowing Senne River (which was open until 1850). Remember that Brussels was once a port, with North Sea boats coming as far as this point to unload their goods. But with frequent cholera epidemics killing thousands of its citizens, the city decided to cover up its stinky river.

Beyond Boulevard Anspach—two blocks past the ugly sky-scrapers—is the charming **Ste. Catherine** neighborhood, clustered around the former fish market and the Church of Ste. Catherine. This village-like zone is the easiest escape from the bustle of downtown Brussels, and features two ideal lunch stops: the Mer du Nord/Nordzee fish bar and the delightful Belgian cheese shop Cremerie de Linkebeek.

• *For efficient sightseeing, consider catching bus #95 from alongside the Bourse (on Rue Henri Maus, in front of Falstaff Café) to the Place Royale, where you can follow my Upper Town Walk (see next chapter), also ending at the* Manneken-Pis. *But if you'd rather stay in the Lower Town, return to the Grand Place.*

From the Grand Place to the *Manneken-Pis*

• *Leave the square kitty-corner, heading south down the street running along the left side of the Town Hall, Rue Charles Buls (which soon changes its name to Stoofstraat). Just five yards off the square, under the*

arch, is a well-polished, well-loved brass statue.

You'll see tourists and locals rubbing a **brass statue** of a reclining man. This was Mayor Evrard 't Serclaes, who in 1356 bravely refused to surrender the keys of the city to invaders, and so was tortured and killed. Touch him, and his misfortune becomes your good luck. Judging by the reverence with which locals treat this ritual, I figure there must be something to it.

A half-block farther (on the left), the **N. Toebac Lace Shop** is a welcoming place with fine lace, a knowledgeable staff, and an interesting three-minute video. Brussels is perhaps the best-known city for traditional lacemaking, and this shop still sells handmade pieces in the old style:

Lace

In the 1500s, lace collars, sleeves, headdresses, and veils were fashionable among rich men and women. For the next 200 years, the fashion raged (peaking in about 1700). All this lace had to be made by hand, and many women earned extra income from the demand. But the French Revolution of 1789 suddenly made lace for men undemocratic and unmanly. Then, in about 1800, machines replaced human hands, and except for ornamental pieces, the fashion died out among women, too.

These days, handmade lace is usually also homemade—not produced in factories, but at home by dedicated, sharp-eyed hobbyists who love their work. Unlike knitting, it requires total concentration as the lacemaker follows intricate patterns. Lacemakers create their own patterns or trace tried-and-true designs. A piece of lace takes days, not hours, to make—which is why a handmade tablecloth can easily sell for €250.

There are two basic kinds of lace: bobbin lace (which originated in Bruges) and needle lace. To make bobbin lace, the lacemaker juggles many different strands tied to bobbins, "weaving" a design by overlapping the threads. Because of the difficulties, the resulting pattern is usually rather rough and simple compared with other techniques.

Needle lace is more like sewing—stitching pre-made bits onto a pattern. For example, the "Renaissance" design is made by sewing a pre-made ribbon onto a pattern in a fancy design. This is then attached as a fringe to a piece of linen—to make a fancy tablecloth, for instance.

In the "Princess" design, pre-made pieces are stitched onto a cotton net. This method is often used to make all sorts of pieces, from small doilies to full wedding veils.

"Rose point"—no longer practiced—used authentic bits of handmade antique lace as an ornament in a frame or to fill a pendant. Antique pieces can be very expensive.

lace clothing, doilies, tablecloths, and ornamental pieces (daily 9:30-19:30, Rue Charles Buls 10). The shop gives travelers with this book a 15 percent discount. For more on lace, the Costume and Lace Museum is a block away and just around the corner (closed Wed).

A block farther down the street on the left (at the little yellow window before the busy street) is the always-popular **Waffle Factory,** where €2 gets you a freshly made take-away "Belgian"

Tapestries

In 1500, tapestry workshops in Brussels were famous, cranking out high-quality tapestries for the walls of Europe's palaces. They were functional (as insulation and propaganda for a church, king, or nobleman) and beautiful—an intricate design formed by colored thread. Even great painters, such as Rubens and Raphael, designed tapestries, which rivaled Renaissance canvases.

To make a tapestry, neutral-colored threads are stretched vertically over a loom. (In Renaissance Belgium, the threads were made from imported English wool.) The design of the tapestry is created with the horizontal weave, from the colored threads that (mostly) overlay the vertical threads. Tapestry-making is much more difficult than basic weaving, as each horizontal thread is only as long as the detail it's meant to create. A single horizontal row can be made up of many individual pieces of thread. Before weaving begins, an artist designs a pattern for the larger picture, called a "cartoon," which weavers follow for guidance as they work.

Flanders and Paris (in the Gobelins workshop) were the two centers of tapestry-making until the art died out, mirroring the decline of Europe's noble class.

(Liège-style) waffle (up to €5 more if you opt for any of the fun toppings).

Across the busy street, step into the **Textilux Center** (Rue Lombard 41, on the left) for a good look at Belgian tapestries—both traditional wall-hangings and modern goods, such as tapestry purses and luggage in traditional designs.

High on the wall to the right, notice the delightful **comic strip panel** depicting that favorite of Belgian comic heroes, Tintin, climbing a fire escape. (For those unfamiliar with this character—beloved by virtually all Europeans—his dog is named Snowy, Captain Haddock keeps an eye out for him, and the trio are always getting into misadventures. Dozens of these building-sized comic-strip panels decorate Brussels (marked on the TI's €0.50 map), celebrating the Belgians' favorite medium. Just as Ireland has its writers, Italy its painters, and France its chefs, Belgium has a knack for turning out world-class comic artists.

• *Follow the crowds, noticing the excitement build, because in another block you reach the...*

Manneken-Pis

Even with low expectations, this bronze statue is smaller than you'd think—the little squirt's under two feet tall, practically the size of a newborn. Still, the little peeing boy is an appropriately low-key symbol for the unpretentious Bruxelloise. The statue was made in 1619 to provide drinking water for the neighborhood. Notice that the baby, sculpted in Renaissance style, actually has

the musculature of a man instead of the pudgy limbs of a child. The statue was actually knighted by the occupying King Louis XV—so French soldiers had to salute the eternally pissing lad when they passed. Sometimes, *Manneken-Pis* is dressed in one of the 700 different costumes that visiting VIPs have brought for him (including an Elvis Pissley outfit).

There are several different legends about the story behind *Manneken*—take your pick. He was a naughty boy who peed inside a witch's house, so she froze him. A rich man lost his son and declared, "Find my son, and we'll make a statue of him doing what he did when found." A bishop cured a nobleman's infertile wife, and when the baby was born, he immediately urinated on the bishop. Or—the locals' favorite version—the little tyke loved his beer, which came in handy when a fire threatened the wooden city: He bravely put it out. Want the truth? The city commissioned it to show the freedom and joie de vivre of living in Brussels—where

happy people eat, drink...and drink...and then pee.

The gathering crowds make the scene more interesting. Hang out for a while and watch the commotion this little guy makes as tour groups come and go. When I was there, a Russian man marveled at the statue, shook his head, and said, "He never stop!"

UPPER TOWN WALK

The Upper Town has always had a more aristocratic feel than the medieval, commercial streets of the Lower Town. With broad boulevards, big marble buildings, palaces, museums, and so many things called "royal," it also seems much newer and a bit more sterile. But the Upper Town has a history that stretches back to Brussels' beginnings.

Use this walk to get acquainted with this less-touristed part of town, sample some world-class museums, see the palace, explore art galleries, and get the lay of the land from a panoramic viewpoint. The tour starts a half-block from the one essential art sight in town, the complex that holds the Royal Museums of Fine Arts of Belgium (museums of ancient and modern art) and the Magritte Museum. Consider a visit while you're here (see next chapter). The Musical Instruments Museum is also in the neighborhood.

Orientation

Length of This Walk: Allow 1.5 hours.

Getting There: The walk begins at Place Royale/Koningsplein in the Upper Town. You have several ways to get there:

    1. From the Grand Place, walk uphill for 15 minutes (follow your map).

    2. From the Bourse, near Falstaff Café, take bus #95, which leaves every few minutes for Place Royale (bus signs call it *Royale/Koning;* buy ticket from driver, validate it in machine).

    3. Catch a taxi (figure €6 from the Bourse).

    4. Hop off here during a hop-on, hop-off bus tour.

Route Overview: From Place Royale, walk south along the

Upper Town Walk

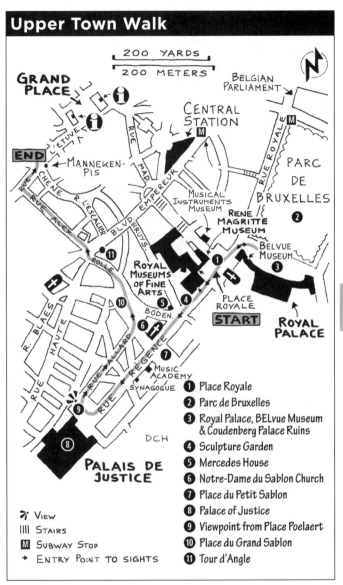

200 YARDS

200 METERS

GRAND PLACE

BELGIAN PARLIAMENT

CENTRAL STATION

RUE MAD.

RUE L'ÉTUVE

END

MANNEKEN-PIS

RUE CHÊNE

R. LESCALIER

BLVD D'RUYS.

BLVD EMPEREUR

MUSICAL INSTRUMENTS MUSEUM

RENE MAGRITTE MUSEUM

RUE ROYALE

PARC DE BRUXELLES

BELVUE MUSEUM

PARC BRUXELLES

RUE ALEX

ROLLE

ROYAL MUSEUMS OF FINE ARTS

BODEN.

PLACE ROYALE

START

ROYAL PALACE

R. BLAES

RUE HAUTE

RUE ALLARD

RUE REGENCE

MUSIC ACADEMY

SYNAGOGUE

RUE

DCH

PALAIS DE JUSTICE

❶ Place Royale
❷ Parc de Bruxelles
❸ Royal Palace, BELvue Museum & Coudenberg Palace Ruins
❹ Sculpture Garden
❺ Mercedes House
❻ Notre-Dame du Sablon Church
❼ Place du Petit Sablon
❽ Palace of Justice
❾ Viewpoint from Place Poelaert
❿ Place du Grand Sablon
⓫ Tour d'Angle

🕊 View
|||| Stairs
Ⓜ Subway Stop
→ Entry Point to Sights

UPPER TOWN WALK

ridge. On the way, pop in to a stained-glass-filled Gothic church, then continue on to reach the towering Palace of Justice, which has the best view of the city. Backtrack a bit and descend through the well-worn tapestry of the Sablon Quarter's antiques stores, art galleries, and cafés, ending down to the *Manneken-Pis* at the foot of the hill.

Starring: Brussels' genteel Upper Town, with its best museums, top views, and a bit of personality poking out from behind its stuffy veneer.

The Walk Begins

❶ Place Royale (Koningsplein)

At the crest of the hill sits Place Royale, encircled by cars and trams and enclosed by white Neoclassical buildings forming a mirror image across a cobblestone square. A big, green statue of a horseman stands in the center.

The **statue** depicts Belgium-born Godfrey de Bouillon, who led the First Crusade (in 1096). He rides forward with his flag, gazing down on the Town Hall spire. If Godfrey turned and looked left down Rue de la Régence, he'd see the domed Palace of Justice at the end of the boulevard. Over his right shoulder, just outside the square, is the Royal Palace, the king's residence.

In the 1800s, as Belgium exerted itself to industrialize and modernize, this area was rebuilt as a sign that Brussels had arrived as a world capital. Broad vistas down wide boulevards end at gleaming white, Greek-columned monuments—this look was all the rage, seen in Paris, London, Washington, DC...and here.

The cupola of the **Church of St. Jacques sur Coudenberg**— the central portion of the square's ring of buildings—makes the church look more like a bank building. But St. Jacques' church goes back much farther than this building (from 1787); the original was built here in the 13th century near a 12th-century castle. Nobles chose to build their mansions in the neighborhood—and, later, so did the king.

The square has several worthwhile museums: the Royal Museums of Fine Arts of Belgium (main entrance a half-block to the right) and the associated Magritte Museum (facing the crusader statue; see tour chapter), and the Musical Instruments Museum, straight downhill from the square—if Godfrey spurred his horse straight ahead, he'd pass it on his right. It's housed in an early 20th-century iron-and-glass former department store. Its Art Nouveau facade was a deliberate attempt to get beyond the retro-looking Greek columns and domes of the Place Royale. Even if you don't visit the Musical Instruments Museum, you can ride the elevator up to the museum café for a superb Lower Town view.

• *Before heading south, exit Place Royale on the north side (to the left as you face Godfrey), which opens up to a large, tree-lined park.*

❷ Parc de Bruxelles

Copying Versailles, the Habsburg empress Maria Theresa of Austria (Marie-Antoinette's mom) had this symmetrical park laid out in 1776, when she ruled (but never visited) the city. This is just one of many large parks in Brussels, which expanded with an awareness of the importance of city planning.

At the far (north) end of the park (directly opposite the Royal Palace, no need to actually walk there) is the Parliament building. Which parliament? The city hosts several: the European Parliament, the Belgian Parliament, and several local, city-council-type parliaments. This is the Belgian Parliament, seen on nightly newscasts as a backdrop for talking heads and politicians.

In 1830, Belgian patriots rose up and converged on the park, where they attacked the troops of the Dutch king. This was the first blow in a short, almost bloodless revolution that drove out the foreign-born king and gave the Belgians independence...and a different foreign-born king.

• *The long building facing the park is the...*

❸ Royal Palace (Palais Royale)

Belgium struck out twice trying to convince someone to be their new king. Finally, Leopold I (r. 1831-1865), a nobleman from Germany, agreed to become "King of the Belgians." Leopold was a steadying influence as the country modernized. His son rebuilt this palace—near the site of earlier palaces, dating back to the 10th century—by linking a row of townhouse mansions with a unifying facade (around 1870).

Leopold's great-great-great-grandnephew, King Albert II, today uses the palace as an office. (His head is on Belgium's euro coins.) Albert and his wife, Queen Paola, live in a palace north of here (near the Atomium) and on the French Riviera. If the Belgian flag (black-yellow-red) is flying from the palace, the king is somewhere in Belgium.

Albert II (born 1932) is a figurehead king, as in many European democracies, but he serves an important function as a common bond between bickering Flemish and Walloon citizens. His son, Prince Philippe, is slated to succeed him, though Philippe—

awkward and standoffish—is not as popular as his wife, Mathilde, also a Belgian native. Their daughter, Elisabeth, born in 2001, will someday become the first Belgian queen.

The bulk of the palace is off-limits to tourists except from late July through early September (see www.opt.be for the latest schedule; gardens open April-May). The adjacent **BELvue Museum** has an impressive exhibit on Belgian history and the royal family, but I'd skip the ho-hum **Coudenberg Palace** ruins (same entry for both).

• *Return to Place Royale, then continue south along Rue de la Régence, noticing the main entrance to the Royal Museums of Fine Arts of Belgium complex. Just past the museums, on the right, you'll see a...*

❹ Sculpture Garden (Jardin de Sculpture)

This pleasant public garden features a statue by Rodin's contemporary, Aristide Maillol, a master of the female form. In *The River* (1938-1943), the moving water is personified as a woman sprawled on her side (and looking terrified, or at least stressed—the statue was originally conceived to represent a victim of war). The wave-like figure teeters on the edge of a pool of water, about to pour in. Or is she just washing her hair? Another copy of this bronze statue sprawls near a pool in the courtyard of New York's Museum of Modern Art.

The garden looks like a great way to descend into the Sablon Quarter, but the gates at the bottom are often locked.

• *About 75 yards farther along Rue de la Régence, on your right at the intersection, is the...*

❺ Mercedes House

This sleek, modern showroom is free to the public, hosting temporary exhibits on cars that change every six months. There's usually a bit of history for classic-car enthusiasts, plus a peek at the latest Mercedes models. The venue also hosts cultural events such as chamber music and jazz (Mon-Sat 10:00-20:00, Fri until 22:00, Sun 10:00-16:00, Rue Bodenbroek 22-24, tel. 02-400-4250, www.mercedeshouse.be). Its classy café/brasserie is open weekdays for lunch and until late on Fridays (closed Sat-Sun).

• *A few yards farther along, you reach the top of the Sablon neighborhood, dominated by the...*

❻ Notre-Dame du Sablon Church

The round, rose, stained-glass windows in the clerestory of this 14th-century Flamboyant Gothic church are nice by day, but are

thrilling at night, when the church is lit from inside and glows like a lantern, enjoyed by locals at the cafés in the surrounding square.

Step inside (enter at the far end, facing the Palace of Justice; free, open daily 8:00-18:00). An artistically carved pulpit stands midway up the nave. The stained-glass windows in the nave are notable for their symmetry—rows

of saints in Gothic niches topped by coats of arms. The glorious apse behind the altar—bathed in colorful light—is what Gothic is all about. The left transept has relics of Karl I, the last Habsburg emperor (1887-1922), who was deposed when Austria became a republic after World War I. Karl's Catholic devotion was legendary, and he was beatified in 2004. Many devoted people pray here, inspired by his patient suffering in exile.

Next to the altar, see a small wooden **statue of Mary** dressed in white with a lace veil. This is a copy, made after iconoclastic Protestant vandals destroyed the original. The original statue was thought to have had miraculous powers that saved the town from plagues. In 1348, when the statue was in Antwerp, it spoke to a godly woman named Beatrix, prompting her to snatch Mary,

board a boat, and steal the statue away from Antwerp. (That's why the church is decorated with several images of boats, including the small **wooden boat** high up in the right transept.) When the citizens of Antwerp tried to stop Beatrix, the Mary statue froze them in their tracks.

When Beatrix and the statue arrived here, the Bruxelloise welcomed Mary with a joyous parade. Not long after, this large church

was erected in her honor. Every summer, in Brussels' famous Ommegang procession, locals in tights and flamboyant costumes re-create the joyous arrival with colorful banners and large puppets. Imagine the scene as they carry Mary from here through the city streets to the parade's climax on the Grand Place.

• *We'll return to the colorful Place du grand Sablon later in the walk.*

For now, head to the other side of Rue de la Régence from the church, where you'll find a leafy, fenced-off garden called the...

❼ Place du Petit Sablon

This is a pleasant refuge from the busy street, part of why this neighborhood is considered so livable. The 48 small statues atop the wrought-iron fence represent the craftsman guilds—weavers, brewers, and butchers—of medieval Brussels. Inside the garden, 10 large statues represent hometown thinkers of the 16th century— a time of great intellectual accomplishments in Brussels. Gerardus Mercator (1512-1594), the Belgian mapmaker who

devised a way to more accurately show the spherical Earth on a flat surface, holds a globe.

• *We'll visit the Sablon neighborhood below the church later, but before losing elevation, let's continue along Rue de la Régence, passing on the left the Music Academy and Brussels' main synagogue—its sidewalk fortified with concrete posts to keep car bombs at a distance—before reaching the long-scaffolded...*

❽ Palace of Justice (Palais de Justice)

This domed mountain of marble sits on the edge of the Upper Town ridge, dominating the Brussels skyline. Built in wedding-cake layers of Greek columns, it's topped with a dome taller than St. Peter's in Rome, rising 340 feet. Covering more than six acres, it's the size of a baseball stadium.

The palace was built in the time of King Leopold II (son of Leo I, r. 1865-1909) and epitomizes the brassy, showy grandeur of his reign. Leopold became obscenely wealthy by turning Africa's Congo region—80 times the size of Belgium—into his personal colony. Whip-wielding Belgian masters forced Congolese slaves to tend lucrative rubber plantations, exploiting the new craze for bicycle tires. Leopold spent much of this wealth expanding and beautifying the city of Brussels.

The building (which stands on the historic site of the town gallows) serves as a Hall of Justice, where major court cases are tried. If you pop in to the lobby, you may see lawyers in black robes buzzing about.

Notice the rack of city bikes. Like many other European cities, Brussels subsidizes a public-bike system. The program, called "Villo," lets locals use bikes scattered all over town (note the map here) for a token €1 per hour. You can pick up a bike in one part of town and drop it off anywhere else. But the scheme doesn't always work as well as intended: These bike racks are often empty, since this is a popular place to grab a bike for the easy ride back down to the Lower Town.

• *One of the best views of Brussels is immediately to the right of the Palace of Justice.*

❾ Viewpoint from Place Poelaert

You're standing 200 feet above the former Senne River Valley. Gazing west over the Lower Town, pan the valley from right (north) to left:

Near you is the stubby **clock tower** of the Minimen Church (which hosts lunchtime concerts in the summer). To the left of that, in the distance past a tall square skyscraper, is the lacy, white Town Hall **spire** (marking the Grand Place).

In the far distance, six miles away, you can see one of the city's landmarks, the **Atomium.** (No doubt, someone atop it is looking back at you.) The Atomium's nine shiny steel balls form the shape of an iron molecule that's the size of the Palace of Justice behind you. Built for the 1958 World's Fair, it's now a middle-aged symbol of the dawn of the Atomic Era.

Next (closer to you) rises the **black clock tower** of the Notre-Dame de la Chapelle church, the city's oldest (from 1134, with a

tower that starts Gothic and ends Baroque). On the distant horizon, see **five boxy skyscrapers,** part of the residential sprawl of this city of 1.8 million, which now covers 62 square miles. Breaking the horizon to the left is a **green dome,** which belongs to the Basilica of Koekelberg (fourth biggest in the world). And finally (panning quickly to the left), you see a **black glass skyscraper** marking the Midi/Zuid/South train station, where you can catch special high-speed train lines, such as the Eurostar, to London.

At your feet lies the **Marolles neighborhood.** Once a funky, poor place where locals developed their own quirky dialogue, today it can be either seedy or colorful, depending on the time of day and your perception. The area is famous for its sprawling flea market (daily 7:00-14:00, best on weekends). Two of the streets just below you—Rue Haute/Hoogstraat and Rue Blaes/Blaesstraat—are lined with secondhand shops. An **elevator** (free, daily 6:00-23:00) connects Place Poelaert with the Marolles neighborhood, which is worth a 10-minute detour to descend to the café-lined square. People who brake for garage sales may want to cut out of this walk early and head to the Marolles from here.

Gazing off into the distance to the far left (south), you can't quite see the suburb of **Waterloo,** 10 miles away. But try to imagine it, because it was there that the tide of European history turned. On the morning of June 18, 1815, Napoleon waited two hours for the ground to dry before sending his troops into battle. That time lag may have cost him the battle. His 72,000 soldiers could have defeated Wellington's 68,000, but the two-hour delay was just enough time for Wellington's reinforcements to arrive—45,000 Prussian troops. Napoleon had to surrender, his rule of Europe ended, and Belgium was placed under a Dutch king—until the Belgians won their independence in the 1830 revolution.

Behind you, in Place Poelaert, is a memorial to the two World Wars, both of which slashed through Belgium with deadly force.

• *Backtrack east, descending to Place du Grand Sablon by walking down Rue Ernest Allard.*

❿ Place du Grand Sablon

The Sablon neighborhood features cafés and restaurants, antiques stores, and art galleries. Chocolatier Wittamer (on the far side of  the square, at #6) often has elaborate window displays. Every weekend, there's an antiques market on the square. On warm summer evenings, the square sparks magic, as sophisticated locals sip apéritifs at the café tables, admiring the church's glowing stained glass.

• *Sloping Place du Grand Sablon funnels downhill into the pedestrian-only street called Rue de Rollebeek, which leads you past fun shops to the busy Boulevard de l'Empereur. To the right on the boulevard, just past the bowling alley, is the...*

⓫ Tour d'Angle

The "Corner Tower" is a rare surviving section of Brussels' 13th-century city wall, and was one of 7 gates along the 2.5-mile-long wall that enclosed Brussels, one of Europe's great cities.

• *Central Station is two blocks directly ahead. To reach the Grand Place, continue downhill two long blocks on Rue des Alexiens (angling off ahead of the bowling alley), and when you hit level ground, turn right on Rue l'Etuve, which leads you directly there. A block along, you'll run into our old friend* Manneken-Pis, *eternally relieving himself (if you're urine-ing to learn more about this leaky little tyke).*

ROYAL MUSEUMS OF FINE ARTS & MAGRITTE MUSEUM TOUR

Musées Royaux des Beaux-Arts de Belgique • Musée Magritte

This museum complex, spread throughout three large buildings, covers the entire history of Western painting. There are technically three museums here: The Museum of Ancient Art (pre-1800), the Museum of Modern Art (post-1800), and—covered by a separate ticket—the Magritte Museum, which celebrates the work of the popular Belgian Surrealist painter. The collections, while enjoyable, can be overwhelming, so this chapter gives you a tour highlighting the museums' strengths: Flemish and Belgian artists. But don't plan your visit around these works—let the museums surprise you.

Orientation

Cost: €8 for Ancient Art and Modern Art museums; €8 for Magritte Museum; €13 combo-ticket covers all three. All are free the first Wed of the month after 13:00. Temporary exhibits (optional) may have an additional charge.

Hours: Tue-Sun 10:00-17:00, closed Mon, last entry 30 minutes before closing. The Magritte Museum stays open Wed until 20:00.

Reservations for the Magritte Museum: A set number of visitors are allowed into the Magritte Museum each hour—you'll reserve an entrance time when you buy your ticket. You must enter the museum during the one-hour window printed on your ticket; the ticket is invalid outside that time. On busy weekends there can be up to a three-hour wait to get in.

If you buy your ticket in advance online (www.musee -magritte-museum.be, no refunds or exchanges), you can skip the wait and enter the Magritte Museum via its doorway on Place Royale/Koningsplein; otherwise, buy your ticket at the main complex entrance at Rue de la Régence 3.

Getting There: The main entrance, with access to all three museums, is at Rue de la Régence 3 in the Upper Town, just a five-minute walk uphill from Central Station (or take bus #38, #71, or #95; or tram #92 or #94). Bus #27 connects this area with the European Parliament and the Park of the Cinquantenaire. You'll also encounter these museums if you take my Upper Town Walk (see previous chapter).

Keep Your Magrittes Straight: Don't confuse this Magritte Museum with the much smaller René Magritte Museum, located in Magritte's former home on the outskirts of Brussels.

Information: Consider the €4 audioguide or the €2.50 tour booklet (*Twenty Masterpieces of the Art of Painting: A Brief Guided Tour,* sold in the museum shop). Ancient Art and Modern Art museums: Tel. 02-508-3211, www.fine-arts-museum.be. Magritte Museum: Tel. 02-508-3333, www.musee-magritte -museum.be.

Length of This Tour: Allow one hour for the ancient and modern art museums, and another hour for the Magritte Museum.

Cuisine Art: The Greshem, a restaurant and tea room, is nearby at Place Royale (daily 11:00-18:00). The museums also have a pricey café and a fancy brasserie on site.

The Tour Begins

Plan your visit to the ancient and modern art museums around your reserved entry time for the Magritte Museum. This tour

assumes you'll visit the ancient and modern art museums first, then the Magritte Museum.

Enter at Rue de la Régence 3 and buy your ticket (advance tickets available online for Magritte Museum—see above). Continue into the large entrance hall and get oriented. The Museum of Ancient Art is on the second floor (in the galleries above you), reached by the staircase directly ahead. The Museum of Modern Art is through the doorway to the right, down several levels. The Magritte Museum is also to the right, through a passageway.

Stop first at the information desk, which has the latest on renovations, room closings, and where paintings are currently located. This is also where you can rent an audioguide. Armed with the museum's free map, make your way through the maze, enjoying whatever you find. Along the way, look for these highlights.

Museum of Ancient Art

• *Go up to the second floor and start with the Flemish masters. Notice how the rooms on the second floor surround a central hall. The art is displayed in (roughly) chronological order, working counterclockwise around the central gallery. In the first room, look for...*

Rogier van der Weyden (c. 1399-1464)—*Portrait of Anthony of Burgundy (Portrait d' Antoine de Bourgogne)*

Anthony was known in his day as the Great Bastard, the bravest and most distinguished of the many bastards fathered by prolific Duke Philip the Good (a Renaissance prince whose sense of style impressed Florence's young Lorenzo the Magnificent, patron of the arts).

Anthony, a member of the Archers Guild, fingers the arrow like a bowstring. From his gold necklace dangles a Golden Fleece, one of Europe's more prestigious knightly honors. Wearing a black cloak, a bowl-cut hairdo, and a dark-red cap, with his pale face and hand emerging from a dark background, the man who'd been called a bastard all his life gazes to the distance, his clear, sad eyes lit with a speckle of white paint.

Van der Weyden, Brussels' official portrait painter, faithfully rendered life-size, lifelike portraits of wealthy traders, bankers, and craftsmen. Here he captures the wrinkles in Anthony's neck and the faint shadow his chin casts on his Adam's apple. Van der Weyden had also painted Philip the Good (in Bruges' Groeninge Museum), and young Anthony's long, elegant face and full lips are a mirror image—pretty convincing DNA evidence in a paternity suit.

Capitalist Flanders in the 1400s was one of the richest, most cultured, and progressive areas in Europe, rivaling Florence and Venice.

• *Continue counterclockwise around the central gallery. As you head up the right side (in the third section), find...*

Hans Memling (c. 1430-1494)—*Martyrdom of St. Sebastian (Volets d'un Triptyque)*

Serene Sebastian is filled with arrows by a serene firing squad in a serene landscape. Sebastian, a Roman captain who'd converted to Christianity, was ordered to be shot to death. (He miraculously survived, so they clubbed him to death.)

Ready, freeze! Like a *tableau vivant* (popular with Philip

the Good's crowd), the well-dressed archers and saint freeze this moment in the martyrdom so the crowd can applaud the colorful costumes and painted cityscape backdrop.

Hans Memling, along with his former employer, Rogier van der Weyden, are called Flemish Primitives. Why "Primitive"? The term comes from the lack of 3-D realism so admired in Italy at the time. Sebastian's arm is tied to a branch that's not arching overhead, as it should be, but instead is behind him. An archer aims slightly behind, not at, Sebastian. The other archer strings his bow in a stilted pose. But Memling is clearly a master of detail, and the faces, beautiful textiles, and hazy landscape combine to create a meditative mood appropriate to the church altar in Bruges where this painting was once placed.

• *Next, head for the far-right corner of Room 68, where paintings by Pieter Brueghel I often are displayed.*

Pieter Brueghel I, the Elder (c. 1527-1569)— *The Census at Bethlehem*

Perched at treetop level, you have a bird's-eye view over a snow-covered village near Brussels. The canals are frozen over, but life

goes on, with everyone doing something. Kids throw snowballs and sled across the ice. A crowd gathers at the inn (lower left), where a woman holds a pan to catch blood while a man slaughters a pig. Most everyone has his or her back to us or head covered, so the figures speak through poses and motions.

Into the scene rides a woman on a donkey led by a man—it's Mary and husband Joseph hoping to find a room at the inn (or at least a manger), because Mary's going into labor.

The year is 1566—the same year that Protestant extremists throughout the Low Countries vandalized Catholic churches, tearing down "idolatrous" statues and paintings of the Virgin Mary. Brueghel (more discreetly) brings Mary down to earth from her Triumphant Coronation in heaven, and places Jesus' birth in the humble here and now. The busy villagers put their heads down and work, oblivious to the future Mother of God and the wonderous birth about to take place.

Brueghel the Elder was famous for his landscapes filled with crowds of peasants in motion. His religious paintings place the miraculous in everyday settings.

In this room you'll see Brueghel's works, as well as those of his less famous sons. Pieter Brueghel II, the younger Pieter, copied his dad's style (and even some paintings, like the *Census at Bethlehem*—displayed to the left). Another son, Jan, was known as the "Velvet Brueghel" for his glossy still lifes of flower arrangements.

• *Circle counterclockwise through the rest of the Ancient Art collection, until you finally reach works by Rubens in Rooms 52 and 53, including the wall-sized...*

Peter Paul Rubens (1577-1640)—*The Ascent to Calvary (La Montée au Calvaire)*

Life-size figures scale this 18-foot-tall canvas on the way to Christ's Crucifixion. The scene ripples with motion, from the windblown clothes to steroid-enhanced muscles to billowing flags and a troubled sky. Christ stumbles—he might get trampled by the surging crowd. Veronica kneels to gently wipe his bloody head.

This 200-square-foot canvas was manufactured by Rubens at his studio in Antwerp. Hiring top-notch assistants, Rubens could crank out large altarpieces for the area's Catholic churches. First, Rubens himself did a small-scale sketch in oil (like many of the studies in Room 52). He would then make other sketches, highlighting individual details. His assistants would reproduce them on the large canvas, and Rubens would then add the final touches.

This work is from late in Rubens' long and very successful career. He got a second wind in his 50s, when he married 16-year-old Hélène Fourment. She was the model for Veronica, who consoles the faltering Christ in this painting.

• *Exit the Rubens room to the left, go into the perpendicular Room 53, and look right to find...*

Jacques-Louis David (1748-1825)—*The Death of Marat (1793)*

In a scene ripped from the day's headlines, Jean-Paul Marat—a well-known crusading French journalist—has been stabbed to

ROYAL MUSEUMS

death in his bathtub by Charlotte Corday, a conservative fanatic. Marat's life drains out of him, turning the bathwater red. With his last strength, he pens a final, patriotic, *"Vive la Révolution"* message to his fellow patriots. Corday, a young noblewoman angered by Marat's campaign to behead the French king, was arrested and guillotined three days later.

Jacques-Louis David, one of Marat's fellow revolutionaries, set to work painting a tribute to his fallen comrade. (He signed the painting: *"À Marat"*—"To Marat.")

David makes it a secular *pietà*, with the brave writer portrayed as a martyred Christ in a classic dangling-arm pose. Still, the deathly pallor and harsh lighting pull no punches, creating in-your-face realism.

David, the official art director of the French Revolution, supervised propaganda and the costumes worn for patriotic parades. A year after finishing this painting, in 1794, his extreme brand of revolution (which included guillotining thousands of supposed enemies) was squelched by moderates, and David was jailed. He emerged later as Napoleon's court painter. When Napoleon was exiled in 1815, so was David, spending his last years in Brussels.

• *To get to the Museum of Modern Art wing, return to the ground floor and the large main entrance hall of the Museum of Ancient Art. From there a passageway leads you to the Modern Art and Magritte museums. You'll pass the entrance to the Magritte Museum, then continue down into the Modern Art wing (entering on Level -3).*

Museum of Modern Art

• *Follow the "Circuit," which leads you down, down, down through several levels on a chronological route through the artwork. Keep an eye out for the following paintings; enlist the help of nearby guards if you can't find a piece.*

Watch Romanticism turn to Impressionism turn to Post-Impressionism. Paul Gauguin and Georges Seurat emerged from Paris' Impressionist community to forge their own styles. Begin on Level -6 by visiting with...

James Ensor (1860-1949)—*Shocked Masks* (1883)

At 22, James Ensor, an acclaimed child prodigy, proudly presented his lively Impressionist-style works to the Brussels Salon for exhibition. They were flatly rejected.

The artist withdrew from public view and, in seclusion,

painted *Shocked Masks,* a dark and murky scene set in a small room of an ordinary couple wearing grotesque masks. Once again, everyone disliked this disturbing canvas and heaped more criticism on him. For the next six decades, Ensor painted the world as he saw it—full of bizarre, carnival-masked, stupid-looking crowds of cruel strangers who mock the viewer.

• *Farther along on Level -6 is something a bit cheerier...*

Georges Seurat (1859-1891)—*The Seine at Grand-Jatte* (*La Seine à la Grande-Jatte,* 1888)

Seurat paints a Sunday-in-the-park view from his favorite island in the Seine. Taking Impressionism to its extreme, he builds the scene out of small points of primary colors that blend at a distance to form objects. The bright colors capture the dazzling, sunlit atmosphere of this hazy day.

• *Behind you is...*

Paul Gauguin (1848-1903)—*Breton Calvary* (*Calvaire Breton,* 1889; a.k.a. *The Green Christ/Le Christ Vert*)

Paul Gauguin returned to the bold, black, coloring-book outlines of more Primitive (pre-3-D) art. The Christian statue and countryside look less like Brittany and more like primitive Tahiti, where Gauguin would soon settle.

• *Level -8 features work by Salvador Dalí, Francis Bacon, and Belgium's own...*

Paul Delvaux (1897-1994)—*Spitzner Museum* (*Le Musée Spitzner,* 1943)

Delvaux, who studied, worked, and taught in Brussels, became famous for his surrealistic paintings of nude women, often wan-

dering through weirdly lit landscapes. They cast long shadows,
wandering bare-breasted among
classical ruins.

• *Belgium has a special affinity for
Surrealist artists, represented in this
museum by the likes of Joan Miró,
Salvador Dalí, Max Ernst, Yves
Tanguy, and Roberto Matta. If you
want more, consider visiting the
Magritte Museum, described next.*

Magritte Museum

Entry to the Magritte Museum is covered by a separate ticket,
which comes with a reserved entry time.

This museum takes you on a chronological route (spread over
several levels of the building) through René Magritte's life and
art. The museum divides his life into three sections, with one floor
devoted to each. At the start of each section is a detailed timeline,
followed by the artist's work. Fascinating quotes from Magritte are
posted around the museum, but only in the original French; pick
up the English translation as you enter.

Magritte's works are perhaps best described in his own
words: "My paintings are visible images which conceal nothing; they evoke mystery and, indeed, when one sees one of my
pictures, one asks oneself this simple question, 'What does
that mean'? It does not mean anything, because mystery means
nothing either, it is unknowable." If that brain-teaser titil-
lates you, you'll love this museum; if it frustrates you, consider
skipping it.

• *From the entrance, you'll board an elevator that takes you up to Level
+3. (Notice the woman's body parts—slowly panning up from the feet to
head—in the window in the back of the elevator.)*

1898-1929 (Level +3)

Born to a middle-class Belgian family, René moved to Brussels at
age 17 to study at the Academy, where he learned to draw meticulously and got a broad liberal-arts education. In the 1920s, he eked
out a living designing advertisements, posters, and sheet music,
and wrote for the avant-garde *7 Arts* magazine (you'll see samples
posted). Meanwhile, he dabbled in Post-Impressionism, Futurism,
and Cubism, in search of his own voice.

In 1922, he married his childhood sweetheart, Georgette,
who became his lifelong companion and muse. It's said that all
the women he would paint (and you'll see many of them in this

René Magritte
(1898-1967)

René Magritte trained and worked in Brussels. Though he's world-famous now, it took decades before his peculiar brand of Surrealism caught on. He painted real objects with photographic clarity, and then jumbled them together in new and provocative ways.

Magritte had his own private reserve of symbolic images. You'll see clouds, blue sky, windows, the female torso, men in bowler hats, rocks, pipes, sleigh bells, birds, turtles, and castles arranged side by side as if the arrangement meant something. He heightens the mystery by making objects unnaturally large or small. People morph into animals or inanimate objects. The juxtaposition short-circuits your brain only when you try to make sense of it. Magritte's works are at once playful and disorienting...and, at times, disturbing.

collection) were versions of Georgette.

Influenced by the Dada and Surrealist movements coming out of Paris (Salvador Dalí, Marcel Duchamp, Giorgio de Chirico), Magritte became intrigued with the idea of painting dreamscapes that capture an air of mystery. You'll see mysterious figures on beaches, inspired by de Chirico's similar canvases.

For Magritte, 1927 was a watershed year, when he painted his first truly Surrealist works. *The Man from the Sea* featured a man on a beach with a wood-block head, pulling a lever. At the far end of the next room, *The Secret Player* perplexed the public (then and now) with a man swinging a bat and missing a flying turtle. In this section, and throughout this floor, you can see Magritte toying with Surrealist thoughts and techniques.

Together, René and Georgette mingled in sophisticated, bohemian circles. Photos show that their creativity went beyond the canvas. Looking at Georgette pose for René's lens (as she often did for his paintbrush), it's touching to think that he had found a soulmate who seemed to truly understand and encourage his weirdness. In the same section, see the series of photos of René, Georgette, and their friends striking wacky tableaux that intentionally distort normal poses. Called *The Fidelity of the Image,* this series was knocking on the door of Magritte's next breakthrough.

He experimented with writing words on the paintings, culminating in *The Treachery of Images.* The original (from 1928-1929, in the Los Angeles County Museum of Art) is Magritte's most famous work—not for its physical appearance, but for the bold conceptual point that it made. It's a photorealistic painting of a pipe with the words (in French) "This is not a pipe." Of course it's not a pipe, Magritte always insisted—it's a *painting* of a pipe. Magritte's wordplay forces the viewer to ponder the relationship between the object and its name—between the "signified" and the "signifier," to quote the deconstructionist philosophy that Magritte's paradoxical paintings inspired. Some credit this work for planting the seeds of postmodernism. At the end of this section you'll see a later ink-and-paper version (1952) with the message (also in French): "This continues not to be a pipe."

• *Head downstairs to...*

1930-1950 (Level +2)

After a few years in Paris, Magritte survived the Depression in Brussels by doing ad work and painting portraits of friends. (You'll see several women on his trademark Surrealist beaches.)

By the late 1930s, he'd refined his signature style: combining two arresting images to disrupt rational thought and produce an emotion of mystery. The paintings' weird titles added another layer of disruption. These were intentional nonsequiturs, which he and his Surrealist friends concocted at Sunday-night naming soirees. Perusing the paintings in here, it's fun to wonder which titles were random...and which meant something. *Forbidden Literature... The Kiss... The Unexpected Answer... God Is No Saint...*

During the World War II years—spent under Nazi occupation—Magritte used birds as a metaphor for the longing to be free *(The Companions of Fear, Treasure Island).*

In 1943, he had a brief Impressionistic period of bright colors and rough brushwork. His characteristic Georgette-inspired nude becomes Technicolor in *The Harvest.* He also took to painting tongue-in-cheek-serious "portraits" of animals *(Stroke of Luck).* Soon after, his series called *Black Magic* continued to colorize women's bodies. But he also created plenty of his distinctive paintings where the background and foreground seem to shift, with plenty of familiar motifs such as clouds and bowler hats.

In the postwar years, Magritte went through a *vache* ("cow") period, where he painted a series of comic-book-inspired paintings (including the green man with rifle-barrel nose, called *The Ellipsis*). Almost childlike, these are a dramatic departure from his normally photorealistic style.

1951-1967 (Level +1)

This floor is divided into two sections (don't overlook the easy-to-miss second one), and feels like a valedictory lap for all of the symbols and styles we've seen so far. At the foot of the stairs, you're greeted by a sculpture of a sleigh bell, curtains, and a blue sky entitled *Mona Lisa*—you'll see more renditions of this in the collection.

Like Picasso (and many other artists) nearing the end of a life of impressive output and experimentation, Magritte had a quiver full of artistic arrows to shoot at the canvas. And yet something feels rote about his final years of work—he seemed to rehash familiar territory, expressing things he'd already mastered—rather than experiment with bold new directions.

The collection culminates at his *Empire of Lights*, which shows how even well-scrubbed suburbia can possess an ominous air of mystery. Magritte loved night-sky tones. He often created several versions of the same work (which explains why there are several *Empire of Lights* canvases in the world).

By the end of his life, Magritte was well-known, especially in America. His use of everyday objects and poster-art style inspired Pop Art.

• *Exit through Level -1, which has a book shop and an appropriately perplexing 50-minute film about Magritte. Descend to Level -2 to find the passageway back to the Royal Museums...and reality.*

ROYAL MUSEUMS

BRUSSELS SLEEPING, EATING, NIGHTLIFE & CONNECTIONS

The capital of Belgium—and of the European Union—Brussels is a great place to spend some time. This chapter provides suggestions for the best places to sleep and eat; tips for after-hours fun; and a rundown of the complicated connections (from the city's three different train stations) to points throughout Belgium, the Netherlands, and beyond, as well as tips for getting to and from the city's two airports.

Sleeping in Brussels

Normal hotel prices are high in central Brussels. A popular business destination, it tends to be busiest, and most expensive, on weekdays. But if you arrive in July, August, or on a Friday or Saturday night, the city's fancy business-class hotels rent rooms for half-price, making them your best budget bet. (Conversely, Bruges—a pleasure destination—has higher demand on weekends. If your trip is flexible, consider arranging your overnights in these two towns with these deal-finding patterns in mind.)

April, May, September, and October are very crowded in Brussels, and finding a room without a reservation can be impossible. The busiest time of year is the European Seafood Exhibition (May 3-5 in 2011, www.euroseafood.com), when the city is awash in seafood-industry employees.

You do have budget options here. The modern hostels, which rent double rooms, are especially good.

Business Hotels with Summer Rates

Brussels' fancy hotels (Db-€150-200) survive because of the business and diplomatic trade. But they're desperately empty most of July and August (sometimes June, too) and on most weekends (Fri,

Sleep Code

(€1 = about $1.40, country code: 32)
S = Single, **D** = Double/Twin, **T** = Triple, **Q** = Quad, **b** = bathroom,
s = shower only. Everyone speaks English and accepts credit
cards. Unless otherwise noted, breakfast is included.

To help you easily sort through these listings, I've divided
the rooms into three categories, based on the price for a
standard double room with bath:

$$$ Higher Priced—Most rooms €100 or more.
  $$ Moderately Priced—Most rooms between €80-100.
    $ Lower Priced—Most rooms €80 or less.

Prices can change without notice; verify the hotel's
current rates online or by email. For other updates, see www
.ricksteves.com/update.

Sat, and, to a lesser extent, Sun nights). During these slow times, rates drop by a third to two-thirds. Three-star hotels in the center abound with amazing summer rates—you can rent a double room with enough comforts to keep a diplomat happy, including a fancy breakfast, for about €60.

There are two ways to get these great rates: You can go through a **booking website** (most Brussels hotels list their rooms through www.booking.com, but you might also find deals on other sites—check www.expedia.com, www.orbitz.com, or your favorite). Or you can book in person (or sometimes by phone or email) at one of Brussels' **TIs.** (Whereas TI booking services in many cities are a bad value, Brussels' is an exception—the TIs here can actually save you some money.) If you simply show up at the TI without a reservation during slow times, they can usually find you a great deal. Because some hotels hold out until the last minute to cut their rates, prices tend to plummet as the date approaches; booking a room a month ahead could cost you substantially more than booking a few days ahead.

Waiting does, however, pose some risks—for example, you might wind up in a less-than-ideal location farther from the action. If waiting seems too risky, do a little homework to gauge what the demand will be when you visit: Check rates online well before your trip. If rates are only slightly discounted, demand is probably pretty strong, so you should book sooner rather than later; if rates are already deeply discounted, consider holding off, to see if they go even lower.

Alternatively, you can contact the TI by email (info@visit flanders.us) or by phone (Town Hall TI room-booking desk is

02-563-6104) and ask which business-class hotels will have special rates during your visit. Ask for the cheapest three-star place near the Grand Place. Historically, the Hotel Ibis Centre Ste. Catherine has double rooms with bath and breakfast for €50 through the summer.

Note that many of the hotels I list below offer these deals. If you prefer to book direct with the hotel (rather than through the TI or a booking website), try this strategy: Check online booking sites to see what your hotel of choice is offering for the dates of your trip. Then contact the hotel directly to see if they'll honor that same price (or give you a better one).

These seasonal rates apply only to business-class hotels. Because of this, budget accommodations, which charge the same throughout the year, may go from being a good value one day (say, a Thursday in October) to a bad value the next (a Friday in October).

Hotels near the Grand Place

$$$ Hotel Ibis off Grand Place, well-situated halfway between Central Station and the Grand Place, is the best of six Ibis locations in or near Brussels. It's a sprawling, modern hotel offering 184 quiet, simple, industrial-strength-yet-comfy rooms (Sb/Db-€145-169 Mon-Thu, generally around €79 Fri-Sun and daily July-Aug, extra bed-€20, breakfast-€14, non-smoking, air-con, elevator, pay Internet access and Wi-Fi, Marché-aux-Herbes/Grasmarkt 100, tel. 02-514-4040, fax 02-514-5067, www.ibishotel.com, h1046 @accor.com).

$$$ Hotel Le Dixseptième, a four-star luxury hotel ideally located a block below Central Station, is an expensive oasis in the heart of town. Prim, proper, and peaceful, with chandeliers and squeaky hardwood floors, its 24 rooms come with all the comforts. Each is decorated with a different theme (Db-€200, Db suites-€270, extra bed-€30, 25 percent off Fri-Sat, often Db-€100 with no breakfast in July-Aug, see their website for deals, air-con, elevator, pay Internet access and Wi-Fi, Rue de la Madeleine/Magdalenasteenweg 25, tel. 02-517-1717, fax 02-502-6424, www .ledixseptieme.be, info@ledixseptieme.be).

$$$ Hotel La Madeleine, on the small "Agora" square between Central Station and the Grand Place, rents 56 plain, dimly lit rooms. It has a great location and a friendly staff (S-€55; Ss-€78, Sb-€108, Db-€115; bigger "executive" rooms: Sb-€125, Db-€130, Tb-€138, family Qb-€180; 20 percent off Fri-Sat, 30 percent off July-Aug—see website for deals, book direct and mention Rick Steves to get the best rates; request a quieter back room when you reserve, non-smoking, elevator, pay Internet access and Wi-Fi, Rue de la Montagne/Bergstraat 22, tel. 02-513-2973,

SLEEPING IN BRUSSELS

Brussels Accommodations

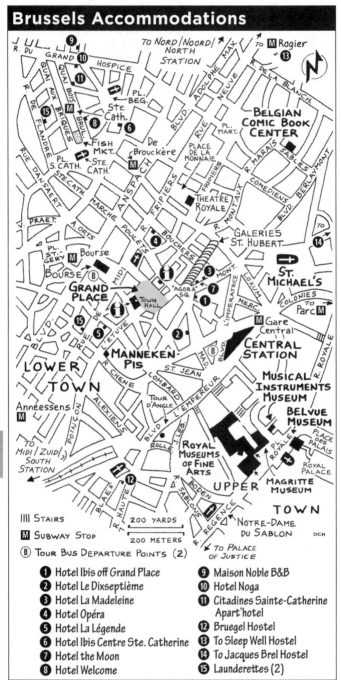

|||| Stairs

Ⓜ Subway Stop

Ⓑ Tour Bus Departure Points (2)

❶ Hotel Ibis off Grand Place
❷ Hotel Le Dixseptième
❸ Hotel La Madeleine
❹ Hotel Opéra
❺ Hotel La Légende
❻ Hotel Ibis Centre Ste. Catherine
❼ Hotel the Moon
❽ Hotel Welcome
❾ Maison Noble B&B
❿ Hotel Noga
⓫ Citadines Sainte-Catherine Apart'hotel
⓬ Bruegel Hostel
⓭ To Sleep Well Hostel
⓮ To Jacques Brel Hostel
⓯ Launderettes (2)

fax 02-502-1350, www.hotel-la-madeleine.be, info@hotel-la
-madeleine.be, Philippe).

$$$ Hotel Opéra, on a people-filled street near the Grand
Place, is professional but standardized, with lots of street noise
and 49 well-worn rooms (Sb-€89, Db-€119 or €85 in July-Aug,
Tb-€135, Qb-€150, 10 percent less with this book in 2011, request
a quieter courtyard room, elevator, free Wi-Fi, Grétry street 53,
tel. 02-219-4343, fax 02-219-1720, www.hotel-opera.be, reception
@hotel-opera.be).

$$$ Hotel La Légende rents 26 small, straightforward rooms
a block from the *Manneken-Pis* statue. Although it's on a busy
road, it has a pleasant courtyard. The furnishings are basic, but the
location and price are right and the rooms are comfortable enough
(prices very flexible—generally Sb-€110, Db-€120, bigger Db-€5-
40 extra, Tb-€145, Qb-€155, 30 percent off on weekends and
July-Aug, request a quieter courtyard room, elevator, free Wi-Fi,
Lombard street 35, tel. 02-512-8290, fax 02-512-3493, www.hotel
lalegende.com, info@hotellalegende.com).

$$ Hotel Ibis Centre Ste. Catherine is a big, impersonal,
perfectly comfortable place with 236 rooms in a great location that
offers very deep discounts during its slow times only through the
TI. Its double rooms, which are reasonable all year (Db-€119 dur-
ing the week, €79-85 on weekends, breakfast-€14), rent for €50
with breakfast through the summer only when booked through the
TI (air-con, elevator, pay Wi-Fi, Joseph Plateau street 2 at Place
Ste. Catherine/Sint-Katelijneplein, tel. 02-513-7620, fax 02-514-
2214, www.ibishotel.com, h1454@accor.com).

$$ Hotel the Moon is a concrete and efficient last resort,
with 17 bare-bones rooms and no public spaces. It has absolutely
no character, the dust bunnies run rampant, and the thin walls and
doors, along with noise from the square out front, can make for a
noisy night. But the location is super-convenient—just steps from
the Grand Place—and it's the cheapest centrally located hotel this
side of a youth hostel (Sb-€55-70, Db-€65-90, Tb-€81-110, lower
prices are for slow times including July-Aug, 10 percent discount if
you book direct with the latest edition of this book, ask for a quieter room in the back, stairs but no elevator, on the small "Agora"
square at Rue de la Montagne/Bergstraat 4, tel. 02-508-1580, fax
02-508-1585, www.hotelthemoon.com, info@hotelthemoon.com).

Hotels in Ste. Catherine, near the Old Fish Market

The next three listings are a 10-minute walk from the intensity
of the old center, near the Ste. Catherine/Sint-Katelijne Métro
stop. This charming neighborhood, called "the village in Brussels,"

faces the canalside fish market and has many of the town's best restaurants.

$$$ Hotel Welcome, owned by an energetic bundle of hospitality named Meester Smeesters, offers outrageously creative rooms, exuberantly decorated with artifacts he's picked up in his world travels. Each of the 16 rooms has a different geographic theme, from India to Japan to Bali: Take a virtual tour of the rooms on their website. Owners Sophie and Michel Smeesters (and their helpers, Vincent and Anna) are the rare hoteliers who actually sleep in their rooms occasionally just to figure out how they can make their guests' experience even better (Sb-€120, standard Db-€125, deluxe Db-€140, large suite-€210, family room, cheaper on weekends, much lower rates in Aug, elevator, free Internet access and Wi-Fi, reasonably priced laundry service, parking-€13, free airport transfer—3 people max—if you book direct and show this book on arrival, 23 Quai au Bois à Brûler/Brandhoutkaai, tel. 02-219-9546, fax 02-217-1887, www.hotelwelcome.com, info@hotelwelcome.com).

$$$ Maison Noble is a charming boutique B&B run by Matthieu and Brendon. This gay-friendly place (the well-hung art gravitates toward male nudes) has three classy, mod rooms, a gorgeous Art Nouveau/Art Deco stained-glass window over the breakfast table, and a free steam room. It's on a dull street just a block off the old fish market (D-€129, big Db-€149, 1-night stay-€10 extra, €10 less for 4 nights or longer, €20 less mid-July-Aug, free Internet access and Wi-Fi, 10 Marcq street, tel. 02-219-2339, www.maison-noble.eu, info@maison-noble.eu).

$$$ Hotel Noga feels extremely homey, with 19 rooms, a welcoming game room, and old photos of Belgian royalty lining the hallways. It's carefully run by Frederich Faucher and his son, Mourad (Sb-€95, Db-€110, Tb-€135, Qb-€160, all rooms about 20 percent off Fri-Sat and in Aug, 5 percent discount if you pay in cash, very quiet, non-smoking, pay Internet access and Wi-Fi, garage-€15, Rue du Beguinage/Begijnhofstraat 38, tel. 02-218-6763, fax 02-218-1603, www.nogahotel.com, info@nogahotel.com).

$$$ Citadines Sainte-Catherine Apart'hotel, part of a Europe-wide chain, is a huge apartment-style hotel with modern, shipshape rooms. Choose from efficiency studios with fold-out double beds or two-room apartments with a bedroom and a fold-out couch in the living room. All 163 units come with a kitchen, stocked cupboards, a stereo, and everything you need to settle right in (official rates: one- or two-person studio-€135, apartment for up to four people-€170, but rates very flexible—check online, much less July-Aug, 15 percent cheaper by the week, breakfast-€13, free Internet access and Wi-Fi, parking-€17, 51 Quai au Bois à Brûler/ Brandhoutkaai, tel. 02-221-1411, fax 02-221-1599, www.citadines .com, stecatherine@citadines.com).

Hostels

Three classy and modern hostels—in buildings that could double as small, state-of-the-art, minimum-security prisons—are within a 10-minute walk of Central Station. Each accepts people of all ages, serves cheap and hot meals, takes credit cards, and charges about the same price. All rates include breakfast and showers down the hall.

$ Bruegel Hostel, a fortress of cleanliness, is handiest and most comfortable, with 135 beds. Of its many rooms, 22 are bunk-bed doubles (S-€32, D-€47, beds in quads or dorms-€20, nonmembers and guests over age 26 pay €3 extra/night, includes sheets and breakfast, open 7:00-10:00 & 14:00-1:00 in the morning, pay Internet access, midway between Midi/Zuid/South and Central stations, behind Chapelle church at Rue de St. Esprit/H. Geeststraat 2, tel. 02-511-0436, fax 02-512-0711, www.youth hostels.be, brussel@vjh.be).

$ Sleep Well Hostel, surrounded by high-rise parking structures, is also comfortable (S-€36, Sb-€46, D-€54, Db-€66, T-€71, Tb-€92, dorm beds-€20-22, includes sheets and breakfast, non-smoking, Internet access and Wi-Fi, lockout 11:00-15:00, Rue de Damier 23, tel. 02-218-5050, fax 02-218-1313, www.sleepwell.be, info@sleepwell.be).

$ Jacques Brel Hostel, with 164 beds, is a little farther out, but it's still a reasonable walk from everything (S-€35, D-€48-52, dorm bed-€17-19, nonmembers and guests over age 26 pay €3 extra/night, includes sheets and breakfast, no curfew, non-smoking rooms, laundry, Rue de la Sablonnière/Zavelput 30, tel. 02-218-0187, fax 02-217-2005, www.laj.be, brussels.brel@laj.be).

Eating in Brussels

For many, the obvious eating tip in Brussels is simply to enjoy the Grand Place. My vote for northern Europe's grandest medieval square is lined with hardworking eateries that serve predictable dishes to tourist crowds. Of course, you won't get the best quality or prices—but, after all, it's the Grand Place. Locals advise eating well elsewhere and enjoying a Grand Place perch for dessert or a drink. While many tourists congregate at the Rue des Bouchers, "Restaurant Row," consider a wander through the new, emerging

EATING IN BRUSSELS

eating zone—gay, ethnic, and trendy—past the Bourse near Place St-Géry/Sint-Goriksplein. Compare the ambience, check posted menus, and choose your favorite.

Brussels is known for both its high-quality, French-style cuisine and for multicultural variety. Seafood—fish, eel, shrimp, and oysters—is especially well-prepared here. As in France, if you ask for the *menù* (muh-noo) at a restaurant, you won't get a list of dishes; you'll get a fixed-price meal. *Menùs*, which include three or four courses, are generally a good value if you're hungry. Ask for *la carte* (lah kart) if you want to see a printed menu and order à la carte, like the locals do. To read local restaurant reviews, check out www.resto.be.

Mussels in Brussels

Mussels *(moules)* are available all over town. For an atmospheric cellar or a table right on the Grand Place, eat at **L'Estaminet du Kelderke.** Its one steamy vault under the square is always packed with both natives and tourists—a real Brussels fixture. It serves local specialties, including mussels (a splittable kilo bucket—just more than 2 pounds—for €20-22; daily 12:00-24:00, Thu-Sat until 2:00 in the morning, no reservations taken, Grand Place 15, tel. 02-513-7344). Also see Restaurant Chez Leon, next.

Rue des Bouchers ("Restaurant Row")

Brussels' restaurant streets, two blocks north of the Grand Place, are touristy and notorious for touts who aggressively suck you in and predatory servers who greedily rip you off. It's a little hard to justify dining here when far better options sit just a block or two away (see later listings). But the area is an exhilarating spectacle and is fun for at least a walk. If you are seduced into a meal here, order carefully, understand the prices thoroughly, and watch your wallet.

Restaurant Chez Leon is a touristy mussels factory, slamming out piles of good, cheap buckets since 1893. It's the original flagship branch of a chain that's now spreading throughout France. It's big and welcoming, with busy green-aproned waiters

Brussels Restaurants

EATING IN BRUSSELS

❶ L'Estaminet du Kelderke
❷ Rest. Chez Leon & Rest. Vincent
❸ Aux Armes de Bruxelles
❹ Restaurant de l'Ogenblik
❺ Belga Queen Brasserie
❻ Le Mokafé
❼ La Maison des Crêpes
❽ Osteria a l'Ombra
❾ De Pistolei Sandwiches
❿ "Pita Street"
⓫ AD Delhaize Grocery
⓬ Super GB Grocery
⓭ Bij den Boer
⓮ La Marie Joseph
⓯ Le Royal Rest.
⓰ La Villette Rest.
⓱ Rest. La Marée
⓲ Rest. Le Pré Salé
⓳ Mer du Nord/Nordzee
⓴ Cremerie de Linkebeek
㉑ Le Pain Quotidien
㉒ A la Mort Subite Bar
㉓ Le Cirio Café
㉔ A la Bécasse Café
㉕ Fin de Siècle & Le Greenwich Bars

offering a "Formula Leon" for €12.90—a light meal consisting of a small bucket of mussels, fries, and a beer. They also offer a €31.30 fixed-price meal that comes with a starter, a large bucket of mussels, fries, and beer (daily 12:00-23:00, kids under 12 eat free, Rue des Bouchers/Beenhouwers 18, tel. 02-511-1415). In the family portrait of Leon's brother Honoré (hanging in the corner), the wife actually looks like a mussel.

Aux Armes de Bruxelles is a venerable restaurant that has been serving reliably good food to locals in a dressy setting for generations. This is another food factory, with white-suited waiters serving an older clientele impressed by the restaurant's reputation. You'll pay a bit more for the formality (€8-18 starters, €16-32 main dishes, €20 fixed-price lunch, €35-46 fixed-price dinner, daily 12:00-23:00, indoor seating only, Rue des Bouchers/Beenhouwers 13, tel. 02-511-5550).

Restaurant Vincent has you enter through the kitchen to enjoy their 1905-era ambience. This place is better for meat dishes than for seafood. Enjoy the engaging old tile murals of the seaside and countryside (€12-19 starters, €20-32 main dishes, €37 fixed-price meal, Mon-Sat 12:00-14:30 & 18:30-23:00, Sun 12:00-15:00 & 18:30-22:30, Rue des Dominicains/Predikherenstraat 8-10, tel. 02-511-2607, Michel and Jacques).

Finer Dining near Rue des Bouchers

These options, though just steps away from those listed above, are more authentic and a better value.

Restaurant de l'Ogenblik, a remarkably peaceful eddy just off the raging restaurant row, fills an early 20th-century space in the corner of an arcade. The waiters serve well-presented, near-gourmet French cuisine. This mussels-free zone has a great, split-table rack of lamb with 10 vegetables (€23-28 plates, Mon-Sat 12:00-14:30 & 19:00-24:00, closed Sun, across from Restaurant Vincent—listed above—at Galerie des Princes 1, tel. 02-511-6151, Yves).

Belga Queen Brasserie bills itself as a "wonderfood place." A huge, trendy, dressy brasserie filling a palatial former bank building, it's *the* spot for Brussels' beautiful people and visiting European diplomats. Although a little more expensive than the alternatives, the "creative Belgian cuisine" is excellent, the service is sharp, and the experience is memorable—from the fries served in silver cones, to the double-decker platters of iced shellfish, to the transparent toilets stalls (which become opaque only after you nervously lock the door). The high-powered trendiness can make you feel a little gawky, but if you've got the money, this is a great splurge. Consider their €33 three-course, fixed-price meal with matching beers (€15-25 starters, €20-30 main dishes,

€30-47 fixed-price meals, daily 12:00-14:30 & 19:00-24:00, call to reserve, bar open all day, Rue Fosse-aux-Loups/Wolvengracht 32, tel. 02-217-2187). The vault downstairs is a plush cigar and cocktail lounge. For just a drink, grab a stool at the white-marble oyster bar.

More Eateries near the Grand Place

Le Mokafé is inexpensive but feels splurgy. They dish up light café fare at the quiet end of the elegant Galeries St. Hubert, with great people-watching outdoor tables (€3-6 sandwiches, €7-11 salads, €8-10 pastas, €9-12 main dishes, daily 8:00-24:00, Galerie du Roi 9, tel. 02-511-7870).

La Maison des Crêpes, a little eatery a half-block south of the Bourse, looks underwhelming but serves delicious €8-10 crêpes (both savory and sweet varieties) and salads. It has a brown café ambience, and even though it's just a few steps away from the tourist bustle, it feels laid-back and local (good beers, fresh mint tea, sidewalk seating, daily 12:00-23:00, Rue du Midi/Zuidstraat 13, mobile 0475-957-368).

Osteria a l'Ombra, a true Italian joint, is perfect for anyone needing a quality bowl of pasta with a glass of fine Italian wine. Across the lane from the TI and just a block off the Grand Place, it's pricey, but the woody bistro ambience and tasty food make it a good value. If you choose a main dish (€14-18), your choice of pasta or salad is included in the price (otherwise €9-13 pasta meals). The ground-floor seating on high stools is fine, but also consider sitting upstairs (Mon-Fri 12:00-15:00 & 18:30-23:30, Sat 18:30-23:30, closed Sun, Rue des Harengs/Haringstraat 2, tel. 02-511-6710).

Cheap Eats near the Grand Place: The super-central square dubbed the "Agora" (officially Marché-aux-Herbes/Grasmarkt, just between the Grand Place and Central Station) is lined with low-end eateries, and is especially fun on sunny days. Pick one of the chain restaurants, or head a few steps up Rue de la Madeleine (toward the train station) to **De Pistolei,** a family-run lunch counter serving tasty made-to-order sandwiches (€3, daily 7:00-20:00, Rue de la Madeleine/Magdalenasteenweg 5, tel. 02-502-9502). At the other end of the Grand Place, Rue du Marché-aux-Fromages/Kaasmarkt—nicknamed "**Pita Street**"—is lined with affordable Turkish and Greek eateries.

Groceries: Two supermarkets are located about a block from the Bourse and a few blocks from the Grand Place. **AD Delhaize** is at the intersection of Anspach and Marché-aux-Poulets/Kiekenmarkt (Mon-Sat 9:00-20:00, Fri until 21:00, Sun 9:00-18:00), and **Super GB** is half a block away at Halles and Marché-aux-Poulets/Kiekenmarkt (Mon-Sat 9:00-20:00, Fri until 21:00, closed Sun). Mini-markets dot the city. Often run by Pakistani and Indian immigrants, they're pricier than supermarkets but handy (open very late, drinks, groceries, phone cards).

In Ste. Catherine, near the Old Fish Market

A 10-minute walk from the old center puts you in "the village within the city" area of Ste. Catherine (Métro: Ste. Catherine/ Sint-Katelijne). The historic fish market here has spawned a tradition of fine restaurants specializing mostly in seafood. The old fish canal survives, and if you walk around it, you'll see plenty of enticing places to eat. Make the circuit, considering these very good, yet very different, options.

Bij den Boer, a fun, noisy eatery popular with locals and tourists, has inviting tables out on the park and feels like a traditional and very successful brasserie. Their specialty: fish (€12-16 starters, €20-30 main dishes, €28 four-course fixed-price meal, Mon-Sat 12:00-14:30 & 18:00-22:30, closed Sun, Quai aux Briques/ Baksteenkai 60, tel. 02-512-6122).

La Marie Joseph, stylish and modern—both the food and the clientele—serves fancy fish and fries, and earns raves from the natives (€16-22 starters, €23-32 plates, Tue-Sun 12:00-15:00 & 18:30-23:00, closed Mon, no reservations taken, Quai au Bois à Brûler/Brandhoutkaai 47, tel. 02-218-0596).

Le Royal is a youthful, rollicking brasserie serving good food. They offer both traditional (and well-executed) Belgian staples and modern fusion dishes—some with a hint of Asian influence. Sit in the high-energy interior, or choose a sidewalk table (€8-15 starters, €13-22 main dishes, €3 sides, daily 12:00-15:00 & 18:00-23:00, later on weekends, Rue de Flandre/Vlaamsesteenweg 103, tel. 02-217-8500).

La Villette Restaurant ("The Slaughterhouse") is a romantic, subdued, seafood-free alternative, serving traditional Belgian cuisine: heavy, meaty stews and dishes with beer. It has a charming red-and-white-tablecloth interior and good outdoor seating facing a small square (€14 two-course fixed-price lunch, €15-22 meals, Mon-Fri 12:00-14:30 & 18:30-22:30, Sat 18:30-22:30 only, closed Sun, Rue du Vieux Marché-aux-Grains/Oude Graanmarkt 3, tel. 02-512-7550, Agata).

Restaurant La Marée is a classic local scene a couple of blocks away from the trendy canalside places. A nontouristy, less trendy bistro with an older clientele, an open kitchen, and an inviting menu, it specializes in mussels and seafood (€19-26 meals, Tue-Sat 12:00-14:00 & 18:30-22:00, closed Sun-Mon, near Rue du Marché aux Porcs/Varkensmarkt at Rue de Flandre/Vlaamsesteenweg 99, tel. 02-511-0040).

Restaurant Le Pré Salé is noisy and family-friendly. A Brussels fixture for its traditional local cuisine, it fills a former butcher shop with happy eaters and a busy open kitchen. Although the service can be spotty, and the place has gone a bit downhill in recent years, it's still a reliable neighborhood choice (big, shareable €21 pots of mussels come with a salad, €13-19 meals, Wed-Sun 12:00-14:30 & 18:30-22:30, closed Mon-Tue, a block off the fish market at Rue de Flandre/Vlaamsesteenweg 20, tel. 02-513-6545).

Cheap, Fast, and Tasty Lunches in Ste. Catherine

Place Ste. Catherine/Sint-Katelijneplein, which branches off from the side of Ste. Catherine Church, is lined with enjoyable cafés with outdoor seating, La Villette (described earlier), and the following two excellent lunch options. (The third place listed below is about a block away, down Dansaert street.)

Mer du Nord/Nordzee is as delicious as it is inexpensive. This seafood bar—basically a grill attached to a fresh fish shop—grills up whatever it catches and serves it on small tapas-like plates with glasses of wine to a very appreciative local crowd. Just belly up to the counter and place your order, then eat it standing at the tables. The €7 *scampi à la plancha* (grilled shrimp) is exquisite (€4-7 small dishes, Tue-Thu 11:00-17:00, Fri-Sat 11:00-18:00, Sun 11:00-20:00, closed Mon, Rue Ste. Catherine/Sint-Katelijnestraat 45, at corner with Place Ste. Catherine, tel. 02-513-1192). The similar **Poissonerie/Vishandel ABC,** across the street, has a comparable operation (closed Sun).

Cremerie de Linkebeek, owned by Jordan (who's part American) and Laurence, is the best place in town to shop for local

Belgian cheeses—rubbed and flavored with beer rather than wine or alcohol. The English-speaking staff is happy to help you explore the options and choose the perfect cheese for your picnic (they also sell baguettes, wine, and crackers—you could assemble a light meal or a snack right here). At midday, they also sell delicious €4 baguette sandwiches to go—grab one before they sell out (Mon 9:00-15:00, Tue-Sat 9:00-18:00, closed Sun, 4 Rue du Vieux Marché aux Grains/Oude Graanmarkt, tel. 02-512-3510).

Le Pain Quotidien ("The Daily Bread") is a popular, upscale, artisan bakery chain selling good sandwiches and other dishes in a rustic yet dignified setting. There's a handy location just below Place Ste. Catherine (Mon-Sat 7:30-19:00, Sun 7:30-18:00, Dansaert street 16A, tel. 02-502-2361). Across the street is **Comocomo,** serving mediocre Basque-style tapas with an innovative twist: on a conveyor belt, sushi bar-style.

EATING IN BRUSSELS

Sampling Belgian Beer with Food and Ambience

Looking for a good spot to enjoy that famous Belgian beer? Brussels is full of atmospheric cafés to savor the local brew. The eateries lining the Grand Place are touristy, but the setting—plush, old medieval guild halls fronting all that cobbled wonder—is hard to beat. I've listed three places a few minutes' walk off the square, all with a magical, old-time feel. If you'd like something to wash down with your beer, you can generally get a cold-meat plate, an open-face sandwich, or a salad.

All varieties of Belgian beer are available, but Brussels' most distinctive beers are *lambic*-based. Look for *lambic doux, lambic blanche, gueuze* (pronounced "kurrs"), and *faro,* as well as fruit-flavored *lambics,* such as *kriek* (cherry) and *framboise* (raspberry—*frambozen* in Flemish). These beers look and taste more like a dry, somewhat bitter cider. The brewer doesn't add yeast—the beer ferments naturally from yeast found floating only in the marshy air around Brussels.

A la Mort Subite, a few steps above the top end of the Galeries St. Hubert, is a classic old bar that has retained its 1928 decor...and many of its 1928 cus-tomers (Mon-Sat 11:00-24:00, Sun 12:00-23:00, Rue Montagne-aux-Herbes Potagères/Warmoesberg 7, tel. 02-513-1318). Named after the "sudden death" playoff that work-ingmen used to end their lunchtime dice games, it still has an unpreten-tious, working-class feel. The decor is simple, with wood tables, grimy yellow wallpaper, and some-other-era garland trim. Tiny metal plates on the walls mark spots where gas-powered flames once flickered—used by patrons to light their cigars. A typical lunch or snack here is a *tartine* (open-face sand-wich, €5) spread with *fromage blanc* (cream cheese) or pressed meat. Eat it with one of the home-brewed, *lambic*-based beers. This is a good place to try the *kriek* (cherry-flavored) beer. The Bruxelloise claim it goes well with sandwiches.

At **Le Cirio,** across from the Bourse, the dark tables bear the skid marks of over a century's worth of beer steins (daily 10:00-1:00 in the morning, Rue de la Bourse/Beursstraat 18-20, tel. 02-512-1395).

A la Bécasse is lower profile than Le Cirio, with a simple wood-panel and wood-table decor that appeals to both poor stu-dents and lunching businessmen. The *lambic doux* has been served in clay jars since 1825. This place is just around the corner from Le

Cirio, toward the Grand Place, hidden away at the end of a court-yard (€3-5 *tartine* sandwiches, €5-9 light meals, daily 11:00-24:00, Tabora street 11, tel. 02-511-0006).

Youthful Fun at Place St-Géry

The classics recommended above are famous among tourists, and understandably so. For a more local and youthful scene, head a few blocks west to Place St-Géry/Sint-Goriksplein. Here you'll find bar and restaurant hangouts that offer a more basic, neighborhood feel. The epicenter is at the northeast corner of the square (intersection of Pont de la Carpe/Karperbrug and Plétinckx street), where you'll find a high concentration of Asian eateries. Rather than recommend a particular place, I'd suggest exploring your options and choosing the menu and indoor ambience or outdoor views you like best.

Perhaps the best options are actually hiding a block away from this lively zone (head up Plétinckx street, turn right up St. Kristoffels street, go one block, then look left). Here you'll find two inviting options: **Fin de Siècle** is a youthful bohemian scene serving basic, unpretentious Belgian/French fare in a classic turn-of-the-century atmosphere (€11-17 meals, daily from 18:00, Rue des Chartreux/Katuizerstraat 9). The adjacent **Le Greenwich** is a chess bar with a rough, circa-1900 former elegance serving good beer and simpler plates (closed Sun, Rue des Chartreux/Katuizerstraat 7, tel. 02-511-4167).

Nightlife in Brussels

After dark, the **Grand Place** becomes even more magical—as day-tripping tourists are gone and the Town Hall spire is floodlit.

Pick up the free *Agenda* and *Brussels Unlimited* magazines from the TI, which list events including opera, symphony, and ballet.

At one time, Brussels had a wide range of characteristic little cinemas. These days, most Bruxelloise flock to the multiplexes; a handy one is the **UGC** cinema on De Brouckère square (look for *v.o.* for the original version; *v.f.* means it's dubbed in French). There's also a small art-house cinema in the Galeries St. Hubert; movies here play in their original language (generally not English, as these are typically international films), with Flemish and French subtitles.

The most interesting neighborhood to explore after-hours

(or any time of day) is just a few steps west of the Grand Place: **Rue du Marché-au-Charbon/ Kolenmarkt** is the center of Brussels' gay scene, with many lively cafés and restaurants with outdoor seating. The trendy eateries, shops, and businesses along here change so fast, the locals can't keep track.

Across the Boulevard Anspach is **Place St-Géry,** where you'll find a raucous collection of lively bars with rollicking interiors and a sea of outdoor tables. Van Praet street, which stretches from

here to the Bourse, is lined with mostly Asian eateries. A five-minute walk northeast is the pleasant **Ste. Catherine** district, with lively local restaurants and hotels huddled around the Church of Ste. Catherine and the old fish market.

Brussels Connections

By Train

Brussels has three train stations: Centraal/Central, Midi/Zuid/ South, and Nord/Noord/North. Most trains stop at all three stations, but high-speed international trains serve only the Midi/ Zuid/South Station.

At any station, as you wait on the platform for your train, watch the track notice board that tells you which train is approaching. Trains zip in and out constantly, so a train with an open door on your train's track—three minutes before your departure time—may well be the wrong train. Anxious travelers, who think their train has arrived early, often board the wrong train on the right track.

Regular Trains to Belgium and the Netherlands

From All Brussels Stations by Train to: Bruges (2/hour, 1 hour, catch InterCity train—direction: Ostende or Knokke-Blankenberge, €12.90), **Antwerp** (5/hour, 40-50 minutes), **Ghent** (3/hour, 35 minutes), **Ypres/Ieper** (hourly, 1.75 hours, some change in Kortrijk), **Amsterdam** (stops at Amsterdam's Schiphol Airport en route, hourly, 2.75 hours), **Haarlem** (hourly, 2.75 hours, transfer

Belgian Train Lines

in Rotterdam), **Delft** (hourly, 2 hours, change in Rotterdam), **The Hague** (hourly, 2 hours).

High-Speed International Trains

Catch the following special, high-speed train lines at Midi/Zuid/ South Station, tracks 1-6. Note that these trains do not stop at the Central or North train stations. For schedules, see http://bahn. hafas.de/bin/query.exe/en.

From Brussels by Thalys Train: The Thalys company has a pricey monopoly on trains to **Paris** (2/hour, 1.5 hours), and runs trains to **Köln,** Germany (9/day, 1.75 hours). They also run special seasonal trains, such as to **Marseille,** France, in the summer and to the **French Alps** in the winter. From Brussels to Paris, a regular second-class Thalys ticket costs about €60-80 second class (compared to about €25 by bus; buy ticket the day before or earlier, as same-day fares are even higher). Railpass-holders need to buy a seat reservation for €26 in second class or €41-54 in first class (first class generally includes a meal). If your railpass covers only France but not BeNeLux, it'll cost you €44 in second class or €69 in first class. Railpasses without France are not accepted on Thalys trains. Train info: Tel. 02-528-2828 (long wait), www.thalys.com.

By TGV Train to France: French TGV trains connect to **Paris' Charles de Gaulle Airport** (7/day, 1.25-1.75 hours, www .tgv-europe.com) and then continue on to various destinations in southern France, including Marseille, Nice, and Bordeaux. Note that since Thalys has exclusive rights for the Brussels-Paris route, TGV trains do not go to downtown Paris—to get there, you must transfer at the airport. All TGV seats are reserved, and railpass-holders pay €5 for a reservation (very limited availability).

By ICE Train to Germany: Germany's InterCity Express trains zip to **Köln** (3/day, 1.75 hours) and **Frankfurt** (3/day, 3 hours). Reservations are not required except for advance-ticket discounts.

To Other Places in Germany: The fastest way to most German destinations, as well as to Vienna, Austria, is to change in Köln (on the Thalys or ICE connection) or in Frankfurt (on the ICE connection).

By Eurostar to/from London: Brussels and London are 2.5 hours apart by Eurostar train (10/day). Trains to London leave from tracks 1 and 2 at Brussels' Midi/Zuid/South Station. Arrive 30 minutes early to get your ticket validated and your luggage and passport checked by British authorities (similar to airport check-in for an international flight).

Fares are reasonable but complicated. Prices vary depending on how far ahead you reserve (up to six months out), whether you can live with restrictions, and whether you're eligible for any discounts (children, youths, seniors, and railpass-holders all qualify). Rates are lowest for round-trips. Fares can change without notice, but typically a **one-way, full-fare ticket** (with no restrictions on refundability) runs about $425 for first class and $310 for second class. Accepting more restrictions lowers the price substantially (figure $90-200 for second class, one-way), but these **cheaper rates** can sell out quickly. Railpasses qualify you for a discount on a Eurostar ticket. Those traveling with a railpass that covers Belgium, France, or Britain should look first at the **passholder** fare (about $90-160 for second-class, one-way Eurostar trips, sold through most agents but not through Eurostar website). See more general info at www .ricksteves.com/eurostar or buy most ticket types at www.eurostar .com (prices in pounds; Belgian tel. 02-528-2828).

Eurostar Routes

ENGLAND
LONDON
EBBS-FLEET
ASHFORD
CALAIS FRETHUN
LILLE
PARIS
AMSTERDAM
NE.TH.
BELG.
BRUSSELS
FRANCE

50 MI
100 KM

—— EUROSTAR
--- CHANNEL TUNNEL
..... OTHER RAIL

More Discounts: A Thalys ticket between Brussels and Paris or a Eurostar ticket between Brussels and London can also cover a regional train connection to/from any Belgian station for a few dollars more, if you choose the "ABS option" at the time of purchase. Just show your ticket when boarding the connecting train(s) within 24 hours of the reserved Brussels arrival or departure (as long as the connecting train is not a Thalys).

All of these fast-train services offer significant price discounts, with restrictions, on tickets reserved in advance (most available 3 months ahead, Eurostar available 6 months ahead). Each company sells e-tickets through its website or through US agents such as www.raileurope.com (prices in dollars, US tel. 800-438-7245). In Europe, you can buy tickets at any major train station in any country or at any travel agency that handles train tickets (expect a booking fee).

By Bus

You can save money—but not time—by traveling by Eurolines bus from Brussels to Paris or London (Eurolines tel. 02-274-1350 in Brussels, www.eurolines.be).

From Brussels by Bus to: Paris (generally €22-26 one-way, €41-44 round-trip, about 4 hours), **London** (generally €35 one-way, €70 round-trip, about 6 hours).

By Plane

Brussels Airport

Brussels' big but well-organized main airport is nine miles north of downtown (many arriving flights pass over the giant, silver molecule-shaped Atomium). The airport is sometimes called "Zaventem," for the nearby town. Departures are at level 3, arrivals are at level 2, buses are at level 0, and the train station is in the basement at level -1. Airport info: Tel. 0900-70000, www .brusselsairport.be.

The clear winner for getting to and from the airport is the **shuttle train** that runs between the airport and all three Brussels train stations (€5, 4/hour, 25 minutes, daily 6:00-23:00). Note that because of a special airport train tax, even if you're using a railpass, you'll have to pay a €2.05 fee to take this train (buy from ticket window or pay conductor directly). If you're connecting the airport with Bruges, take this shuttle train and transfer at Brussels' North Station (about 1.5 hours total). For a **taxi,** figure on spending around €40 between downtown Brussels and the airport.

Thrifty Brussels Airlines flies between Brussels and several European cities, including Athens, Milan, Florence, Zürich, Nice, Lisbon, Barcelona, Madrid, and more (Belgian tel. 07-035-

BRUSSELS CONNECTIONS

1111, www.brusselsairlines.com). Bmi british midland has inexpensive flights from Brussels to London and the British Isles (www.flybmi.com). Non-discount airlines, such as Lufthansa (www.lufthansa.com), Finnair (www.finnair.com), and Alitalia (www.alitalia.com), offer daily flights from Brussels Airport.

Brussels South Charleroi Airport

Discount airlines Ryanair (www.ryanair.com) and Wizz Air (www.wizzair.com) use this smaller airport, located about 30 miles from downtown Brussels in the town of Gosselies, on the outskirts of the city of Charleroi.

The easiest way to connect to downtown Brussels is to take the **shuttle bus** to Brussels' Midi/Zuid/South Station (2/hour, about 1 hour, runs 4:00-22:30, €13; stops right in front of airport terminal; if you're taking the bus from Brussels' South Station, look for it outside at the corner of Rue de France/Frankrijkstraat and Rue de l'Instruction/Onderwijsstraat, www.voyages-lelan.be). You can also take a **bus-plus-train** connection: Bus #A connects Charleroi Airport and Charleroi Station (2/hour, 18 minutes), where you can take the train to all three Brussels train stations (2/hour, 40 minutes). It's costly by taxi (figure around €85-90); depending on traffic, it can take between 45 minutes and 1.5 hours to drive between downtown Brussels and Charleroi Airport. Airport info: Tel. 07-125-1211, www.charleroi-airport.com.

ANTWERP

Antwerpen

Antwerp (Antwerpen in Flemish, Anvers in French) is one of Europe's great once-drab, now-reborn port cities—ranking right up there with Liverpool, Barcelona, and Gdańsk. It's the biggest city and de facto capital of Flanders, with an illustrious history, a collection of top-tier museums, and a unique urban grittiness (some might say seediness) mingling with avant-garde fashion and a youthful trendiness. Its big-city bustle is the yang to Bruges' cutesy-village yin. Once Europe's most important trading city, later the hometown of accomplished painter Peter Paul Rubens, destroyed by World War II and then reborn, and recently emerging as a European fashion capital, Antwerp is more than the sum of its parts.

In the late 15th century, as Bruges' harbor silted up, Antwerp became a major trading center and the Low Countries' top city of the Baroque period. As the Age of Exploration dawned, Portuguese and Spanish ships returning from the New World laden with exotic goods docked here in Antwerp. During Antwerp's 16th-century Golden Age, it became Europe's wealthiest city, with a population of about 100,000.

In the mid-16th century, Antwerp was pulled into the Eighty Years' War between the Dutch rebel Protestants and the ruling Spanish Catholics. In 1576, after growing impatient at not being paid by Habsburg King Philip II, Spanish troops relentlessly sacked Antwerp for three days—massacring thousands of its residents and destroying hundreds of homes. The outraged public response to this so-called "Spanish Fury" elevated Antwerp to the capital of the Dutch Revolt. (Meanwhile, the event irrevocably damaged Antwerp's trade ties with partners who wanted no business with a war zone.) But the crushing, Spanish-led Siege of Antwerp (July 1584 through August 1585) wore down the independence

Antwerp

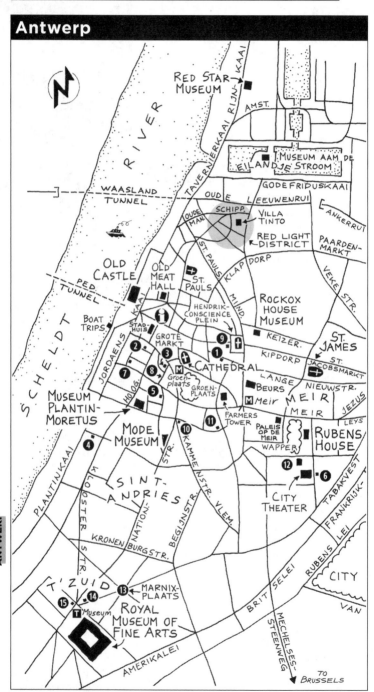

ANTWERP

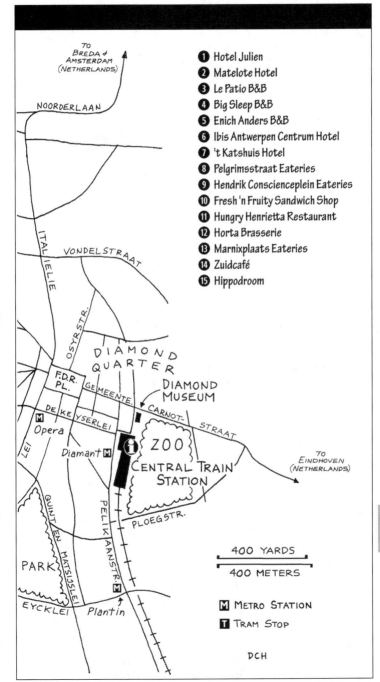

TO BREDA & AMSTERDAM (NETHERLANDS)

NOORDERLAAN

ITALIELIE

VONDELSTRAAT

OSYR STR.

DIAMOND QUARTER

F.D.R. PL.

GEMEENTE.

DIAMOND MUSEUM

DE KEYSERLEI

CARNOT-STRAAT

Opera

Diamant M

ZOO

CENTRAL TRAIN STATION

TO EINDHOVEN (NETHERLANDS)

LEI

QUINTEN MATSIJSLEI

PELIKAANSTR.

PLOEGSTR.

PARK

EYCKLEI

Plantin

1 Hotel Julien
2 Matelote Hotel
3 Le Patio B&B
4 Big Sleep B&B
5 Enich Anders B&B
6 Ibis Antwerpen Centrum Hotel
7 't Katshuis Hotel
8 Pelgrimsstraat Eateries
9 Hendrik Conscienceplein Eateries
10 Fresh 'n Fruity Sandwich Shop
11 Hungry Henrietta Restaurant
12 Horta Brasserie
13 Marnixplaats Eateries
14 Zuidcafé
15 Hippodroom

400 YARDS
400 METERS

M METRO STATION
T TRAM STOP

DCH

ANTWERP

movement, and the city fell under Spanish/Catholic control. More than half of the city's population fled to Amsterdam, where they restarted their businesses. Amsterdam's ensuing Golden Age was, in many ways, a direct result of talent and resources that Antwerp lost during this postwar "brain drain."

Seeking to rehabilitate its image in the aftermath of the bloody warfare, the Catholic Church invested mightily in building and decorating churches in Antwerp. A local artist named Peter Paul Rubens (1577-1640)—while arguably less talented than some of his contemporaries—found himself in the right place at the right time, and was a brilliant salesman who allied himself with the Church to win big commission after big commission. Rubens' style epitomized exactly what the Church was looking for: bold, bombastic images trumpeting the glory of God (and his Church on earth).

The treaty that ended the Eighty Years' War in 1648 imposed rigid regulations on shipping on the Scheldt River, restricting Antwerp's outlet to the North Sea. This caused the city to become more of a regional port than an international one. Antwerp's industry, led by an elite group of pro-Catholic traders, began to specialize in luxury goods—cabinets, paintings, tapestries, and so on. The city would languish as a Catholic backwater and second-rate shipping city for centuries, although its industry was kick-started by Napoleon, then by Belgian independence, in the early 1800s. By the 20th century, Antwerp ranked as Europe's second-busiest port (just after Dutch rival Rotterdam). Damaged in both World Wars, Antwerp has only recently begun to enjoy a new gentrification that's making it one of Europe's most exciting young cities.

Antwerpenaars (as locals are called) have a love of life. If funky urbanity is your thing, Antwerp is one of Europe's most intriguing cities. It's a great place for browsing without a sightseeing agenda. But its sights are easily on par with Brussels' and Bruges': Antwerp boasts a wide range of well-presented museums with exciting new exhibits opening all the time, interesting churches packed with great art, and fun-to-explore neighborhoods. And compared to stodgy, bureaucratic Brussels, Antwerp has a colorful personality that respects its storied past even as it embraces a bright future.

Planning Your Time

While Antwerp could easily fill a day or two, it's worth at least a few hours (as a side-trip from Brussels—less than an hour away by train—or on the way between Brussels and Amsterdam). Take my self-guided walk from the train station to the Old Town (by way of the Rubens House), tour the cathedral, ogle the Grote Markt, and pay a quick visit to other sights that intrigue you. (Historians enjoy the Museum Plantin-Moretus, art-lovers savor the Rockox House, fashionistas love the ModeMuseum and nearby window-shopping, and gem-and-jewelry fans covet the sparkle at the Diamond Museum.) Then zip back to the train station on the metro. If you have more time, Antwerp's diverse restaurant scene and lively nightlife make it worth considering for an overnight. With a different variety of quirky boutiques and cafés on each street, it's a delightful place to linger. As in most of Belgium, be aware that most Antwerp museums are closed on Mondays.

Orientation to Antwerp

Belgium's "second city" (with 460,000 people), Antwerp sits along the east bank of the Scheldt River (Schelde in Flemish). The main tourist area is fairly compact. On a quick trip, narrow your focus to these main zones: the **Old Town** along the river; the **train station area** and **Diamond Quarter** to the east, and the **Meir** shopping district between the Old Town and train station; the newly rejuvenated **Little Island** (Eilandje) zone and the red light district to the north; and, to the south, the **Sint-Andries** fashion district and, beyond that, the happening nightlife zone aptly called **'t Zuid** ("The South"). All of these areas are within about a 30-minute walk (or a quick tram or taxi ride) of one another.

Tourist Information

Antwerp's TI has two branches: in the train station (at the head of the tracks, on level 0), and right on the Grote Markt (both open Mon-Sat 9:00-17:45, Sun 9:00-16:45; tel. 03-232-0103, phone answered Mon-Sat 9:00-17:50, not on Sun; www.visitantwerp .be). Peruse their racks of fliers and pick up a free town map. The **Museum Card,** which covers public transportation and entry to most museums and churches (plus discounts on special exhibits), will easily save a busy sightseer some money (€20/48 hours, sold at TI or participating sights).

The Grote Markt TI also has a desk where you can get information and buy tickets for musical events (€1 service charge, Tue-Fri 10:00-16:50, Sat 12:00-17:00, closed Sun-Mon).

Arrival in Antwerp

By Train: Antwerp's Central Station (Antwerpen Centraal)—with a grand century-old shell recently refurbished and expanded with a modern underground zone—is one of Europe's most impressive. With tracks on three levels (connected by escalators and elevators), the station can be tricky to navigate—follow posted signs, or pick up a copy of the free station map. Tracks 1-6 are on level +1, above ground; tracks 11-14 are on level -1, below ground; and tracks 21-24 are on level -2, even deeper underground.

The ground floor's atrium (on level 0) is the hub of activity, where escalators funnel passengers from all three track levels. At the front of this area is the large TI, and behind that (through the passage, tucked under the stairs) are luggage lockers (€3-4). Continuing past the lockers, you emerge into the great hall, a gorgeously restored temple of travel. Here you'll find ticket windows. Exiting straight ahead out the front door puts you in the vast and somewhat seedy Koningin Astridplein, with the Diamond Museum and the city's zoo on your right.

To get to the Old Town and most sights, you have two basic options: You can walk (see my self-guided walk, facing page); or, if you're in a hurry (or the weather's bad) and you want to make a beeline to the Grote Markt, ride the **metro** (actually an underground tram line). From next to the TI, take the escalator marked *metro* to the underground tracks. Buy a ticket from the automated machines, and take tram #2 or #15 in the direction of *Linkeroever*; get off at the Groenplaats stop for the Grote Markt and the historical center. Note: The train station's metro stop is named Diamant (for the surrounding Diamond Quarter).

Getting Around Antwerp

Sprawling Antwerp is walkable, but using the city's good public-transit network saves time and sweat. For visitors, the handiest option is the misnamed "metro," which is actually a tram line running underground through the town center. The metro's tracks carry various numbered trams, including #2 and #15, which conveniently connect many of the city's most important sights. Stops on these lines include (from east to west) Diamant (train station), Opera (at east end of Meir shopping street), Meir (at west end of Meir shopping street, a block from the Rubens House), and Groenplaats (near the cathedral and Grote Markt). Other trams (such as #8, which runs between Groenplaats and the Museum stop in 't Zuid) and buses round out your options.

Tickets (€1.20) are easy to buy at automated machines at each stop, or you can pay €2 to buy one on board. If you'll be using public transit a lot, invest in a day pass (€6/1 day, €10/3 days) or a shareable 10-ride ticket (€8, just €0.80 per ride). Information: Toll tel. 070-220-200, €0.30/minute; www.delijn.be.

Tours in Antwerp

Walking Tours—The TI organizes a historical **walking tour** through town, in both English and French (€6 if you book at least a day in advance at the TI, €8 same-day ticket, July-Aug daily at 14:00, Sept-June Sat-Sun only, departs from TI on Grote Markt).

Local Guide—The TI can arrange a private guide for an afford-able city tour (€65/2 hours, tel. 03-338-9539, gidsenwerking @stad.antwerpen.be). One of their excellent guides, **Ariane Van Duytekom,** tells Antwerp's story well, with a knack for psycho-analyzing its complicated history. If Ariane isn't available, they can arrange another good guide for you.

Self-Guided Walk

▲From Antwerp's Train Station to the Old Town

You can zip from the train station to the historical center by metro, but it's a short (25-30 minute) and enjoyable stroll that takes you through an interesting and diverse stretch of Antwerp—and passes one of the city's top sights (the Rubens House).

The **train station** itself is a work of art. It was built around the turn of the 20th century, and was thoroughly renovated a few years

ago. If you didn't arrive by train—or haven't yet seen its remarkable main hall—step inside to take a look.

From inside the station, in the atrium at the head of the tracks, face the TI and exit the door to your left (marked *Keyserlei/ Meir/Centrum*). You'll walk basi-cally straight ahead on this street all the way to the Old Town.

The area around the train station is known as the **Diamond Quarter**—one of the world's top centers where diamonds are both sold and cleaved (split into smaller pieces to prepare them for cut-ting). Although the industry is highly secretive, experts guess that four out of every five of the world's rough diamonds pass through Antwerp at some point. The diamond industry is located in the train-station neighborhood for good reason: If you're carrying mil-lions of dollars worth of precious jewels in your briefcase through a strange city, you don't want to have to venture too far to reach a trader or diamond-cutter.

Beginning in the 16th century, the diamond industry in Antwerp was dominated by Sephardic Jews from Spain, but under Catholic rule, they fled to Amsterdam. Then, in the late 19th century, Hasidic Orthodox Jews fleeing the pogroms in Russia settled here and took up the industry. In the streets around the train station, you'll likely see men wearing tall hats, black coats, long beards, and curly locks at their temples, and women with long dresses and hair-covers. More recently, the diamond trade here is increasingly dominated by Indians. As it's a center for trade rather

ANTWERP

than tourism, there's little to actually see in this district, but if you want to learn more about the local diamond trade, visit the Diamond Museum (fronting the square in front of the train station, and described later, under "Sights in Antwerp").

Head three blocks up the bustling, tree-shaded boulevard called **De Keyserlei,** lined with chain restaurants and shops. You'll  run into the big boulevard called Frankrijklei, which marks the former course of the town wall. Continue straight across the street, then between the twin grand facades that exemplify the style called Historicism. All the rage in the late 19th century, this school of architectural thought borrowed the best, most bombastic bits and pieces from past styles to wow the viewer.

Passing between the facades, you enter a delightful pedestrians-only shopping zone. Bear left as the road curves at the statue of Anthony Van Dyck (1599-1641), a talented Antwerp artist who became the court painter for English King Charles I, and whose works now appear in many local museums. This puts you on **the Meir** (pronounced "mare"),  Antwerp's showcase shopping zone. (Meir is the name of both the street and the neighborhood.) A block later, on the left, notice the grand Stadsfeestzaal shopping mall (with the gold niche over the door). Venture inside for a look at its astonishing interior.

One block later, the big gap in the buildings on your left marks the square called Wapper; a half-block down this square on the left is one of the city's top sights, the **Rubens House** (described later). Just beyond the end of the square is a remarkable **Art Nouveau Hall** called Horta (for the renowned Belgian architect Victor Horta). Like Brussels, Antwerp has a proud Art Nouveau tradition, as the local shipping industry was spurring city growth just as that style was becoming popular in the early 20th century. Today the hall houses a recommended café with a pricey menu but an opportunity to enjoy a coffee or a meal immersed in slinky Art Nouveau. A block farther past the Art Nouveau Hall is Antwerp's new **City Theater** (Stadsschouwburg), with a gigantic rain-shield overhang that seems to cover the entire square.

Back on the Meir, the ornate building on the left-hand corner just after Wapper is the **Paleis op de Meir,** a gorgeous Rococo-style palace built in 1745 by a local aristocrat who died before he could actually move in. Later, Napoleon purchased the home and decorated the interior in Empire Style. With Belgium independence in 1830, this became an official residence of the King of the Belgians. Around 1900, the "builder king" Leopold II spiffed it up even more—you'll see his double-cursive-L monogram everywhere. Finally, in 1969, the royal family donated it to the government of Flanders, who recently refurbished it and opened it to the public. You can enjoy the gourmet chocolate shop and chandeliered tea room on the ground floor, or pay to go upstairs and tour the apartments (guided tours only, €8 to join a 1.5-hour Flemish-only tour, Sun-Fri at 15:00, Sat at 11:00, for English you must hire your own private guide for €145, Meir 50, tel. 03-206-2121, www.paleisopdemeir.be).

From here Rubens fans can detour a block north to **St. James' Church** (Sint-Jacobskerk) to see his tomb. Go up Lange Klarenstraat (across from the Paleis op de Meir), then turn right onto Lange Nieuwstraat to enter the church through its right transept. True to its name, this church was a stop for pilgrims on the Camino de Santiago, walking from here all the way to the shrine of St. James in northwest Spain. Rubens' tomb is in the chapel behind the high altar (€2, daily 14:00-17:00, Lange Nieuwstraat 73-75).

Continue along the Meir, passing the Meir metro stop. Then cross the tram tracks and continue straight, bearing right on Eiermarkt around the giant Art Deco, Gotham City-style **Farmers Tower** (Boerentoren, marked for its current occupant, KBC). Completed in 1932, this was considered the first American-style skyscraper in Europe, and held the title of Europe's tallest skyscraper for 20 years.

After two blocks on Eiermarkt, you come to the square called **Groenplaats,** with its statue of Rubens and the cathedral spire hovering just beyond.

Sights in Antwerp

Antwerp offers visitors an eclectic array of sightseeing. If you have just one day (or less), you'll need to be selective: art, churches, history, fashion, and so on. I've listed these sights in the order you might encounter them, beginning at the train station.

Near the Train Station

▲**Diamond Museum (Diamantmuseum)**—This small museum offers you a good look at one of Antwerp's most famous and important industries. Each year, the city trades some $29 billion in diamonds—representing 8 percent of Belgium's entire export market. That's a lot of glittering stones. Because the museum sits on the big square directly in front of the train station, a visit here is easy—you could drop in before catching your train (lockers are provided at the entry). Ride the elevator up to the third floor, then wind your way down through the sleek, almost futuristic, but fairly dry exhibit (with English descriptions and an included audioguide).

The history of the diamond trade focuses on Africa, where diamond-seekers dug the world's biggest manmade hole, the Kimberley Crater in South Africa. (In some parts of Africa, the exploitative conditions for finding these gems haven't improved much since the early days of Belgian colonialism. A strict new diamond-certification process, introduced here in Antwerp in 2000, attempts to block the sale of so-called "blood diamonds"— sold by rebels fighting governments in war zones in central and western Africa.) Peruse the remarkable collection of diamond jewelry, but don't linger too long or take photos...these security guys are se-ri-ous. Watch an actual diamond-cutter shaping and polishing a stone. By the end, you'll find out where we get the "karat" measurement for diamonds, why diamond-cutters use strobe lights, and what the only material is that's hard enough to cut a diamond.

Cost and Hours: €6, includes audioguide, Thu-Tue 10:00-17:30, closed Wed, Koningin Astridplein 19-23, tel. 03-202-4890, www.diamantmuseum.be.

Between the Train Station and the Old Town

▲▲**Rubens House (Rubenshuis)**—The most popular sight in town, this former home of Peter Paul Rubens does a fine job of introducing visitors both to the artist's works (several of which are displayed here) and to his lifestyle. There are better places in Antwerp to see Rubens' paintings, but this exhibit offers you a unique opportunity to also learn about how he lived and the methods he employed—interesting even to people who think Peter Paul Rubens is the guy who plays Pee-Wee Herman.

Though the house looks untouched, after Rubens' death in 1640, his heirs sold it, and it was updated and remodeled over the years. In the 1940s, it was restored to its original condition. As you tour the place, keep in mind that it's basically a replica of where Rubens lived (for more authentic period houses, visit the home of Rubens' friend at the Rockox House Museum).

ANTWERP

Peter Paul Rubens
(1577-1640)

Born in Germany in 1577, Rubens moved with his family to Antwerp at age 12, where he was apprenticed to a local painter. Showing great promise, Rubens went to study in Italy  during his twenties. After eight years, in 1608, he returned to Antwerp to care for his dying mother. He married Flemish aristocrat Isabella Brant and settled down here, buying today's Rubens House in 1610, and living in it for the next 25 years. He added on to the house, turning it into a workshop that churned out painting after painting.

In Rubens' work, everything is on a larger-than-life scale. Many canvases almost fill entire walls—you can see the seams where the cloth pieces were stitched together. Rubens famously did not actually paint all of the approximately 2,500 canvases that bear his name. As was standard at the time, his assistants, students, and colleagues did much of the work, then Rubens would swoop in at the last minute, add a flourish or two, and sign it.

Rubens distinguished himself not necessarily with his technical ability, but as a smart businessman who knew how to provide wealthy benefactors (such as the Catholic Church) with exactly what they wanted. During those Counter-Reformation days, when the Church was eager to win back fans after their ruthlessness in the Eighty Years' War, Rubens' flashy and fleshy Baroque style was perfect. His fascination with plus-size models, and his skill at capturing their rippling folds of fat, introduced the term "Rubenesque" into the English language. These chubby damsels were inspired by Hélène Fourment, 37 years Rubens' junior, whom the artist married in 1630 after his first wife died. A true Renaissance man in the Baroque Age, Rubens was also an accomplished diplomat, who helped to negotiate peace between England and Spain (and was knighted by the kings of both countries in appreciation).

Cost and Hours: €6, includes essential audioguide, Tue-Sun 10:00-17:00, last entry 30 minutes before closing, closed Mon, Wapper 9-11, tel. 03-201-1555, www.rubenshuis.be. The house is between the train station and the Old Town—to walk here, follow my self-guided walk, described earlier. To get here quickly, you can ride the metro to the Meir stop, then walk one long block east (back toward the station).

◑ **Self-Guided Tour:** Buy your ticket at the glass pavilion in the middle of the square in front of the house, then head inside. The excellent, included 1.5-hour audioguide explains all the details (or you can pick up a booklet with detailed descriptions). Here are the highlights:

In the **courtyard,** you can see the original 16th-century house (on the left), the studio that Rubens added on to the complex (on the right), and the elaborate Michelangelo-flavored portico that connects them. An architect as well as a painter, Rubens designed the additions himself. The influence of his time in Italy is evident: Notice the dramatic contrast between the traditional Flemish home and the flamboyant Italian palazzo-style studio.

Now go inside the **house** and follow the one-way route through the various rooms. Many of the paintings are not by Rubens, but by other artists he admired; in fact, his personal art collection was the biggest in the Low Countries. In the dining room (with leather-tooled walls) is a rare self-portrait of Rubens in his fifties—one of only four known Rubens self-portraits. Facing him from across the room is a portrait (not by Rubens) of his second wife, Hélène Fourment. After his first wife died, Rubens married the much younger Hélène for love instead of entering into a strategic marriage with a noblewoman. Upstairs in his bedroom is a short, carved-wood bed like the one Rubens likely used—people slept sitting up in those days. Nearby is Rubens' portrait of his top student, Anthony Van Dyck, a prodigiously talented painter whose skill eclipsed that of his teacher. Van Dyck's deservedly self-confident air, masterfully captured here, probably bugged Rubens even as it provoked his begrudging respect.

Continue into the **studio,** where Rubens and his students produced thousands of paintings. Lingering over the selection of canvases displayed here helps you understand their production process. In general, Rubens' paintings came about in one of three ways: For an important commission, he'd paint the entire thing himself. More often, he'd paint an original, then have his school make many copies of it for him to sell on a wide scale (each one would just get a few personal highlights from the master...only Rubens himself could create just the perfect twinkle in an eye, or glimmer of light on that cellulite). And other times, he would simply do a rough oil sketch of what he wanted, then enlist experts in certain areas (such as flowers or portraits) to fill in the blanks. Then he'd sweep through at the end to finalize the work.

In the main hall, peruse the paintings counterclockwise,

beginning with the canvases to the right as you enter. In the two early (pre-Italy) Rubens canvases of *St. Sebastian* and *Adam and Eve,* notice that the colors are subdued, and the bodies aren't as developed—lacking the rippling muscles and folds of fat that would later become Rubens' trademark.

The end of the room is flanked by twin portraits of the Spanish monarchs of the Netherlands, **Archduke Albert** and **Infanta Isabella.** Rubens was this couple's official court painter,

and these original Rubens works were copied in large numbers by his assistants. The monarchs' time was valuable, so Rubens worked quickly. To pose for the painting of herself dressed in a nun's habit, Isabella reportedly came to Antwerp for only one night; Rubens sketched her face quickly, just enough to capture her likeness, then filed in the details later.

High on the wall between the Spanish rulers is *The Annunciation,* with an Italian-inspired dynamism typical of the master.

The unfinished **battle scene,** *Henry IV at the Battle of Ivry,* illustrates Rubens' collaborative process. Rubens never completed this oil sketch, but you can see—at the top of the canvas—where the battle specialist has already filled in his section.

The Feast of St. Martin was actually painted by a lesser-known artist, then purchased by Rubens, who added his own touches to make it his own. Rubens enjoyed doing this as a fun pastime, to get a painting just right for his own collection—not to sell.

Finally is **a portrait by Anthony Van Dyck.** While Rubens got the lion's share of the fame, some of his students were even more talented than he was—and Van Dyck was a verifiable genius, who prodded Rubens to become a better painter. And yet Van Dyck was just a painter...whereas Rubens was also an architect, an aristocrat, and a diplomat—a true jack of all trades.

In and near the Old Town

These sights are listed roughly in the order you'll reach them, whether you come from the train station on the metro (Groenplaats stop) or by foot (see my self-guided walk, earlier).

Groenplaats—This urban-feeling square, with a handy metro stop, is dominated by a larger-than-life sculpture of Antwerp's favorite son, Peter Paul Rubens. Bear left up "Little Italy Lane"—the narrow street at the top of the square (Jan Blomstraat), passing a row of Italian restaurants—until you pop out at Handschoenmarkt in front of the cathedral.

▲▲Cathedral of Our Lady (Onze-Lieve-Vrouwekathedraal)—Antwerp's biggest church has a

spire that shoots 400 feet up from the middle of the Old Town, like a Gothic rocket...the tallest church steeple in the Low Countries. Its cavernous interior is packed with fine artwork, including four paintings by Peter Paul Rubens. You'd normally only see copies of these pieces, but while the Museum of Fine Art is closed for renovation (through late 2017), you'll see the original canvases *in situ* (in the setting for which they were intended).

Cost and Hours: €5, Mon-Fri 10:00-17:00, Sat 10:00-15:00, Sun 13:00-16:00, free English tours daily at 11:00 and 14:15, €2 audioguide, Handschoenmarkt, tel. 03-213-9951, www.dekathedraal.be.

Ⓞ Self-Guided Tour: Stepping inside, notice how remarkably wide the cathedral is, with seven aisles (three on either side of the nave). Looking up, you'll see that the Gothic design is also dramatically vertical—everything stretches upward, toward heaven. In the Middle Ages, the interior was filled with thousands of candles, and this was the only place to find bright light after dark. The stained-glass windows (some of them still original) color-

ANTWERP

ized the light emanating from inside, drawing worshippers like moths to a flame.

The cathedral has a dynamic, troubled history—in fact, it's amazing the place has survived at all. Built over many generations in the Middle Ages (1352-1521), two tragedies befell it soon after completion: In 1533, it was scorched by fire; and in 1566, it was gutted by iconoclastic Protestants, who stripped it of its medieval decoration. (Though most of the interior was whitewashed, you can still see fragments of some very colorful murals on the underside of the vaults, where the iconoclasts couldn't reach.) After the Catholics came to power here, in 1585, they decorated the church in bubbly Baroque, including several pieces by Rubens. Each local guild had their own private altar area (at the base of each pillar), where they celebrated baptisms, weddings, and funerals—this was truly a community church.

When Napoleon's troops arrived in the late 18th century, they again emptied the church of its decorations, turned the building into a stable, and had plans to destroy it entirely before Napoleon was defeated. Once again needing to redecorate the place, church leaders bought a hodgepodge of ecclesiastical art from other churches and monasteries throughout the region, which Napoleon had also shut down.

In the left transept is Rubens' famous ***Raising of the Cross*** (1610-1611). Biblical bodybuilders strain to upright the cross,

which is heavy with the swooning body of Christ. The painting is emotive, sumptuous, and almost sensual, especially considering its painful theme. Having just returned from eight years in Italy—where he'd studied the works of Michelangelo and Caravaggio (both of whose influence is evident here)—Rubens was eager to show off his mastery of musculature and human skin. Notice how lifelike Jesus' skin appears—a Rubens forte. The bold diagonal composition, thickly muscled bodies in motion, bright (almost garish) colors, and illusion of movement are vintage Rubens. The painting is the inner panel of a hinged altarpiece; it was normally kept closed, and opened to reveal this scene only on special occasions—when its color and motion must have been even more striking to churchgoers unaccustomed to this sort of spectacle.

Duck in to the chapel behind this painting, where you'll see some of the church's oldest stained glass. Find the wood-carved **medieval altarpiece** (actually a replica—the original was destroyed by iconoclasts). Notice that it's drab and hard to see from far away, making it difficult to grasp and emotionally connect with the story it presents. If the purpose of church art is to excite the congregation, this is a failure—no wonder Rubens' bombastic approach was a perfect fit for the Counter-Reformation Catholics.

Continue farther into the church, and go into the choir area. Over the main altar is another Rubens painting, *The Assumption* (1626), showing the moment that the cathedral's namesake was brought up to heaven. Beneath Mary are the twelve apostles (after the Resurrection, the faithful disciple Matthias replaced Judas) and the three women who were present at her death. The role of Mary in church doctrine was one of the major dividing lines between Catholics and Protestants; whereas the Catholic Church considered her a saint to be venerated, the Protestants embraced the notion that she was an ordinary woman called to do God's work. The gauzy heroine-worship of this canvas makes it clear who finally controlled the turf here.

On the right side of the church, in a red chapel, is a less impressive Rubens painting, *The Resurrection of Christ* (unfortunately, it's likely covered by scaffolding).

Circle back up into the right transept to see another Rubens canvas, *Descent from the Cross* (1612-1614). Rubens' diagonal composition is the mirror image of the one we saw earlier, across the nave. It's a freeze-frame of an action-packed moment...just as workers strained to erect the cross with Christ's limp body, now they struggle to lower him from it. But at this somber moment, the subjects seem to be moving more slowly, methodically. Notice the pale pallor of Christ's dead skin—a strong contrast to the lifelike luster of the other painting. The details make the poignancy of this moment come to life: the man in the top-right corner who's holding onto the shroud with his teeth; Mary's outstretched arm, in a tender matronly effort to comfort her son even in death; and, in the lower-right section, a blood-filled bronze basin holding the crown of thorns and the nails.

• *After visiting the cathedral, head straight out from the main entrance and squeeze out through the little gap at the far end of the square. Bearing right, you'll wind up in the...*

▲**Grote Markt**—Antwerp's main square is dominated by the looming tower of the cathedral at one end, and the stately Town Hall at the other. With a facade dating from Antwerp's Golden Age (16th century), the **Town Hall** (Stadhuis) is adorned with flags from many different countries—representing the importance of international trade to the city.

The other buildings fronting the square are **guild houses,**

celebrating the trade associations of each of the city's industries. Each one is topped with a golden statue, which typically represents that guild's patron saint. The many ground-floor cafés are a good place for a drink with a view. Locals say that when the outdoor terraces open up, they know it's summertime in Antwerp.

The **fountain** in the middle of the square illustrates a gruesome story from Flemish folklore. Supposedly a giant named

Druon Antigoon collected tolls along the Scheldt River. If someone was unable or unwilling to pay, the giant would sever their hand. His reign of terror was finally ended when a brave young Roman soldier named Silvius Brabo defeated Antigoon, then cut off the giant's own hand and threw it into the river. Here we see Brabo on the windup to toss Antigoon's hand, which spouts blood. Tour guides love to explain that *hand werpen* ("to throw a hand") evolved into "Antwerpen"...though scholars prefer less glamorous alternatives: *an 't werf,* "on the wharf"; or *ando verpis,* "where land is thrown up against land" (the river has long deposited sludge along the bank here).

• *From the Grote Markt, you can head toward the waterfront by going up the big street called Suikerrui.*

Waterfront—Though historically important, Antwerp's waterfront is now dingy and drab. From the Grote Markt, Suikerrui street leads you to the busy riverfront street and, beyond it, a long parking lot, a tiny park, and a forgotten castle. Cross the street and stand along the river.

This now-derelict waterfront, with its priceless access to where the Scheldt River spills into the North Sea, is where the shipping settlement of Antwerp began in the Middle Ages. All that's left from those glory days is the forlorn **castle** (to the right), which was once part of a city wall that fortified the heart of town. While this building once housed a museum, its collection has been folded into the new Museum aan de Stroom (MAS) at Little Island (described later)...so for now, it sits empty. This is representative of how Antwerp has turned its back on the river that once made it wealthy. When a train station opened across town in 1836, it pushed the city to the east. The shipping ports to the north are still busy, but most of the city is happy to ignore its river.

But the river doesn't always cooperate. Notice the orange **flood gates**—with long, heavy, waist-high steel doors that can roll open and closed on railroad tracks. Because the Scheldt is a tidal river, there's a huge risk of flooding—made more serious because of the town center's proximity to the river. Plans are afoot to replace the ugly portside wall with walkable dikes.

Gloomy as it seems, the broad **embankment** is a popular place for Antwerpenaars to walk, and young people enjoy hanging out along the river on warm summer evenings. Notice the 19th-century, Industrial-Age-style steel canopies that line the waterfront. These formerly functioned as warehouses; now they're used for other purposes: as you face the river, the stretch to the left is covered parking; to the right is an impressive array of seafaring vessels that were once part of the Maritime Museum inside the castle. The fancy elevated terrace, across the little park from the castle, provides a view of the river (notice I didn't say "good" view), and has WCs below; this is also the cruise-ship terminal.

• *To reach the Old Meat Hall (described next), cross the busy street from the castle and head a few steps downriver (with the water on your left) to Repenstraat, which leads in two blocks up to the...*

Musical Instruments Museum at the Old Meat Hall (Museum Vleeshuis)—This recently restored brick palace, erected to house

meat during Antwerp's glory days, now houses a fine collection of musical instruments. The Klank van de Stad ("Sound of the City") exhibition presents two floors of instruments and old music manuscripts (don't miss the cellar). English information is limited (unless you buy a €3.50 booklet with descriptions), and even the included touchscreen audioguide is mostly in Flemish—but at least it lets you hear some of the instruments. And though the collection itself isn't too exciting, it's fun to see the impressive brick vaults inside; consider just ducking into the entry area for a peek (it's a fine place to use the bathroom, or to warm up on a cold day).

Cost and Hours: €5, Tue-Sun 10:00-17:00, closed Mon, last entry 30 minutes before closing, Vleeshouwersstraat 38-40, tel. 03-233-6404, www.museumvleeshuis.be. To get here from the Grote Markt, face the Town Hall and turn right up Braderijstraat, take the first left on Kuipersstraat, then look right.

Nearby: My self-guided stroll through the red light district, ending at the up-and-coming Little Island district, begins from right in front of this building.

▲**Hendrik Conscienceplein**—Nicknamed "Antwerp's Piazza," this delightful square, tucked in an attractive maze of lanes in

the town center, dates from the Counter-Reformation period when the Catholic Church was keen to demonstrate its worthiness. Dominating the square is the very Italian-looking, early 16th-century, Jesuit **Church of Carolus Borromeus** (Carolus Borromeuskerk). Compared with Antwerp's many grand Gothic churches, such as the big-and-bold cathedral, notice how this church is more horizontal than vertical— melting into its neighborhood. You don't even see it until you're right on top of it. After the ruthless, deadly "persuasion" of the Inquisition, the Catholic Church wanted to soften its image and entice worshippers without coming on too strong. While a Gothic steeple—reaching dramatically up toward heaven—is meant to intimidate, this Baroque church's delicate facade is designed to invite people in without overwhelming them. Once inside, its sumptuous interior seals the deal by re-creating heaven here on earth. Rubens himself designed many decorations for the original interior of the church—including 39 paintings—but these were completely destroyed in a 1718 fire (free entry, Mon-Sat 10:00-12:30 & 14:00-17:00, closed Sun). Near this square are some of the city's most appealing restaurants (see "Eating in Antwerp," later).

▲**Rockox House Museum (Museum Rockoxhuis)**—Nicolaas Rockox (1560-1640) was a mayor of Antwerp and a friend and sponsor of Peter Paul Rubens. Today his house—buried in a residential zone a 10-minute walk northeast of the cathedral and Grote Markt—is a lovely museum. Here you can get a truly authentic look at an aristocratic home from the period (unlike the Rubens House, which was rebuilt), while viewing impressive artwork. The house also has interesting themed exhibits (which highlight, for example, period food or clothing). Rounding out the experience is a fine furniture collection and a beautiful period garden/courtyard.

While the walls were originally covered from floor to ceiling with paintings, these days the curator is more selective; he regularly assembles good temporary exhibits that draw from Rockox's vast personal art collection. People decorated with art as a way of expressing themselves—their values, the people they knew, and so on—so viewing the collection lets you psychoanalyze Rockox. Highlights include an original Rubens canvas of Mary looking tenderly over Baby Jesus (modeled after Rubens' own first wife and son), and Van Dyck's study of two old men's heads. David Teniers the Younger's *Village Feast* evokes the action-packed canvases of the Brueghels (in fact, Teniers—a contemporary of Rubens—married into that prolific clan).

Though the collection is always good, it's particularly worth seeing while the Museum of Fine Arts is closed for restoration

(through late 2017); during this time, the Rockox House is displaying Rubens' *Doubting Thomas* triptych, the left panel of which features a portrait of Nicolaas Rockox (who commissioned the work for the chapel where he was ultimately entombed). It's clear that Rubens really knew this man, as the portrait truly captures his personality. Nearby are usually displayed two replicas, in which Rockox's gaze is less intense—clearly executed by a lesser artist.

Another highlight—and just plain fun to look at—is Peter Brueghel the Younger's *The Proverbs* (actually a copy of his father's earlier work), which strives to make literal more than a hundred Flemish sayings of the day. Try to find some of the examples: "armed to the teeth," "banging your head against the wall," "the die is cast," "going against the tide," "the blind leading the blind," and dozens of others that make no sense in English ("Who knows why the geese go barefoot?").

Cost and Hours: €2.50, Tue-Sun 10:00-17:00, closed Mon, Keizerstraat 10-12, tel. 03-201-9250, www.rockoxhuis.be.

▲▲**Museum Plantin-Moretus**—More interesting than it sounds, this museum about the history of the local printing industry offers an engaging look at Antwerp's 16th-century Golden Age. You'll find out how Antwerp became one of Europe's most important printing cities. Every Flemish kid comes here on a field trip to ogle the old printing presses, smartly decorated aristocratic rooms, and fine collection of antique manuscripts. The excellent, included audioguide tells the whole story. You'll need at least an hour or two to really see the place.

The museum is named for two influential Antwerp printers: Frenchman Christoffel Plantin, who began a printing business here in 1546; and his son-in-law Jan Moretus, who carried on the family business. Eventually their business became the official court printer for the Spanish monarchs of the Low Countries. This building was both the family's home and their workshop, and, since the family was wealthy enough to maintain the property, it's a remarkably well-preserved look at 16th- and 17th-century aristocratic life. The sprawling complex surrounds a pleasant garden, with wings dating from different periods. You'll follow the one-way, counterclockwise tour route through the ground floor, then head upstairs. Sprinkled throughout these rooms are ample samples of period manuscripts and maps, a Gutenberg Bible, and more.

The ground floor is devoted mostly to the printing shop, starting with the reception rooms. In the bookshop, look for the list of

books forbidden by the Catholic Church—the list was printed by, and includes books sold by, Christoffel Plantin. In the proofreaders' room, you can imagine diligent editors huddled around the shared oak desk, debating the 17th-century equivalent of whether "email" takes a hyphen. The publisher's private leatherbound office is a class act. In the print shop you'll see some of the oldest printing presses in the world (c. 1600); neatly stacked in the back room are some 10 tons of lead letters.

Upstairs is the residence, showing off how the upper crust lived 300 years ago—tapestry wall hangings, high-beamed ceilings, leather-tooled walls, and so on. The 18th-century library displays a polyglot bible, with five languages on one page, printed by Christoffel Plantin. The Rubens Room is a reminder that the famous painter was an old family friend.

Cost and Hours: €6, includes audioguide, Tue-Sun 10:00-17:00, closed Mon; last entry 30 minutes before closing—but give yourself at least an hour; Vrijdagmarkt 22, tel. 03-221-1450, www.museumplantinmoretus.be.

Nearby: The museum is on a charming square called Vrijdagmarkt, where there really is a "Friday market" each week with an auction of secondhand stuff.

North of the Old Town
▲**"Little Island" (Eilandje) at the Old Dockyards**—Antwerp's formerly derelict and dangerous old port area, just a 15-minute walk from the Grote Markt, has been rejuvenated and redeveloped. Built by Napoleon in the early 1800s, and filled with brick warehouses around the turn of the 20th century, this part of town became deserted in the 1950s and 1960s, when the city's shipping industry relocated to the larger ports farther north. In the

mid-1980s, city leaders decided it was time to reclaim this prime real estate, and invested heavily in a systematic gentrification program. Today it's a youthful Soho-type area, home to a tidy little yacht marina, a row of desirable condos, some trendy restaurants, and—soon—a pair of the city's top museums.

Perched on the Little Island in the middle of the harbor area is the area's main attraction: The new **Museum aan de Stroom** (Museum on the River), or **MAS** for short. It's housed in a purpose-built, 210-foot-tall blocky tower, encased in hand-cut red stone, and speckled with silver hands (the symbol of Antwerp). Designed to resemble the spiraling stacks of goods in an old maritime warehouse, the museum emphasizes the way that Antwerp's status as a shipping center has made it a crossroads for people from around the world. The collections of several smaller Antwerp museums—including the maritime, ethnographic, and folklore museums—have been brought together in  this brand-new facility. Billed as a "museum of, for, and about the city and the world," MAS includes four semi-permanent exhibits (on the fourth through the eighth floors) that emphasize connections between people by juxtaposing old items in new ways, temporary exhibits, and a top-floor restaurant with panoramic views. The building's many windows also offer great views over Antwerp—and you're welcome to come inside even if you're not paying for the museum (€5 for permanent collection, €8 for temporary exhibits, €10 for both; Tue-Sun 10:00-17:00, closed Mon, Hanzestedenplaats 1, tel. 03-338-4434, www.mas.be).

A five-minute walk beyond the MAS (north, past the greenish skyscraper) is another promising, brand-new exhibit that's scheduled to open in 2012: the **Red Star Line Museum** (a.k.a. People on the Move), which promises to show the "other end" of the Ellis Island experience. During the great migration to the US and Canada between 1873 and 1935, the Red Star shipping line brought some two million emigrants to New York City, and those steamers began their journey here in Antwerp. In addition to "steerage-class" peasants, the line also transported luxury travelers and cargo. By the 1930s, many of the emigrants were Jews fleeing the Nazi regime in Germany. In these red-brick warehouses, emigrants were given humiliating health exams, had their clothes and luggage fumigated, and nervously waited while clerks processed their paperwork. Today, the same buildings are being turned into a museum documenting the experience of the people who said their final farewell to Europe right here. The exhibit traces the history of the Red Star Line and its passengers, displays actual artifacts from the emigrants, and shows off evocative artwork depicting emigrants poignantly waiting for a steam ship to whisk them off to the New World in pursuit of the American Dream (cost and hours not yet set, Rijnkaai 15, tel. 03-206-0350, www.redstarline.org).

Red Light District Walk—On your way to or from the Little Island area, you might want to pass through (or avoid) Belgium's biggest hub of legalized prostitution. This zone lacks the touristy patina of Amsterdam's...which makes it feel that much creepier. You'll see fewer rowdy "stag parties" making a racket, but lots of lonely men silently prowling the pedestrian zone. As with other red light districts, this area is not as dangerous as it might initially seem—the mayor actually encourages visitors to stroll here—but it's also not entirely safe. If you're curious to see it, wander here during the day (combined with a visit to the Little Island area described earlier). If you're wary, or if it's after dark, this neighborhood is best avoided.

Begin in the Old Town, in front of the Old Meat Hall (housing the Musical Instruments Museum). Head up the street called **Vleeshouwersstraat,** walking along the drab brick "projects"—subsidized housing built during the 1970s. These sterile rows of buildings replaced a very run-down, overpopulated, and lively old quarter that some residents miss—notice there are no pubs or shops along here.

Cut diagonally through the square and continue up Nosestraat, passing a church...and some sex-toys shops. You'll wind up at the square called **Sint-Paulusplein,** which used to be a medieval harbor, then a dangerous wasteland, and then a bustling sailors' quarter with red lights in the windows. While you'll still see sex workers, peep shows, and tattoo parlors, this area also has its share of trendy restaurants.

Head up Oudemanstraat, which becomes **Vingerlingstraat,** in the heart of the red light district. Here you'll really begin to see ladies shimmying in windows. In the 19th century, Antwerp's red light district was known (or notorious) the world over; these days, it's a much tamer place...but still provocative.

Bear right on Blauwbroekstraat/Schippersstraat. Halfway down the block on the right is **Villa Tinto,** a modern-looking mall, designed by prominent artist Arne Quinze, where you can window-shop for sex. It's considered one of Europe's most high-tech brothels, with a system of "panic buttons" for sex workers to call for help if necessary. Notice the police station right in the middle of the complex. In Belgium, as throughout the Low Countries, prostitution is pragmatically integrated into the larger society without blushing. City leaders firmly believe that concentrating prostitution in this small neighborhood makes things safer both for the sex workers and for city residents at large.

Pass all the way through Villa Tinto, then bear left (or, to skip the Villa Tinto experience, just continue on Schippersstraat). You'll pop out on a long, narrow square called **Falconplein.** This used to be dubbed "Red Square," for its Russian-dominated illegal activity (Russian mafia-style thugs selling designer knock-offs...and worse). Nervous about sketchy stuff just a few steps from its up-and-coming museum scene, spunky city leaders recently cracked down, evicted the worst offenders, and spiffed up the square.

Turn left and walk up Falconplein, then cross the big, tree-lined Brouwersvliet (which used to be a canal). This puts you right at the old docklands in the heart of the Little Island.

South of the Old Town
Sint-Andries Fashion District

Worth ▲▲▲ for lovers of couture, Antwerp's fashion district is fun for anybody to window-shop. It's mostly in the Sint-Andries

area, a few minutes' walk south of the Old Town, centered on the street called Nationalestraat. In the shops along the streets of Sint-Andries, you'll find everything from top-name international designers to funky hole-in-the-wall boutiques to vintage shops to jewelers. (For tips on shopping here, see "Shopping in Antwerp," facing page.) Antwerp's status as a fashion mecca is a relatively recent development. In 1988, six students from the Royal Academy of Fine Arts' Fashion Department (www.antwerp-fashion.be) traveled to a London show, where they got a lot of attention. Because their Flemish names were too challenging to pronounce, the English press simply dubbed them the "Antwerp Six." Each one opened a shop here in Sint-Andries, which at the time was a very poor neighborhood. They put this area on the map, other designers began to move in, and now it's one of Europe's top fashion zones. The academy is still up and running; it has a small enrollment and a strong focus on creativity.

▲**ModeMuseum ("MoMu")**—The collection here, like fashion itself, is always changing...but it's also always good. Housed in the modern ModeNatie facility in the heart of the Sint-Andries fashion zone, this museum presents good rotating exhibits about big-name designers, with a new exhibit every six months. The building is also home to the Antwerp Fashion Academy, a library with books about fashion, a good bookshop, and—on the ground floor near the ticket desk—a gallery of works by students. Everything is (no surprise) very stylishly presented.

Cost and Hours: €7, Tue-Sun 10:00-18:00, closed Mon, last entry 30 minutes before closing, a five-minute walk south of Groenplaats at Nationalestraat 28, tel. 03-470-2770, www.momu.be.

▲▲ 't Zuid

Literally "The South," 't Zuid (pronounced "tzowd") has emerged as Antwerp's trendiest zone. It's the best place to go for fun and funky boutiques, and a wide array of lively restaurants and bars. With the multiyear closure of the Royal Museum of Fine Arts, there's little sightseeing here, but it's the best place to head in the evenings to stroll and find an enticing place for a meal (for suggestions, see "Eating in Antwerp," later).

To get to 't Zuid from the Old Town, you can either hop on a tram (#8, from Groenplaats, to Museum stop in front of the Royal Museum of Fine Arts), or walk about 20-25 minutes. From the Grote Markt, head down Hoogstraat, which turns into Kloosterstraat, lined with lots of fun antiques stores, retro-style boutiques, and so on.

Royal Museum of Fine Arts of Antwerp (Koninklijk Museum voor Schone Kunsten Antwerpen, a.k.a. KMSKA)—Currently closed for an extensive renovation (through late 2017), this museum normally collects many of Antwerp's most exciting art treasures under one roof. While it's out of commission, many of its items are on display at other museums around town (Leopold De Waelplaats 2, tel. 03-238-7809, www.kmska.be).

Shopping in Antwerp

As a capital of both fashion and avant-garde culture, Antwerp is a shopper's delight, with a seemingly endless array of creative little corner boutiques selling unique items, as well as outlets for big-name international designers. The fanciest shops are on the boulevard called **the Meir,** between the train station and Old Town. The **Sint-Andries** district, just to the west along Nationalestraat, is the center of the fashion scene (described earlier).

As you explore, you'll discover that each street has its own personality and specialties. For example, Schuttershofstraat and Hopland are where you'll find famous-label international couture, while Kammenstraat is better for young, trendy, retro-hipster fashions. For antiques, head to Kloosterstraat (to the west) and Leopoldstraat (to the east); for more antiques and home decor near Leopoldstraat, check out Sint-Jorispoort and Mechelsteenweg.

Sleeping in Antwerp

$$$ Hotel Julien, an extremely chic boutique hotel, is Antwerp's most enticing splurge. Located in a renovated 16th-century building on a drab street just outside the Old Town, its 22 rooms are a perfectly executed combination of old and new. The public areas, with high ceilings and lots of unfinished wood, feel like an art gallery (Db-€170-290 depending on size and amenities, air-con in most rooms, elevator, free Internet access and Wi-Fi, spa in basement, Korte Nieuwstraat 24, tel. 03-229-0600, www.hotel-julien .com, info@hotel-julien.com).

$$$ Matelote Hotel ("Fisherman") is a less pretentious boutique hotel, with a central location on a characteristic street deep in the Old Town. Its 10 rooms have artistic decor and some nice touches (small "cozy comfort" Db-€80-130—usually €90-100, deluxe Db-€100-150—usually €120, breakfast-€12.50, free Internet access and Wi-Fi, Haarstraat 11a, tel. 03-201-8800, www .hotel-matelote.be, info@matelote.be).

$$ Le Patio is the best B&B I found in Antwerp, with three comfortable, thoughtfully appointed ground-floor rooms around a little courtyard on the restaurant-lined Pelgrimstraat (Db-€95, Tb-€120, 20 percent less for 3 nights or more, free Wi-Fi, Pelgrimstraat 8, tel. 03-232-7661, www.lepatio.be, info@lepatio .be, Nicole and Roger).

$$ Big Sleep B&B, between the Old Town and 't Zuid, has two very mod rooms in an old warehouse, with lots of minimalist white and frosted glass—a little too transparent if privacy is a priority (Sb-€55, Db-€80, includes breakfast in your room, cash only, free Wi-Fi, Kromme-Elleboogstraat 4, mobile 0474-849-565, www.intro04.be/thebigsleep, els.hubert@skynet.be, Els Hubert).

$$ Enich Anders B&B is well-priced and nicely located above an art gallery around the corner from Vrijdagmarkt, in the heart of town (Sb-€66, Db-€72, Tb-€88, Qb-€104, €5 cheaper per night with two-night stay, includes breakfast served in your own kitchenette, cash only, free Wi-Fi, tight and steep stairs, Leeuwenstraat 12, mobile 0476-998-601, www.enich-anders.be, Ine and Jan).

$$ Ibis Antwerpen Centrum, the cookie-cutter standby, has 150 predictable rooms sharing the big Oudevaartplaats square with the modern City Theater, just south of the Meir and the Rubens House between the train station and Old Town (Sb/Db-€92-109 depending in demand, as low as €59 in slow times if you book online 3 weeks ahead, breakfast-€14/person, air-con, elevator, free Wi-Fi in lobby, pay Wi-Fi in rooms, Meistraat 39, tel. 03-231-8830, www.ibishotel.com, h1453@accor.com).

$ 't Katshuis is a very rough-around-the edges budget option, with nine sketchy but affordable rooms in two buildings right in the heart of town. Because central Antwerp doesn't yet have an official youth hostel (though one is planned soon), this last resort has the best-located cheap beds in town (Ss-€35, Ds-€50, Db-€55, includes coffee but not breakfast, cash only, Grote Pieter Potstraat 18 and 19—reception at #19, mobile 0476-206-947, www.katshuis .be, katshuis@gmail.com).

Eating in Antwerp

This trendy, youthful city is changing all the time, and the range of options is impressive. Because what's good one year is old news the next, it's risky to recommend any particular place. Instead, I suggest poking around the neighborhoods described next and choosing the menu and ambience that appeal to you the most. Exploring this evolving scene is actually enjoyable—a fun part of the Antwerp experience. Ask your hotelier for pointers.

If you're dining in the Old Town area, simply accept that anywhere you go will cater at least partly to tourists. But since Antwerp isn't overrun by visitors, these places also entertain their share of locals. For a more authentic Antwerp experience, head south to 't Zuid.

In the Old Town
Touristy restaurants with outdoor seating abound on the Grote Markt and Handschoenmarkt, the square in front of the cathedral. Choose your view and overpay for mediocre food. Better yet, venture a few blocks away to one of these neighborhoods.

Pelgrimsstraat: Just a block south of the cathedral, this delightful, cobbled, traffic-free lane is still a tourist zone—but a bit more respectable than the high-profile squares. You'll find a staggering variety along here: Italian and tapas, sushi and Thai, rustic taverns and chic bars. Keep an eye out for these (coming from the cathedral): **Pasta Hippo** has a reputation for good pasta (Mon-Sat for lunch and dinner, Sun only for dinner). On the right at #4, go through the doorway to discover a series of narrow alleyways (called **Vlaeykensngang**) that twist through the middle of the block, passing a trio of well-regarded restaurants en route. Back on the main drag, on the left is **Pelgrom,** a tavern in a

cozy brick cellar that oozes atmosphere. Farther down on the right is **Lollapalooza,** with a fun, eclectic menu, a rocker-grrl pink-and-tattoos ambience, and a charming little brick grotto across the street. Two nearby streets (Grote Pieterpotstraat and Haarstraat) are similar, but less developed and more bar-oriented.

Near "Antwerp's Piazza": The streets branching off from Hendrik Conscienceplein (about a block northeast of the cathedral), with its very Italian-feeling Baroque Jesuit church, are a charming cobbles-and-red-brick maze of alleys with intriguing little eateries. Two good, upscale choices are kitty-corner in the heart of this neighborhood: **Aurelia** (French and Belgian, cozy, white-tablecloth but rustic, under low wooden beams, €13-18 starters, €25-30 main dishes, €55 fixed-price meals, Thu-Mon 18:00-22:30, closed Tue-Wed, Wijngaardstraat 22, tel. 03-233-6259) and **Neuze Neuze** (French, gastronomic, dressy, white stucco and old beams, €20-30 starters and mains, Mon-Sat 12:00-14:00 & 19:00-21:30, closed for lunch Wed and Sat and all day Sun, Wijngaardstraat 19-21, tel. 03-232-2797). This area is fun to stroll, whether or not you dine here.

Just South and East of the Old Town

In Sint-Andries: The area called Sint-Andries, the center of the fashion district, has its share of enjoyable bars and restaurants. For a quick lunch, try **Fresh 'n Fruity,** selling good €2-5 baguette sandwiches and fresh-squeezed fruit juice (closed Sun, Kammenstraat 19, tel. 03-231-1308). **Hungry Henrietta,** tucked away in a nondescript, businesslike neighborhood just south of Groenplaats, has mod black decor and good Belgian food (€9-15 starters, €20-26 main dishes, €15 daily specials, daily 12:00-14:00 & 18:00-21:00, Lombardenvest 19, tel. 03-232-2928).

In the Meir: **Horta** is a brasserie with a pricey menu located in a gorgeously restored Art Nouveau hall a few steps south of the Rubens House. Come here not for the food, but for the remarkable setting, with its glassy spaciousness and iron adornments (€10-15 light meals served until 17:00, €13-18 starters, €16-30 main dishes, daily 11:30-22:00, until 23:30 on weekends, Hopland 2, tel. 03-203-5660).

In 't Zuid

Literally "The South," this zone is emerging as Antwerp's top restaurant and nightlife zone. Frequented mostly by urbanites, this is where you'll find most of the city's hot new restaurants. Options are scattered around a several-block area, with one or two tempting eateries on each block. The long parking lot that runs parallel to the river a block inland (between Waalsekaai and Vlaamsekaai) is lined with several options.

At **Marnixplaats,** the confluence of eight streets creates a circle of corner buildings made-to-order for restaurants with outdoor seating. **Fiskebar** is done up like a fish market (as its name implies), and lists a wide range of seafood specialties on its chalkboard menu high on the wall (€7-10 starters, €15-25 main dishes, €17-20 specials, open daily, Marnixplaats 12-13, tel. 03-257-1357). **Osteria Casa Zaga** dishes up Italian food in one long room that stretches along the open kitchen (€16-18 pastas and salads, €23 main dishes, open daily, Marnixplaats 10, tel. 03-216-4616).

Although the Royal Museum of Fine Arts is closed for renovation, the area in front of it is still lined with several good options. **Zuidcafé** is a lively, youthful spot with an eclectic menu (€10-12 pastas and salads, €13-15 main dishes, open daily, Volkstraat 69, tel. 03-248-8189). **Hippodroom** also has a varied menu, but feels a bit more upscale (€11-17 starters, €19-30 main dishes, closed Sun, Leopold De Waelplaats 10, tel. 03-248-5252).

Antwerp Connections

From Antwerp by Train to: Brussels (5/hour, 40-50 minutes), **Ghent** (3/hour, 50-55 minutes), **Bruges** (2/hour, 1.5 hours, half change in Ghent), **Ypres/Ieper** (hourly, 2.25 hours, change in Kortrijk), **Amsterdam** (about hourly on Thalys, 1.25 hours; also possible on slower but still direct IC, some with a transfer at Schiphol Airport—see next, 2 hours total), Amsterdam's **Schiphol Airport** (hourly on IC, 1.75 hours), **Delft** (hourly, 1.5 hours, change in Rotterdam), **Paris** (about hourly direct on Thalys, 2 hours; more possible with a transfer at Brussels Midi/Zuid/South to Thalys, 2.5 hours). In Belgium, dial 050-302-424 for train information—press 4 for English, www.b-rail.be.

GHENT

Gent

Made terrifically wealthy by the textile trade, medieval Ghent was a powerhouse—for a time, it was one of the biggest cities in Europe. It erected grand churches and ornate guild houses to celebrate its resident industry. But, like its rival Bruges, eventually Ghent's fortunes fell, leaving it with a well-preserved historic nucleus surrounded by a fairly drab modern shell.

Ghent doesn't ooze with cobbles and charm, as Bruges does; this is a living, thriving city—home to Belgium's biggest university. In contrast to the manicured-but-empty back lanes of Bruges, Ghent enjoys more urban grittiness and a thriving restaurant and nightlife scene. It's also a browser's delight, with a wide range of fun and characteristic little shops and boutiques that aren't aimed squarely at the tourist crowds. Simply put, Ghent feels more real than idyllic. Visitors enjoy exploring its historic quarter, ogling the breathtaking Van Eyck altarpiece in its massive cathedral, touring its impressive art and design museums, strolling its picturesque embankments, basking in its finely decorated historic gables, and prowling its newly revitalized Patershol restaurant quarter.

Planning Your Time

Ghent is ideally located, about halfway between Brussels and Bruges. It's easy to get the gist of the town in a few hours (either toss your bag in a locker at Ghent's train station on your way between those two cities, or side-trip here from either one). With limited time, focus on the historical center: Follow my self-guided walk, tour the cathedral, and dip into any museums that intrigue you. With more time or a strong interest in art, also visit the art museums closer to the train station. Be aware that nearly all museums in Ghent are closed on Mondays (though the cathedral and other churches remain open).

If you'd like to home-base in Belgium, Ghent couldn't be more handy—just a half-hour from either Brussels or Bruges and 50 minutes from Antwerp (though be aware that most Ghent hotels are a tram ride away from the train station).

Orientation to Ghent

Although it's a mid-sized city (pop. 240,000), the tourist's Ghent is appealingly compact—you can walk from one end of the central zone to the other in about 15 minutes. Its Flemish residents call it Gent (gutturally: hhhent), while its French name is Gand (sounds like "gone").

Tourist Information

Ghent's TI is in the process of moving; if it's not in its original home, on the ground floor of the Cloth Hall beneath the Belfry, you'll find it in the newly renovated Fish Market (Vismijn) building next to the Castle of the Counts (daily mid-March-mid-Oct 9:30-18:30, off-season 10:30-17:30, tel. 09-266-5232, www.visit gent.be). They also hope to open branches in the train station and the City Museum (STAM). At any TI, you can pick up a free town map and a pile of brochures (including a good self-guided walk; vegetarian info; and lists of hotels, B&Bs, bars, and restaurants).

The **Gent Museum Card,** which includes public transit and entrance to all the major museums and monuments in town, is worth the price if you'll be visiting four or more sights (€20/3 days, sold at TI, hotels, and museums).

Arrival in Ghent

By Train: Ghent's main train station, called Gent-Sint-Pieters, is about a mile and a half south of the city center. As the station is undergoing an extensive renovation (through 2020), you might find things different than described. The left-luggage desk (daily 6:15-21:30) is across the hall from the Travel Centre ticket office, and lockers are just down the same hall on the right (€3-4/day for either bag-storage option).

It's a dull 30-minute **walk** to the city center. Instead, take the **tram:** Buy a ticket from the Relay shop just inside the train station exit, then head outside to find the stop for tram #1 (likely out the front door and to the left; the location might change depending on the renovation—ask around or look for signs). Board tram #1 in the direction of Wondelgem/Evergem (departs about every 10 minutes, ride into town takes 10-15 minutes, €1.20 if you buy the ticket in advance at a shop or automated machine, €2 from the driver; you can also get a shareable 10-ride ticket for €8). Get off at the Veldstraat stop; continue two blocks straight ahead to Korenmarkt, where you can see most of the city's landmark towers (St. Michael's Bridge, where my self-guided walk begins, is just to the left). Figure €10 for a **taxi** into town.

To reach the art museums in Citadelpark, simply exit the station straight ahead, then bear right at the end of the square (onto Koningin Astridlaan).

By Car: Exit the E40 expressway at the Gent Centrum exit, then follow the *P-route* (parking route) to various pay garages in town; the most central include P1 (Vrijdagmarkt) and P5 (Kouter).

Helpful Hints

Festivals: Ghent is proud of its Gentse Feesten (Ghent Festivities), which last for 10 days and begin around the city holiday of July 21. This open-air music festival, featuring different types of music in venues around town, books up hotels—reserve ahead. Other events include a jazz festival (the week before the big festival), and a film festival each mid-October.

Market Day: Sunday is the main market day in Ghent, with small markets filling squares around town: a flower market at Kouter, secondhand books along Ajuinlei, clothes and pets on Vrijdagmarkt, and more. There are also smaller markets on Fridays and Saturdays.

Laundry: A handy, unstaffed coin-op launderette is in the heart of the Patershol restaurant neighborhood...handy for multitaskers (daily 7:00-22:00, corner of Oudburg and Zwaanstraat, mobile 0475-274-686).

Tours in Ghent

Walking Tours—Guided two-hour tours of Ghent (in English and sometimes also other languages) depart daily from the TI (€7, May-Oct daily at 14:30, Sun only off-season, reserve at the TI or by calling 09-233-0772).

Local Guide—**Toon Van den Abeele** enthusiastically shares Ghent's charms (€65/2-hour tour, book through Gidsenbond Gent agency: tel. 09-233-0772, www.gidsenbond-gent.be, info @gidsenbond-gent.be).

Self-Guided Walk

Welcome to Ghent

This walk takes in the historic center of Ghent. Begin at the bridge in the heart of town, next to the bustling Korenmarkt square.

St. Michael's Bridge (Sint-Michielsbrug)

This viewpoint offers Ghent's best 360-degree panorama. The city was founded at the confluence (the origin of the word "Ghent")

of two rivers: the Lys (Leie in Flemish) and the Scheldt (Schelde in Flemish, Escaut in French). Ghent boomed in the Middle Ages, when the wool trade made it wealthy. By the 14th century, Ghent's population was around 65,000—positively massive in an age when most of Europe was rural farmland. Two-thirds of the city's population were textile workers, making Ghent arguably Europe's first industrial city. The waterway in front of you—now plied by tourist-laden boats—was the city's busy harbor. Lining the embankment on the right are several ornately decorated guild houses—meeting halls for the town's industries (such as corn traders or seamen). Straight ahead is the newly renovated Fish Market (the new home of the TI, likely sometime in 2011), which marks the start of the seedy-chic Patershol zone (a residential district sprinkled with great restaurants); behind that is the imposing Castle of the Counts. (We'll circle through town and end near there.)

• *Turn to the right and walk to...*

Korenmarkt

This "Corn Market" is one of many small squares throughout the city. Whereas many Belgian cities (including Brussels, Bruges, and Antwerp) have a single "Great Market" (Grote Markt), Ghent was too big for just one such square. Instead it had a smattering of smaller squares that specialized in different areas of commerce. They retain these traditional names today.

The big building on the left is the former **post office** (now the Post Plaza mall). While it seems to match the classic medi-

eval style of old Ghent, it's much newer—Neo-Gothic, from the early 20th century. As throughout Europe, the late 1800s and early 1900s were a time of powerful nationalism, when smaller minority groups (such as the Flemish) rose up against the

more dominant groups (such as the French-speaking Belgians) to assert their worth. There was a flurry of Neo-Gothic construction, hearkening back to a time when the Flemish had more power.

Ghent

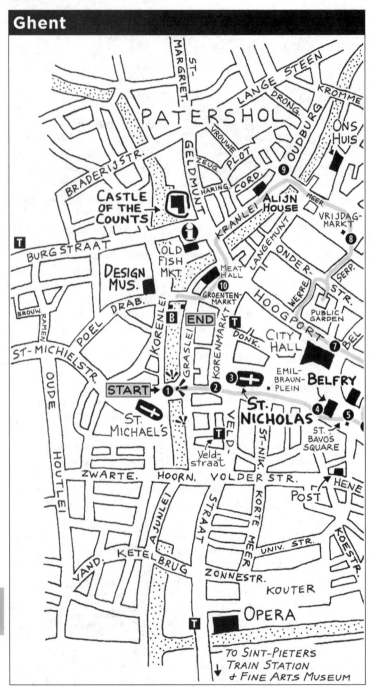

GHENT

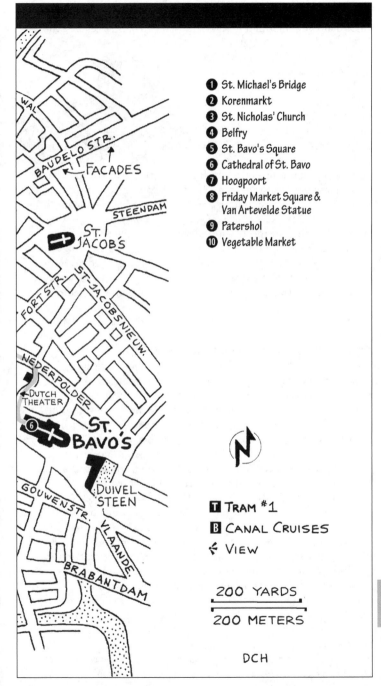

1. St. Michael's Bridge
2. Korenmarkt
3. St. Nicholas' Church
4. Belfry
5. St. Bavo's Square
6. Cathedral of St. Bavo
7. Hoogpoort
8. Friday Market Square & Van Artevelde Statue
9. Patershol
10. Vegetable Market

T TRAM #1
B CANAL CRUISES
← VIEW

200 YARDS
200 METERS

DCH

Looking straight ahead, you can see the spires of Ghent's three main buildings (left to right): the Church of St. Nicholas, the Belfry, and St. Bavo's Cathedral.

As you tour Ghent, you can play amateur archaeologist to quickly deduce the age of various buildings. Before the year 1400, when Ghent was rolling in wool money, they built with valuable, imported gray limestone. Between 1400 and 1500, as the economy slowed, they used yellow sandstone, which was quarried nearby. And after 1500—when competition from Brussels and England, combined with very conservative guild leadership that was slow to adapt to the changing markets, caused Ghent's economy to tank—they resorted to the cheapest material: locally produced red brick. Even in a single building—such as these old churches—you can spot several centuries of construction at a glance. (People from Ghent gleefully point out that their rival, Bruges, is built mostly of brick—indicating that city's lowlier economic status in medieval times.)

• *Turn your attention to the big church at the end of the square.*

St. Nicholas' Church (Sint-Niklaaskerk)

This stout church is made mostly of gray limestone, indicating that it dates from a boom time for Ghent. Before entering, look around the left (north) side of the church, where the facade appears more like cinderblock than the rough stonework of the rest of the building. Looking more closely, you'll see that it's covered with an inch-thick layer of plaster, and the "gaps" between the "blocks" are painted on. This was the fashion in the Middle Ages, when painted plaster facades were considered superior to naked stone... especially the asymmetrical stonework of this church.

Now go inside (free, daily 10:00-17:00). You can tell it was built from the back to the front, as the gray limestone transitions to the yellow sandstone. While the building itself is Gothic, the decorations inside—like most in Ghent—are much newer. As this region was at the forefront of the Protestant Reformation in the 16th century, the interior of Ghent's churches suffered at the hands of the iconoclasts—Protestants who stripped churches of all adornments to unclutter their communion with God. The church was later partly redecorated by Catholics, who installed the very Baroque altar, with modern stained glass above (representing the seven sacraments).

• *Exiting the church, look straight ahead and notice the stepped gable of the **Masons' Guild House**. This 15th-century facade was only revealed* *in the 1980s, when workers peeled back a more modern layer on top of it. They restored the building, added the decorations at the tops of the gables (bottom row: humans; middle row: devils; top row: angels), then added a very modern section behind it (notice the glass–and–steel structure down St.-Niklaasstraat).*

The square beyond St. Nicholas, **Emil-Braunplein,** *is in transition; they recently excavated the brick foundations of humble buildings that once stood here, and hope to build a grassy park and a new market hall; expect some construction work around here.*

The next tall building is the...

Belfry

Although most of this tower has stood here since the 14th century, the Neo-Gothic top spire (from the gargoyles up) was added when Ghent proudly hosted a World's Fair in 1913. The tower was originally built to house and protect the parchment record of Ghent's favored privileges, granted to the city by the Counts of Flanders in exchange for financial support. The dragon topping the spire symbolizes not the devil (as was typical in the Middle Ages), but a protector who never sleeps as it watches over the city's rights. It was also a fire watchtower, represented by the four sentries positioned at the corners. The carillon in the tower plays the Ghent town anthem each hour.

Visitors enjoy ascending the belfry for a view over town. It's just a couple of flights of stairs, then an elevator most of the way (€5, borrow English explanations as you enter, daily 10:00-18:00, last entry 30 minutes before closing, www.belfortgent.be). On the way, you'll pass a modest exhibit about the history of the building, including models of former spires that topped it.

The long building at the base of (and behind) the belfry is the **Cloth Hall,** which was important to this textile center. The TI is located here, unless it has already moved across town to the Fish Market.

• *The square beyond the Belfry is...*

St. Bavo's Square (Sint-Baafsplein)

This square became a symbolic battleground during the period of Flemish nationalism in the early 20th century. Previously, when Belgium gained its independence from the Netherlands in 1830, it was ruled by its Francophone (French-speaking) aristocracy, even though the Flemish-speakers were in the majority. Flemish people felt mistreated by their Francophone overlords. (It took a century after independence for Ghent's prestigious university to finally start offering classes in Dutch; to mark that day in 1930, the Francophone-aristocracy-owned electric company spitefully cut power to mourn the university's end of "enlightened" thinking.)

The ornate building on the square is the **Dutch Theater** (Koninklijke Nederlandse Schouwburg, a.k.a. NT Gent), built in 1899 to provide the town's Flemish speakers a place to perform

plays of their own. By embracing Dutch as a language worthy of theater, the spunky Flemish were asserting their cultural legitimacy. The golden mosaic depicts Apollo returning to Mount Parnassus, much as the Flemish felt they were coming home to their beloved language.

Circle around for a look at the far side of the **statue** in the middle of the square. The relief on the base (facing the theater) depicts Jan Frans Willems, one of the founders of the Flemish move-

ment. The man and woman in the statue represent the resurrection of the Dutch (Flemish) language—notice the lion, a symbol of Flanders, on their flag.

As you face the theater, look to the left to see **Van Hoorebeke Chocolatier,** a producer of fine pralines. Peek in the window (or go in the shop and look through the glass floor) to see the chocolate-makers hard at work (€4/100 grams—about 7 pieces, daily 10:00-18:00, tel. 09-221-0381).

• *At the end of the square is Ghent's top sight...*

▲▲Cathedral of St. Bavo (Sint-Baafskathedraal)

The main church of Ghent, this also houses three of the city's art treasures: the exquisite *Adoration of the Mystic Lamb* altarpiece, by Jan Van Eyck and his brother, Hubert; an elaborately carved pulpit; and an altar painting by Rubens depicting the town's patron saint (and the church's namesake).

Cost and Hours: Free, Mon-Sat 9:30-16:45, Sun 13:00-16:30, later in summer. During busy times, volunteer guides can show you around.

◒ Self-Guided Tour: Step inside. This giant Gothic cathedral was built over many centuries—notice the telltale three materials: gray stone (choir), red brick (nave), and yellow stone (tower). As in St. Nicholas' Church, all of the decorations and stained glass date from the 19th century (following the iconoclasm of the 16th century).

Below, I've first described the great altarpiece, and then the rest of the church. Note that there are two opportunities to see the altarpiece: You can view a replica in the chapel that originally contained the piece (at the front-right corner of the church) for free. Or you can pay €4 to see the original, in a small room in the back-left corner of the church (€1 audioguide). The locations of both the original and the replica are explained under "The Rest of the Church," later.

The Adoration of the Mystic Lamb: The highlight of the church (and, for art-lovers, of all Ghent) is Jan and Hubert Van Eyck's *Adoration of the Mystic Lamb* altarpiece. Hubert Van Eyck (c. 1385-1426) began the painting, but after his death, his better-known younger brother, Jan (1395-1441), picked up the brush and completed Hubert's vision. Finished in 1432, this altarpiece represents a monumental stride in Northern European art from medieval stiffness to Renaissance humanism, with a closely observed attention to detail. The first work signed by Jan Van Eyck, it's also considered one of the first works of the Flemish Primitives (characterized by a precise dedication to detail, if an imperfect mastery of perspective).

During the wave of iconoclasm in the 16th century, the altar was hidden in the cathedral tower. And later, during World War II, the altar was on its way to safe storage at the Vatican when it was caught up in the fighting and squirreled away in the French Pyrenees, then swiped by Hitler and stored in a Bavarian castle, then a salt mine, before being returned here by US forces at war's end.

The altarpiece has a dozen separate paintings on each side (front and back). On weekdays, the altarpiece was closed to show only the outside panels; it was opened up on Sundays and holidays to reveal the scenes inside. (On the replica, you can actually open and close the panels; on the original, you'll have to circle around back to see them in their open state.)

First, look at the **outside panels,** showing the Annunciation—when the archangel Gabriel comes to Mary to tell her she will bear God's child. Gabriel, holding a lily (representing purity), says to Mary, "Hail Mary, full of grace." Mary (with the Holy Spirit above her) replies, "I am the servant of the Lord." Notice that Mary's words are upside-down—intended for God above. Through the windows, we get a glimpse of medieval Ghent, and in the niche is a medieval "bathroom" (with a pitcher and basin). Below are the kneeling couple who commissioned the work for their private chapel, and statues of St. John the Baptist (holding the lamb) and St. John the Evangelist (holding the cup of poison). Above are two sibyls (pagan prophets) flanked by the Old Testament prophets Zechariah (on the left) and Micah (on the right)—all of whom prophesied the coming of Christ.

Now get the full feast-day effect of the **inside panels.** The main scene, playing out at the bottom, depicts the adoration of the lamb (representing Jesus) at the Revelation. The scene is a big Christ-celebrating party, and everyone's here: angels, church teachers, holy virgins, Old Testament prophets (in the left-foreground), the 12 apostles (in the right-foreground),  saints, popes, pagan writers, Jewish prophets, knights and judges (on the left panel) and pilgrims and hermits (on the right panel)... all coming to worship their savior. Notice the diversity of the people assembled, wearing all different styles of clothing and headwear—from Asia, India, and the entire known world at the time. Hovering overhead is a dove (the Holy Spirit), and in the foreground is the well of life, spewing water and jewels. As in Christian tradition, the lamb at the very center is a stand-in for Christ—but it also has a special meaning here in Ghent, whose wool trade put it on the map. It's too bad that the lamb itself—which scholars suspect was later retouched by a lesser artist—isn't particularly well-depicted. He looks more like a sheep...and is that an extra right ear I see?

Above this scene are (from left to right) Mary, the resurrected Christ (or is it God himself, wearing a triple-tiara to represent the Trinity?), and John the Baptist (wearing a garment of camel hair, per biblical descriptions). On the upper outside panels are angels playing music, and a pair of famous portraits of **Adam and Eve**—which scholars believe were the first Renaissance-era nudes painted north of the Alps. The tiny, wedge-shaped panels above them tell the story of Cain and Abel.

Take a moment to simply bask in the astonishing level of detail. You can see each hair on Adam's legs (and notice the not-quite-perfectly executed, Italian-inspired perspective—with Adam's toes breaking the plane as they seem to emerge from the panel). Hymnals of the time indicated which face a singer should make when singing a particular note; today's experts can guess which notes the angels are singing from their expressions. The countryside scenes are decorated with dozens of different, identifiable species of plants and flowers, and the angels around the lamb in the lower panel have feathers from a variety of actual birds (peacocks, pigeons, and swallows). And in the amulet around the neck of the angel by Adam, you can actually see a faint reflection of the stained-glass window that decorated the chapel where this altarpiece originally stood.

The Rest of the Church: Go for a counterclockwise spin around the cathedral's interior. Along the way, you'll have a chance to see both the replica and the original of the altarpiece described above.

Begin in the back-right corner of the church (to the right as you enter). Near the information desk, see the panels showing **Adam and Eve with clothes**—added to cover Van Eyck's nudes during the puritanical 19th century (1825-1896). Instead of discreetly covering their nudity, now they just look like they're scratching their privates through their clothes. Is this really an improvement?

Along the right wall of the church, near the shop, find the chapel with a statue of **Pater Damiaan** (Father Damien, 1840-1889), a Flemish missionary who went to Hawaii to care for lepers, but after 16 years died of leprosy himself. Canonized in 2009, he's a rare saint with a connection to the United States, and an important figure both to Belgians and to Hawaiians.

Inside the main nave, on the right-hand side, you can't miss the elaborately carved, remarkable Rococo **pulpit,** representing the tree of life and the tree of knowledge. Notice the golden serpent entwined around the top of the pulpit; follow its body to find the pudgy, winged baby (a sure sign of Rococo) prying the apple of sin from the snake's

mouth. The Carrara marble statues just beneath the pulpit drive home a Counter-Reformation message: The woman on the right (with the quill, representing faith) wakes up the winged old man on the left (representing time): It's time to wake up to the Catholic faith. The goody-two-shoes angels at the bases of the staircases offer a lesson in appropriate worship: The angel on the left watches the pulpit intently, and the one on the right points up to the pulpit while glancing scoldingly to the back of the church: Hey, you in the back row—pay attention!

Go up the right aisle toward the front of the church. Above the main altar is **St. Bavo,** the beloved local saint, on his way to heaven. This seventh-century saint was once a wealthy and rambunctious young soldier, but became a born-again Christian after the death of his wife. Bavo rejected his life of materialism and became a monk, living for a time in a hollow tree. He is also the patron saint of Haarlem, the Netherlands.

In the front-right part of the church (just to the right, as you face the main altar) is the Vijdt Chapel, housing the **replica of the Van Eyck altarpiece** (described earlier). Van Eyck painted the altarpiece specifically to be displayed in this room—in fact, the light and subtle reflections in his work are designed to complement this space.

Circling around the back of the church to the left transept, you'll find another great work of art, **Peter Paul Rubens'** *Entrance of St. Bavo into the Monastery of Ghent,* depicting the moment this local-boy-done-good started on his righteous course. Notice the parallel, diagonal composition: On the top, Bavo, in the red cloak (and with the face of the painter, Rubens—a rare self-portrait), kneels before the abbot. The lower group shows Bavo's estate manager distributing his belongings to the poor. The women on the left, representing Bavo's daughter and her servant, are modeled after Rubens' two wives—his older first wife, wearing the giant hat; and his much younger, more  voluptuous second wife, Hélène Fourment, in the red dress. (The Flemish like to say, with a wink, "An old billy goat loves a young leaf.") Compare the very static composition of Van Eyck's altarpiece (1432) with this dynamic canvas, pregnant with motion (1624)—illustrating the contrast between staid medieval and exuberant Baroque.

Across from this canvas is the entrance to the **crypt,** where you can see some of the building's Romanesque foundations and various chapels decorated with ecclesiastical art both old and modern.

Circling back to the entrance, you reach the chapel with the **original Van Eyck painting.** If you want a closer look at this remarkable work in its original form, you can pay €4 to see it now.

• *Exiting the cathedral, turn right and head down the narrow, twisty*

Biezekapelstraat. You'll pass the turrets and other medieval-looking features of the back of the Achtersikkel mansion, the home of a powerful aristocratic family. The music you might hear is provided by students rehearsing at the nearby music college. Exiting this narrow street, turn left and head up...

Hoogpoort

This "High Gate" street connects Ghent's two rivers. As you walk, notice you're on a slight hill; Ghent was founded at a high point between two rivers, which people made ample use of for trade.

Crossing Belfortstraat, you'll see the giant, eclectic, slightly run-down **City Hall** on your left. Onto the ornate Gothic core of

the building, from the early 16th century, have been grafted many centuries of additions (for example, the blocky Renaissance-style section just down Belfortstraat). Continue along Hoogpoort, observing the many facets of this one building.

At the end of the City Hall, watch (on the right) for the narrow, covered lane called Werregarn Straat. Once used to drain water away from this high ground, today it has a different purpose and nickname: **Graffitistraat.** Walk down the lane, enjoying the artwork provided by the people

of Ghent. This is a typically pragmatic Belgian solution to a social problem: Rather than outlawing graffiti entirely, the police have designated this one street to give would-be artists a legal, controlled outlet for their impulses. Halfway down the

lane, notice the beautiful fenced-in garden on your right. This restful, picnic-perfect space is open to the public: When you emerge from Graffitistraat, turn right on Onderstraat; on the right, at #22, you can go through the giant green door (if it's open) into this city-owned garden courtyard.

• *Roughly across the street from #22—and just before the worth-a-peek **Flamingo's Pub**, with its avant-garde, funky-kitsch interior and Barbie chandelier—head down Serpentstraat, which is lined with some fun boutiques and colorful secondhand stores. When you pop out, turn left and you'll be in...*

Friday Market Square (Vrijdagmarkt)

While these days, the primary market day is Sunday, this square's name indicates its history. The church a block beyond the square is **St. Jacob's** (Sint-Jacobskerk), a pilgrimage stop for those walking from here to northwest Spain on the Camino de Santiago (the Camino's telltale scallop-shell symbol is at the church's entrance).

The statue in the square depicts a different Jacob: **Jakob Van Artevelde,** a clever businessman who saved the day in the 14th century, when the Hundred Years' War between France (which then controlled Ghent) and England (which provided Ghent with much-needed wool) threatened local industry. When the English king refused to export his wool to Ghent, Van Artevelde—not an aristocrat, but an ordinary citizen—boldly negotiated directly with the king to keep Ghent neutral in the conflict and keep the wool coming in. Largely forgotten by history, Van Artevelde's memory was resurrected during the nationalism of the late 19th century, as a symbol of the Flemish people of Ghent asserting their independence from the Francophones. Today he's still celebrated by the people of Ghent, who sometimes call their city "Artevelde-Stad."

Behind the statue is the eclectic **"House of the People"** (Ons Huis), the headquarters for the region's socialist movement. Not surprisingly for a city with a long industrial heritage, Ghent is a hotbed of left-leaning politics, and the birthplace of the Belgian Labor Party. Above the door on the right, notice the rooster—crowing to wake up the workers.

Farther to the right, peek up the street called **Baudelostraat** for some particularly beautiful gables.

• *Go down the narrow street that Van Artevelde is pointing down (Meerseniersstraat). In a block you reach a bridge. Notice the giant red cannon on the left. Several different tour-guide stories have circulated about this giant piece of artillery, but most are probably made up.*

Cross the bridge to enter the district called...

Patershol

Once a dingy and deserted danger zone, this neighborhood has turned into one of Ghent's trendiest. And though it's predominantly residential, Patershol is also a great place for restaurant-hunting (see "Eating in Ghent," later).

Looking straight ahead as you cross the bridge, you'll see two particularly fine (and symbolism-packed) gabled **facades.** The red one on the right features five panels showing the five senses, each one represented by an animal that exemplifies it (taste =

monkey; sight = eagle; hearing = deer; smell = dog; and touch = humans, since we have no hair on our hands). The building on the left has panels demonstrating six virtuous acts (the seventh—burying the dead—was deemed too gruesome to depict, so it's symbolized by the urn on top). The ground floor of this building houses a favorite old-fashioned candy shop, **Temmerman,** with some unique Ghent treats, including Wippers—toffee with sugar coating; Lieve Vrouwkens—in the shape of the Virgin Mary; and the local favorite, raspberry-flavored Cuperdons (Wed-Sat 11:00-18:00, closed Sun-Tue, Kraanlei 79, tel. 09-224-0041).

• *Turn left and walk along Kraanlei, passing the Alijn House (with a tourable interior—see next page). Continue along the embankment, curving right with the road. Pause at the next intersection.*

At the corner on the right, notice the brasserie called 't Stopkje ("The Noose"). The people of Ghent are called **"noose-wearers"** *(Stopkens).* This dates back to the time of King Charles V, who had been born here in Ghent but ruled from Spain. In 1540, he demanded a huge tribute from the people of Ghent. When they refused and revolted, he came here personally to enforce his authority. The leaders of Ghent had to beg on their knees with nooses around their necks for his forgiveness.

Across the street, the imposing **Castle of the Counts** is worth touring, if you have time (described later, under "Sights in Ghent").

Across the little square from the castle is the fancy arched facade of the **Old Fish Market** (Oude Vismijn). Deserted for years, this is now being renovated to house the TI, a conference center, and a café. Study the facade: That's Neptune on top; below him are Ghent's two rivers: Scheldt (male) and Lys (female). It's said that Ghent is the child of these two rivers.

• *Now cross the bridge to one final stop.*

Vegetable Market (Groentenmarkt)

The long, white **Meat Hall** (Groot Vleeshuis) looks like it's seen better days, but it's worth a peek inside to see its impressive wooden vault (built entirely without nails, and clearly employing

ship-builders' expertise). You'll see local cured ham hanging from the rafters. The shop inside sells specialty products from East Flanders (Tue-Sun 10:00-18:00, closed Mon).

Back out on the square are more snacking opportunities. Across the square from the Meat Hall is a good traditional bakery (Himschoot); next to that, a café selling delicious take-away waffles; and to the right of that, the **Tierenteyn Verlent mustard shop.** Made in the cellar, then pumped into a barrel in the back of the shop, the mustard is some of the horseradish-hottest you'll ever sample. They use no preservatives, so you'll need to refrigerate it—or use it for today's picnic (Mon-Fri 8:30-18:00, Sat 9:00-18:00, closed Sun, Groentenmarkt 3, tel. 09-225-8336, www.tierenteyn -verlent.be).

• *Head to the far end of the Meat Hall, then the building beyond it. The bridge here affords another good view of Ghent's canals. Just across the bridge and to the right is the good **Design Museum** (described later). Near this bridge, various companies sell 40-minute **cruises** around the canals of Ghent (€6, includes commentary). Or you can backtrack (turn right along the river) to the **Castle of the Counts** or the **House of Alijn.** Most of what's worth seeing in Ghent is within a few steps of right here. Enjoy.*

Sights in Ghent

Most of Ghent's sights cluster in one of two areas: in the historic city center, or at a park two long blocks from the train station.

In the Historic Center
The House of Alijn (Huis van Alijn)—This museum shows how everyday Belgian lifestyles evolved over the course of the 20th

century. It assembles an intriguing collection of bric-a-brac from various themes and walks of life (including an old pharmacy, grocery, and candy shop). However, the museum administration has chosen not to include much in the way of description, to encourage visitors to experience the place on their own—making the fine collection difficult to appreciate. And though this place could be fascinating with a good audioguide or regularly scheduled guided tour, neither is available; instead you'll borrow generalized explanations in each section. It's exhibited in several buildings around a tranquil courtyard, which used to be a refuge for poor elderly people (similar to a begijnhof). The courtyard

GHENT

hosts an authentic Ghent pub where you can sample *jenever*, or gin *('t plumeetse)*.

Cost and Hours: €5, Tue-Sat 11:00-17:00, Sun 10:00-17:00, closed Mon, Kraanlei 65, tel. 09-269-2350, www.huisvanalijn.be.

▲**Castle of the Counts (Gravensteen)**—Built in 1180 by Philip of Alsace, this fortress was designed not to protect the people of

Ghent, but to intimidate the city's independence-minded citizens. Built outside the city walls, it's morphed over the centuries, and was partly destroyed by an accidental explosion (when it served as a textile factory), then restored. It's impressive from the outside, but explanations and exhibits inside are pretty modest. Still, it's a fun opportunity to twist through towers and ramble over ramparts. You'll see a sparse armory collection, a better torture museum, paintings and photos that explain the history of the place, an 18-foot-deep dungeon, and great views from the tops of the towers (be prepared for lots of climbing up claustrophobic stairs). Although good explanations would help bring this mostly empty shell to life, instead you get a few perfunctory words. Admission includes a pointless, portable "movieguide," with corny dramatizations of actual historic events in each room (45 minutes; you watch clips as you walk through the grounds).

Cost and Hours: €8, dry €1.50 guidebook tells the history of the place, daily May-Sept 9:00-18:00, Oct-April 9:00-17:00, last entry one hour before closing, tel. 09-225-9306.

▲**Design Museum**—Worth ▲▲▲ for those interested in decorative arts and design, and enjoyable to anybody, this collection cel-

ebrates the Belgian knack for design. It combines a classic old building with a creaky wood interior, with a bright-white, spacious, and glassy new hall in the center. You'll cross back and forth between these sections, seeing both old-timey rooms

and exquisite pieces of Art Nouveau, Art Deco, and contemporary design. Just explore: Everything is clearly explained in English and easy to appreciate. The temporary exhibits are well-presented and interesting. Don't miss the 18th-century dining room, with a remarkable wood-carved chandelier. If you visit the bathroom—in a courtyard around back—walk around a bit to discover that the little building is in the shape of a giant roll of toilet paper.

Cost and Hours: €5, Tue-Sun 10:00-18:00, closed Mon, Jan Breydelstraat 5, tel. 09-267-9999, www.designmuseumgent.be.

Near the Train Station

These museums cluster closer to the train station than to the historical center—making them ideal to visit on your way into or out of Ghent (lockers are at the station).

Getting There: To reach the two art museums from the train station (about a 10-minute walk), exit straight ahead to the modern sculpture in the middle of the plaza. Turn right and walk up the tree- and bike-lined Koningin Astridstraat about five minutes, then cross the road and enter Citadel Park. Walk straight ahead, then curl around the left side of the big, modern building at the center of the park; as you round the far side, the Neoclassical entrance to the Fine Arts Museum is across the small street, and the SMAK is on your right.

▲**Fine Arts Museum (Museum voor Schone Kunsten)**—This museum offers a good, representative look at Northern European art. It's one of the most user-friendly collections of Low Countries art you'll find in Belgium, with lesser-known yet fun works by artists such as Bosch, Rubens, Van Dyck, and Magritte. As you enter, to the right (in numbered rooms) are older works, and to the left (in lettered rooms) are 19th- and 20th-century works and temporary exhibits. The €2.50 audioguide is both essential and excellent.

Cost and Hours: €5, Tue-Sun 10:00-18:00, closed Mon, in Citadelpark along Fernand Scribedreef street, tel. 09-240-0700, www.mskgent.be.

Highlights: Turn right from the entrance, and take a counterclockwise, chronological spin though the collection, keeping an eye out for these fine pieces.

In room 2, **Hieronymus Bosch's** jarring *Christ Carrying the Cross* (1515-1516) features a severe-looking Jesus surrounded by

grotesque faces. Typical of the Middle Ages, Bosch believed that evil was ugly—and all but three faces on this canvas (forming a diagonal, from lower-left to upper-right) are hideous. The serene woman to the left of Christ is Veronica, who has just wiped his face. In the upper-right, with an ashen complexion, is the stoic good thief, flanked by a doctor and a taunting monk. Meanwhile, in the lower-right, the orange-tinged unrepentant thief sneers back at his hecklers. Nearby, Bosch's portrait of St. Jerome

(c. 1505)—who was his personal patron saint—shows the holy hermit having discarded his clothes. Just above his legs, notice the owl (representing evil) sinisterly eyeing a titmouse (good). Also in this room, in **Rogier Van der Weyden**'s *The Virgin with a Carnation* (1480), the Baby Jesus makes a benediction gesture with his little hand. This painting was designed as a focal point for meditation.

Room 5 displays **Peter Paul Rubens'** altarpiece painting of *St. Francis of Assisi Receiving the Stigmata,* with Francis' brother Leo staring in amazement from below. According to Church accounts, an angel appeared to Francis in the form of a six-winged seraphim.

In Room 7, Rubens' student **Anthony Van Dyck** depicts the mythological story of *Jupiter and Antiope*—a horned-and-horny god about to inseminate a sleeping woman.

Room 8 features **Pieter Brueghel the Younger**'s copy of his more famous father, Pieter Brueghel the Elder's, much-loved

Peasant Wedding in a Barn. The elder painter trained his kids to carry on the family business. But Brueghel the Younger was a talented painter in his own right: In his *Village Lawyer,* we see the attorney behind a desk piled with papers, as peasants bring items to barter for his services.

Circle into the modern (lettered) wing. Near the front of this section, in Room B's *Portrait of Physician Ludwig Adler,* Viennese Secessionist painter **Oskar Kokoschka** uses dynamic, expressionistic brushstrokes to capture the personality, rather than a precise reproduction, of his subject.

In Room F you'll find works by homegrown Belgian modernist **René Magritte.** His clever *Perspective II*—part of a larger series—wryly replaces the four subjects on Edouard Manet's famous *Balcony* with coffins.

Stedelijk Contemporary Art Museum (Stedelijk Museum voor Actuele Kunst, a.k.a. SMAK)—This art gallery is constantly changing, both the "permanent" collection and many temporary exhibits. It's worth a visit only for art-lovers, and is conveniently located just across the street from the Fine Arts Museum (€6, more for special exhibits, Tue-Sun 10:00-18:00, closed Mon, tel. 09-240-7601, www.smak.be).

Ghent City Museum (Stadsmuseum Gent, a.k.a. STAM)—This new facility, which opened in October of 2010, explains the history of Ghent. It's housed in a beautiful 14th-century Gothic abbey complex called Bijloke and in a modern annex. The permanent exhibit traces the city's history with high-tech exhibits (€6, Tue-Sun 10:00-18:00, closed Mon, Godshuizenlaan 2, tel. 09-267-1400, www.stamgent.be). In addition to the exhibit, officials plan to eventually have a TI desk here, provide bike rentals, and offer boat trips up the canal and into the town center.

From the train station, it's about a 15-20-minute walk: Exit straight ahead, then angle left up the busy tram-tracks-lined Koningin Maria Hendrikaplein. After the bridge, turn right on Godshuizenlaan. Or, from the station, you could ride tram #1, #4, #21, or #22 to the STAM stop.

Sleeping in Ghent

A convention town, Ghent is busiest in spring (April-June) and fall (Sept-mid-Dec); things are quieter (and prices lower) in July and August, and even more so in the winter.

$$$ Chambre Plus is a three-room B&B run with an impeccable French flair for design by Mia (a cook) and Hendrik (a chocolatier, who makes chocolates in the basement). They say the "Plus" is for the personal touch they put into their B&B. This place, with a cozy lounge and an inviting garden, oozes class with a contemporary touch (rooms are €95 or €115; cottage out back is €165; air-con, free Internet access and cable Internet in rooms, Hoogpoort 31, tel. 09-225-3775, www.chambreplus.be, chambre plus@telenet.be).

$$$ Hotel Harmony is a pricey, classy, four-star, family-run boutique hotel with modern style and 25 rooms ideally located on the embankment in the town center (Db-€150-225 depending on size and amenities, Sb for €15 less, air-con, elevator, pay Internet access and Wi-Fi, very medieval breakfast room and music room/parlor, heated outdoor pool in summer, Kraanlei 37, tel. 09-324-2680, fax 09-324-2688, www.hotel-harmony.be, info@hotel -harmony.be).

$$ B&B King, hiding in a nondescript residential area a 10-minute walk from the main tourist zone, is a find. Charmingly run by Sarah and Dominiek, this mod B&B has two rooms and artistic flair, with modern art exhibited in the halls (Sb-€75, Db-€80, free Wi-Fi, Brouwersstraat 22, mobile 0489-572-909, www.bbking.be, info@bbking.be). From Drabstraat/Poelstraat, swing right onto the big street, then turn immediately right again on Ramen, then left on Brouwersstraat; it's the last house on the right.

$$ Erasmus Hotel, well-run by Peter, has 12 well-maintained rooms around a creaky wooden staircase in a classic 400-year-old building. It's on a boring street, just a short walk from the embank-

---

Sleep Code

(€1 = about $1.40, country code: 32)

S = Single, **D** = Double/Twin, **T** = Triple, **Q** = Quad, **b** = bathroom, **s** = shower only. Everyone speaks English. Unless otherwise noted, breakfast is included and credit cards are accepted.

To help you easily sort through these listings, I've divided the rooms into three categories, based on the price for a standard double room with bath:

$$$ Higher Priced—Most rooms €100 or more.
$$ Moderately Priced—Most rooms between €50-100.
$ Lower Priced—Most rooms €50 or less.

Prices can change without notice; verify the hotel's current rates online or by email. For other updates, see www .ricksteves.com/update.

---

ment (Sb-€79, Db-€99, large Db-€120, prices can flex depending on demand, no elevator, pay Wi-Fi, Poel 25, tel. 09-224-2195, fax 09-233-4241, www.erasmushotel.be, info@erasmushotel.be)

$$ Ibis Gent Centrum St-Baafs Kathedraal is a good branch of the Europe-wide chain, offering affordable, predictable cookie-cutter comfort in 120 rooms right next door to the cathedral (Db-€79-109—generally €82 in summer, €99 in high season, and €109 for special events; breakfast-€14, elevator, free Internet access, pay Wi-Fi, Limburgstraat 2, tel. 09-233-0000, www.ibishotel.com, h1455-re@accor.com).

$$ *Other B&Bs:* Other good rooms in the town center include **In's Inn** (1 room, in Patershol, Db-€85, Corduwaniersstraat 11, tel. 09-225-1705, mobile 0494-361-861, insinn@telenet.be), **Simon Says** (2 rooms over a colorful café at the far end of Patershol, Db-€95, Sluizeken 8, tel. 09-233-0343, www.simon-says.be, info @simon-says.be), and **Brooderie** (3 rustic, woody rooms sharing a single bathroom over a café along the embankment in the heart of town, D-€70-75, Jan Breydelstraat 8, tel. 09-225-0623, www .brooderie.be, brooderie@pandora.be).

$ De Draecke, Ghent's very institutional HI youth hostel, has 106 beds—including some private rooms—in a residential zone a short walk from the castle (all rooms have private bathrooms inside, €18 for a dorm bed, Sb-€32, Db-€45, €3 extra for nonmembers, about €2-3 extra for guests older than 26, includes breakfast and sheets, towel rental extra, pay Internet access and Wi-Fi, Sint-Widostraat 11, tel. 09-233-7050, www.vjh.be, gent @vjh.be).

Ghent Accommodations and

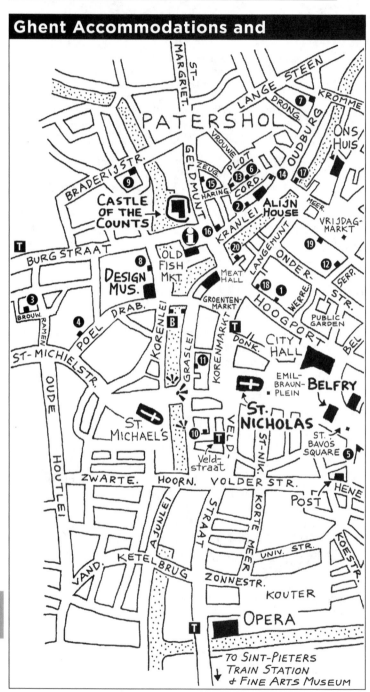

Restaurants

1. Chambre Plus B&B
2. Hotel Harmony
3. B&B King
4. Erasmus Hotel
5. Ibis Gent Centrum St-Baafs Kathedraal
6. In's Inn
7. Simon Says Rooms
8. Brooderie Rooms
9. De Draecke Hostel
10. Pakhuis Restaurant
11. Belga Queen
12. Marco Polo Trattoria
13. Bij den Wijzen en den Zot Restaurant
14. Valentijn Restaurant
15. Avalon Restaurant
16. 't Stropke Brasserie
17. Souplounge
18. Tasty World
19. De Dulle Griet Bar
20. 't Dreupelhof Bar

T TRAM #1
B CANAL CRUISES
VIEW

200 YARDS
200 METERS

DCH

Eating in Ghent

All of my listings are in the city center. Ghent prides itself on being a particularly vegetarian-friendly city. Especially on Thursdays, most restaurants offer a veggie option.

Pakhuis is a gorgeously restored, late 19th-century warehouse now filled with a classy, lively brasserie and bar. In this light, airy, two-story, glassed-in birdhouse of a restaurant, they serve up good traditional Belgian food with an emphasis on locally sourced and organic ingredients. It's tucked down a nondescript brick alley, but it's worth going a few steps out of your way for (€12 weekday two-course lunch menu is a great deal, otherwise €9-14 starters, €14-30 main dishes, €25-42 fixed-price meals, Mon-Sat 12:00-23:00, closed Sun, Schuurkenstraat 4, tel. 09-223-5555).

Belga Queen, an outpost of a similarly popular eatery in Brussels, is the most enticing of the restaurants with seating sprawling along the embankment in the picturesque core of Ghent. The food is "Belgian-inspired international," and the interior is extremely trendy and minimalist/industrialist (with three floors of seating, plus a top-floor lounge). While pricey, the place is packed with locals and visitors (€16 lunches, €15-22 starters, €21-35 main dishes, €33-42 fixed-price dinners, daily 12:00-14:30 & 19:00-22:30, Graslei 10, tel. 09-280-0100).

Marco Polo Trattoria is a good choice for Italian-style "slow food" (specializing in fish) at reasonable prices. It fills one long, cozy, tight room with warm, mellow music and tables crowded by locals celebrating special occasions. Reservations are smart (€9-14 antipasti, €14-19 pastas, €10-15 pizzas, Tue-Sun 18:00-22:00, Fri also 12:00-15:00, closed Mon, Serpentstraat 11, tel. 09-225-0420).

In Patershol

For decades this former sailors' quarter was a derelict and dangerous no-man's land, where only fools and thieves dared to tread. But a generation ago, restaurateurs began to reclaim the area, and today it's one of Ghent's most inviting and happening neighborhoods for dining. Stroll the streets and simply drop in on any place that looks good. Continue north beyond the end of Oudburg to find Sleepstraat, which is lined with cheap Turkish eateries (locals recommend Gok Palace).

It's hard to go wrong in Patershol, but here are some particularly well-regarded favorites:

Bij den Wijzen en den Zot ("By the Wise One and the Crazy One") was the first restaurant that opened in Patershol, back when people figured you were either a genius or a madman to open up shop in such a sketchy area (traditional Belgian with some French, €11-15 starters, €20-30 main dishes, Tue-Sat 12:00-14:00 & 18:30-

22:00, closed Sun-Mon, Hertogstraat 42, tel. 09-223-4230).

Valentijn, in the heart of the district, has a romantic, dressy interior and a no-fuss menu of classics (€20-25 main dishes, €33 meals, Mon-Wed and Fri-Sat from 18:30, closed Thu, Sun open for lunch only, Rodekoningstraat 1, tel. 09-225-0429).

Avalon, across the street from the castle, offers tasty vegetarian fare (€11-13 main dishes, €16-19 specials, daily 11:30-14:30, lunch only, Geldmuntstraat 32, tel. 09-244-3724).

't Stropke ("The Noose"), down the street from Avalon, is a brasserie with bright, woody, rustic ambience and a treehouse floor plan. They serve Belgian and French food, with Ghent specialties, such as the creamy soup called *waterzooi* (€8 sandwiches served until 18:00, €10-14 starters, €16-20 main dishes, Fri-Wed 9:00-22:00, closed Thu, Kraanlei 1, tel. 09-329-8335).

Fast and Cheap

These centrally located options are suitable for a quick lunch.

Souplounge is basic, but cheap and good. They offer four daily soups, along with salads; a bowl of soup, two rolls, and a piece of fruit runs just €3.50. Eat in the mod interior, or at the outdoor tables overlooking one of Ghent's most scenic stretches of canal (also €5 salads, daily 10:00-19:00, Zuivelbrugstraat 6, tel. 09-223-6203).

Tasty World serves up decent €5 veggie burgers with various toppings, plus a wide range of fresh fruit juices and salads (Mon-Sat 11:00-20:00, closed Sun, Hoogpoort 1, tel. 09-225-7407).

Bar Scene

Two touristy bars in the center are worth considering if you want to sample a wide range of Belgian favorites: beer or gin.

De Dulle Griet, on Vrijdagmarkt, serves up 249 types of beer in a cozy, sprawling bar with beer glasses hanging from the ceiling. The local beer, Gruut, is made with no hops; instead, it's flavored with a medieval (pre-hops) mix of herbs that brewers call *gruit* (Tue-Sat 12:00-1:00 in the morning, Sun 12:00-19:00, Mon 16:30-1:00 in the morning, Vrijdagmarkt 50, tel. 09-244-2455).

't Dreupelhof is a cozy little bar along the river, helmed by chain-smoking Pol, who offers a lukewarm welcome and 100 different types of Dutch and Flemish gin, or *jenever* (€2-5 shots, daily from 16:00, or from 18:00 in July-Aug, open until late, Groentenmarkt 12, tel. 09-224-2120).

Ghent Connections

From Ghent by Train to: Brussels (3/hour, 35 minutes), **Bruges** (4/hour, 30 minutes), **Antwerp** (3/hour, 50-55 minutes), **Ypres/ Ieper** (hourly, 1.25 hours, transfer in Kortrijk), **Paris** (2/hour,

2-2.5 hours, change at Brussels Midi/Zuid/South to Thalys train), **Amsterdam** (hourly, 2.25 hours, transfer in Antwerp), **Delft** (2/hour, 2-2.5 hours, transfer in Antwerp and Rotterdam). In Belgium, dial 050-302-424 for train information—press 4 for English, www.b-rail.be.

PRACTICALITIES

This section covers just the basics on traveling in Belgium (for more information, see *Rick Steves' Amsterdam, Bruges & Brussels*). You can find free advice on specific topics at www.ricksteves.com/tips.

Money

Belgium uses the euro currency: 1 euro (€) = about $1.40. To convert prices in euros to dollars, add about 40 percent: €20 = about $28, €50 = about $70. (Check www.oanda.com for the latest exchange rates.)

The standard way for travelers to get euros is to withdraw money from a cash machine (called a *geldautomaat* in Flemish, or a *retrait de billets* or *distributeur de billets* in French) using a debit or credit card, ideally with a Visa or MasterCard logo. Before departing, call your bank or credit-card company: Confirm that your card will work overseas, ask about international transaction fees, and alert them that you'll be making withdrawals in Europe.

To keep your valuables safe, wear a money belt. But if you do lose your credit or debit card, report the loss immediately to the respective global customer-assistance centers. Call these 24-hour US numbers collect: Visa (410/581-9994), MasterCard (636/722-7111), and American Express (623/492-8427).

Dealing with "Chip and PIN": Belgium (and much of northern Europe) is adopting a "chip-and-PIN" system for credit cards. These "smartcards" come with an embedded microchip, and cardholders enter a PIN code instead of signing a receipt. If your US card is rejected, a cashier will probably be able to process your card the old-fashioned way. A few merchants might insist on the PIN code—making it helpful for you to know the code for your credit card (ask your credit-card company before your trip). The easiest solution is to pay for your purchases with cash you've withdrawn from an ATM. Your US credit card may not work at Belgium's automated pay points, such as ticket machines at train and subway stations, toll booths, parking garages, luggage lockers, and self-serve pumps at gas stations. But in many of these cases, a cash-only payment option is available.

Phoning

Smart travelers use the telephone to reserve or reconfirm rooms, reserve restaurants, get directions, research transportation connections, confirm tour times, phone home, and lots more.

To call Belgium from the US or Canada: Dial 011-32 and then the local number, minus its initial zero. (The 011 is our international access code, and 32 is Belgium's country code.)

To call Belgium from a European country: Dial 00-32 followed by the local number, minus its initial zero. (The 00 is Europe's international access code.)

To call within Belgium: Just dial the local number.

To call from Belgium to another country: Dial 00 followed by the country code (for example, 1 for the US or Canada), then the area code and number. If calling European countries whose phone numbers begin with 0, you'll usually have to omit that 0 when you dial.

Tips on Phoning: To make calls in Belgium, you can buy two different types of phone cards—international or insertable—sold locally at newsstands. Cheap international phone cards, which work with a scratch-to-reveal PIN code at any phone, allow you to call home to the US for pennies a minute, and also work for domestic calls within Belgium. Insertable phone cards, which must be inserted into public pay phones, are reasonable for calls within Belgium (and work for international calls as well, but not as cheaply as the international phone cards). Calling from your hotel-room phone is usually expensive, unless you use an international phone card. A mobile phone—whether an American one that works in Belgium, or a European one you buy when you arrive—is handy, but can be pricey. For more on phoning, see www.ricksteves.com/phoning.

Emergency Telephone Numbers in Belgium: For English-speaking **police** help, dial 101 or 112. To summon an **ambulance** or **fire truck,** call 100 or 112. For other concerns, get advice from your hotel. For passport problems, call the **US Embassy** (in Brussels, tel. 02-508-2111; for after-hours emergencies, call and ask to be connected to the duty officer) or the **Canadian Embassy** (in Brussels, tel. 02-741-0611).

Making Hotel Reservations

To ensure the best value, I recommend reserving rooms in advance, particularly during peak season. Email the hotelier with the following key pieces of information: number and type of rooms; number of nights; date of arrival; date of departure; and any special requests. (For a sample form, see www.ricksteves .com/reservation.) Use the European style for writing dates: day/month/year. For example, for a two-night stay in July, you could request: "1 double room for 2 nights, arrive 16/07/12, depart 18/07/12." Hoteliers typically ask for your credit-card number as a deposit.

In general, hotel prices can soften if you do any of the following: offer to pay cash, stay at least three nights, or travel at off-peak times (business-class hotels in Brussels often have discounts on weekends). You can also try asking for a cheaper room (for example, with a bathroom down the hall), or offer to skip breakfast.

Eating

In addition to its fine restaurants, Belgium has other types of eateries. Cafés are all-purpose establishments, serving light meals at mealtimes, and coffee, drinks, and snacks at other times. An *eetcafé* is a simple restaurant serving basic, traditional meals in a straightforward setting. A *proeflokaal* is a bar (with snacks) for tasting wine, spirits, or beer. And there's no shortage of stand-up, take-out places serving Flemish fries, pickled herring, sandwiches, and all kinds of quick ethnic fare—including falafels (fried chickpea balls in pita bread), *shoarmas* (lamb tucked in pita bread), and *döner kebabs* (Turkish version of a *shoarma*).

Good service is relaxed (slow to an American). You won't get the bill until you ask for it. Most restaurants include a 15 percent service charge in their prices, but an additional tip of about 5-10 percent is a nice reward for good service. In bars, rounding up to the next euro ("keep the change") is appropriate if you get table service, but not necessary if you order at the bar.

For more on Belgian food (and beer), see the Belgium chapter.

Transportation

By Train: Hourly trains connect Bruges, Brussels, Antwerp, and Ghent faster and easier than driving. Just buy tickets as you go. You don't need advance reservations to ride a train between these cities. If you're coming from Amsterdam, note that the Amsterdam–Brussels Thalys train is pricey but avoidable; plenty of regular trains also make this run. To research train schedules, visit Germany's excellent all-Europe website, http://www.bahn .de, or Belgium's www.b-rail.be. For more extensive travels beyond

Belgium, you may want to study your railpass options (see www
.ricksteves.com/rail). For more specifics, see the "Connections"
section for each city.

By Car: It's cheaper to arrange most car rentals from the
US. For tips on your insurance options, see www.ricksteves.com
/cdw. Bring your driver's license. For route planning, try www
.viamichelin.com. A car is a worthless headache in cities (including Bruges and Brussels)—get tips from your hotel on where to
park safely.

Helpful Hints

Time: Belgium uses the 24-hour clock. It's the same through 12:00
noon, then keep going: 13:00, 14:00, and so on. Belgium, like most
of continental Europe, is six/nine hours ahead of the East/West
Coasts of the US.

Holidays and Festivals: Belgium celebrates many holidays,
which can close sights and attract crowds (book hotel rooms ahead).
For more on holidays and festivals, check Belgium's website: www
.visitbelgium.com. For a simple list showing major—though not
all—events, see www.ricksteves.com/festivals.

Numbers and Stumblers: What Americans call the second
floor of a building is the first floor in Europe. Europeans write
dates as day/month/year, so Christmas is 25/12/12. Commas are
decimal points and vice versa—a dollar and a half is 1,50, and
there are 5.280 feet in a mile. Belgium uses the metric system: A
kilogram is 2.2 pounds; a liter is about a quart; and a kilometer is
six-tenths of a mile.

Language: Belgium is linguistically divided. The northern
part of the country (including Bruges, Antwerp, and Ghent)
speaks Flemish, which is very closely related to Dutch. The southern part of the country (including Brussels) speaks French. Many
people throughout the country also speak English. But just in case,
I've included both Flemish and French survival phrases later in
this book.

Resources from Rick Steves

This Snapshot guide is excerpted from *Rick Steves' Amsterdam,
Bruges & Brussels, 8th edition,* which is one of more than 30 titles
in my series of guidebooks on European travel. I also produce
a public television series, *Rick Steves' Europe,* and a public radio
show, *Travel with Rick Steves.* My website, www.ricksteves
.com, offers free travel information, a Graffiti Wall for travelers'
comments, guidebook updates, my travel blog, an online travel
store, and information on European railpasses and our tours of

Europe. If you're bringing a mobile device on your trip, you can download free information from **Rick Steves Audio Europe,** featuring travel interviews and other audio content about Belgium (via www.ricksteves.com/audioeurope, iTunes, or the Rick Steves Audio Europe free smartphone app).

Additional Resources
Tourist Information: www.visitbelgium.com
Passports and Red Tape: www.travel.state.gov
Packing List: www.ricksteves.com/packlist
Cheap Flights: www.skyscanner.net
Airplane Carry-on Restrictions: www.tsa.gov/travelers
Updates for This Book: www.ricksteves.com/update

How Was Your Trip?
If you'd like to share your tips, concerns, and discoveries after using this book, please fill out the survey at www.ricksteves.com /feedback. Thanks in advance—it helps a lot.

Flemish Survival Phrases

Northern Belgium speaks Flemish—closely related to Dutch. You won't need to learn Flemish, but knowing a few phrases can help. Taking a few moments to learn the pleasantries (such as please and thank you) will improve your connections with locals.

To pronounce the difficult Flemish "g" (indicated in phonetics by hhh), make a hard, guttural, clear-your-throat sound, similar to the "ch" in the Scottish word "loch."

Hello.	**Hallo.**	hol-LOH
Good day.	**Dag.**	dahhh
Good morning.	**Goeiemorgen.**	hhhoy-ah-MOR-hhhen
Good afternoon.	**Goeiemiddag.**	hhhoy-ah-MIT-tahk
Ma'am	**Mevrouw**	meh-frow
Sir	**Meneer**	men-ear
Yes	**Ja**	yah
No	**Nee**	nay
Please	**Alstublieft**	AHL-stoo-bleeft
Thank you.	**Dank u wel.**	dahnk yoo vehl
You're welcome.	**Graag gedaan.**	hhhrahhk hhkeh-dahn
Excuse me.	**Pardon.**	par-DOHN
Do you speak English?	**Spreekt u Engels?**	spraykt oo ENG-els
Okay.	**Oké.**	"okay"
Goodbye.	**Tot ziens.**	toht zeens
one / two	**een / twee**	ayn / t'vay
three / four	**drie / vier**	dree / feer
five / six	**vijf / zes**	fife / ses
seven / eight	**zeven / acht**	say-fen / ahkht
nine / ten	**negen / tien**	nay-hhhen / teen
What does it cost?	**Wat kost?**	vaht kost
I would like...	**Ik wil graag...**	ik vil hhhrahhhk
...a room.	**...een kamer.**	un kah-mer
...a ticket.	**...een kaart.**	un kart
...a bike.	**...een fiets.**	un feets
Where is...?	**Waar is...?**	vahr is
...the station	**...het station**	het sta-tsee-on
...the tourist info office	**...de VVV**	duh vay vay vay
left / right	**links / rechts**	links / rechts
open / closed	**open / gesloten**	"open" / hhhe-sloh-ten

PRACTICALITIES

In the Restaurant

The Belgians have an all-purpose word, *alstublieft* (AHL-stoo-bleeft), that means: "Please" or "Here you are" (if handing you something), or "Thanks" (if taking payment from you), or "You're welcome" (when handing you change). Here are other words that might come in handy at restaurants:

I would like...	Ik wil graag...	ik vil hhhrahhk
...a cup of coffee.	...kopje koffee.	kop-yeh "coffee"
non-smoking	niet-roken	neet roh-ken
smoking	roken	roh-ken
with / without	met / buiten	met / bow-ten
and / or	en / of	en / of
bread	brood	broht
salad	sla	slah
cheese	kaas	kahs
meat	vlees	flays
chicken	kip	kip
fish	vis	fis
egg	ei	eye
fruit	vrucht	frucht
pastries	gebak	hhhe-bak
I am vegetarian.	Ik ben vegetarish.	ik ben vay-hhhe-tah-rish
Tasty.	Lekker.	lek-ker
Enjoy!	Smakelijk!	smak-kuh-luk
Cheers!	Proost!	prohst

French Survival Phrases

When using the phonetics, try to nasalize the <u>n</u> sound.

Good day.	**Bonjour.**	boh<u>n</u>-zhoor
Mrs. / Mr.	**Madame / Monsieur**	mah-dahm / muhs-yur
Do you speak English?	**Parlez-vous anglais?**	par-lay-voo ah<u>n</u>-glay
Yes. / No.	**Oui. / Non.**	wee / noh<u>n</u>
I understand.	**Je comprends.**	zhuh koh<u>n</u>-prah<u>n</u>
I don't understand.	**Je ne comprends pas.**	zhuh nuh koh<u>n</u>-prah<u>n</u> pah
Please.	**S'il vous plaît.**	see voo play
Thank you.	**Merci.**	mehr-see
I'm sorry.	**Désolé.**	day-zoh-lay
Excuse me.	**Pardon.**	par-doh<u>n</u>
(No) problem.	**(Pas de) problème.**	(pah duh) proh-blehm
It's good.	**C'est bon.**	say boh<u>n</u>
Goodbye.	**Au revoir.**	oh vwahr
one / two	**un / deux**	uh<u>n</u> / duh
three / four	**trois / quatre**	twah / kah-truh
five / six	**cinq / six**	sa<u>n</u>k / sees
seven / eight	**sept / huit**	seht / weet
nine / ten	**neuf / dix**	nuhf / dees
How much is it?	**Combien?**	koh<u>n</u>-bee-a<u>n</u>
Write it?	**Ecrivez?**	ay-kree-vay
Is it free?	**C'est gratuit?**	say grah-twee
Included?	**Inclus?**	a<u>n</u>-klew
Where can I buy / find...?	**Où puis-je acheter / trouver...?**	oo pwee-zhuh ah-shuh-tay / troo-vay
I'd like / We'd like...	**Je voudrais / Nous voudrions...**	zhuh voo-dray / noo voo-dree-oh<u>n</u>
...a room.	**...une chambre.**	ewn shah<u>n</u>-bruh
...a ticket to ___.	**...un billet pour ___.**	uh<u>n</u> bee-yay poor
Is it possible?	**C'est possible?**	say poh-see-bluh
Where is...?	**Où est...?**	oo ay
...the train station	**...la gare**	lah gar
...the bus station	**...la gare routière**	lah gar root-yehr
...tourist information	**...l'office du tourisme**	loh-fees dew too-reez-muh
Where are the toilets?	**Où sont les toilettes?**	oo soh<u>n</u> lay twah-leht
men	**hommes**	ohm
women	**dames**	dahm
left / right	**à gauche / à droite**	ah gohsh / ah dwaht
straight	**tout droit**	too dwah
When does this open / close?	**Ça ouvre / ferme à quelle heure?**	sah oo-vruh / fehrm ah kehl ur
At what time?	**À quelle heure?**	ah kehl ur
Just a moment.	**Un moment.**	uh<u>n</u> moh-mah<u>n</u>
now / soon / later	**maintenant / bientôt / plus tard**	ma<u>n</u>-tuh-nah<u>n</u> / bee-a<u>n</u>-toh / plew tar
today / tomorrow	**aujourd'hui / demain**	oh-zhoor-dwee / duh-ma<u>n</u>

In the Restaurant

I'd like / We'd like...	**Je voudrais / Nous voudrions...**	zhuh voo-dray / noo voo-dree-oh<u>n</u>
...to reserve...	**...réserver...**	ray-zehr-vay
...a table for one / two.	**...une table pour un / deux.**	ewn tah-bluh poor uh<u>n</u> / duh
Non-smoking.	**Non fumeur.**	noh<u>n</u> few-mur
Is this seat free?	**C'est libre?**	say lee-bruh
The menu (in English), please.	**La carte (en anglais), s'il vous plaît.**	lah kart (ah<u>n</u> ah<u>n</u>-glay) see voo play
service (not) included	**service (non) compris**	sehr-vees (noh<u>n</u>) koh<u>n</u>-pree
to go	**à emporter**	ah ah<u>n</u>-por-tay
with / without	**avec / sans**	ah-vehk / sah<u>n</u>
and / or	**et / ou**	ay / oo
special of the day	**plat du jour**	plah dew zhoor
specialty of the house	**spécialité de la maison**	spay-see-ah-lee-tay duh lah may-zoh<u>n</u>
appetizers	**hors-d'oeuvre**	or-duh-vruh
first course (soup, salad)	**entrée**	ah<u>n</u>-tray
main course (meat, fish)	**plat principal**	plah pra<u>n</u>-see-pahl
bread	**pain**	pa<u>n</u>
cheese	**fromage**	froh-mahzh
sandwich	**sandwich**	sah<u>n</u>d-weech
soup	**soupe**	soop
salad	**salade**	sah-lahd
meat	**viande**	vee-ah<u>n</u>d
chicken	**poulet**	poo-lay
fish	**poisson**	pwah-soh<u>n</u>
seafood	**fruits de mer**	frwee duh mehr
fruit	**fruit**	frwee
vegetables	**légumes**	lay-gewm
dessert	**dessert**	duh-sehr
mineral water	**eau minérale**	oh mee-nay-rahl
tap water	**l'eau du robinet**	loh dew roh-bee-nay
milk	**lait**	lay
(orange) juice	**jus (d'orange)**	zhew (doh-rah<u>n</u>zh)
coffee	**café**	kah-fay
tea	**thé**	tay
wine	**vin**	va<u>n</u>
red / white	**rouge / blanc**	roozh / blah<u>n</u>
glass / bottle	**verre / bouteille**	vehr / boo-teh-ee
beer	**bière**	bee-ehr
Cheers!	**Santé!**	sah<u>n</u>-tay
More. / Another.	**Plus. / Un autre.**	plew / uh<u>n</u> oh-truh
The same.	**La même chose.**	lah mehm shohz
The bill, please.	**L'addition, s'il vous plaît.**	lah-dee-see-oh<u>n</u> see voo play
tip	**pourboire**	poor-bwar
Delicious!	**Délicieux!**	day-lee-see-uh

For more user-friendly French phrases, check out *Rick Steves' French Phrase Book and Dictionary* or *Rick Steves' French, Italian & German Phrase Book*.

INDEX

INDEX

INDEX

INDEX

Audio Europe

RICK STEVES AUDIO EUROPE

Rick's free app and podcasts

The FREE **Rick Steves Audio Europe**™ app for iPhone, iPad and iPod Touch gives you 29 self-guided audio tours of Europe's top museums, sights and historic walks—plus more than 200 tracks filled with cultural insights and sightseeing tips from Rick's radio interviews—all organized into geographic-specific playlists.

Let **Rick Steves Audio Europe**™ amplify your guidebook.

With Rick whispering in your ear, Europe gets even better.

Thanks Facebook fans for submitting photos while on location! From top: John Kuijper in Florence, Brenda Mamer with her mother in Rome, Angel Capobianco in London, and Alyssa Passey with her friend in Paris.

Find out more at ricksteves.com

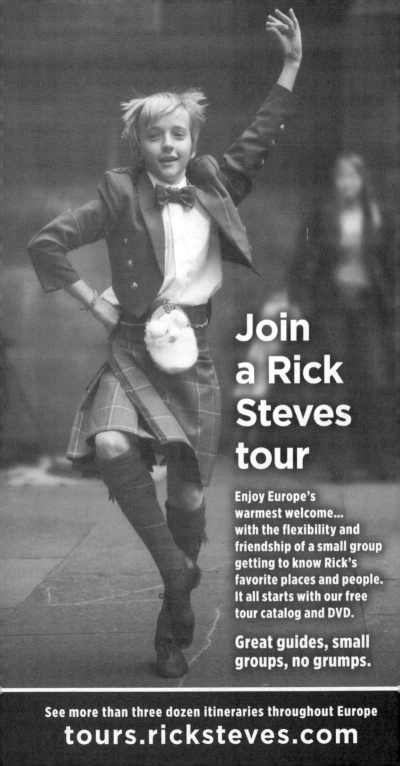

Join a Rick Steves tour

**Enjoy Europe's warmest welcome...
with the flexibility and
friendship of a small group
getting to know Rick's
favorite places and people.
It all starts with our free
tour catalog and DVD.**

**Great guides, small
groups, no grumps.**

Start your trip at

Free information and great gear to

▶ Plan Your Trip

Browse thousands of articles and a wealth of money-saving tips for planning your dream trip. You'll find up-to-date information on Europe's best destinations, packing smart, getting around, finding rooms, staying healthy, avoiding scams and more.

▶ Eurail Passes

Find out, step-by-step, if a railpass makes sense for your trip—and how to avoid buying more than you need. Get free shipping on online orders

▶ Graffiti Wall & Travelers Helpline

Learn, ask, share—our online community of savvy travelers is a great resource for first-time travelers to Europe, as well as seasoned pros.

Rick Steves' Europe Through the Back Door, Inc.

Rick Steves.

www.ricksteves.com

EUROPE GUIDES
Best of Europe
Eastern Europe
Europe Through the Back Door
Mediterranean Cruise Ports

COUNTRY GUIDES
Croatia & Slovenia
England
France
Germany
Great Britain
Ireland
Italy
Portugal
Scandinavia
Spain
Switzerland

CITY & REGIONAL GUIDES
Amsterdam, Bruges & Brussels
Budapest
Florence & Tuscany
Greece: Athens & the Peloponnese
Istanbul
London
Paris
Prague & the Czech Republic
Provence & the French Riviera
Rome
Venice
Vienna, Salzburg & Tirol

SNAPSHOT GUIDES
Barcelona
Berlin
Bruges & Brussels
Copenhagen & the Best of
    Denmark
Dublin
Dubrovnik
Hill Towns of Central Italy
Italy's Cinque Terre
Krakow, Warsaw & Gdansk
Lisbon
Madrid & Toledo
Munich, Bavaria & Salzburg
Naples & the Amalfi Coast
Northern Ireland
Norway
Scotland
Sevilla, Granada & Southern Spain
Stockholm

POCKET GUIDES
London
Paris
Rome

TRAVEL CULTURE
Europe 101
European Christmas
Postcards from Europe
Travel as a Political Act

Rick Steves guidebooks are published by Avalon Travel,
a member of the Perseus Books Group.

NOW AVAILABLE:
eBOOKS, APPS & BLU-RAY

eBOOKS

Most guides are available as eBooks from Amazon, Barnes & Noble, Borders, Apple, and Sony. Free apps for eBook reading are available in the Apple App Store and Android Market, and eBook readers such as Kindle, Nook, and Kobo all have free apps that work on smartphones.

RICK STEVES' EUROPE DVDs

10 New Shows 2011–2012
Austria & the Alps
Eastern Europe
England & Wales
European Christmas
European Travel Skills & Specials
France
Germany, BeNeLux & More
Greece & Turkey
Iran
Ireland & Scotland
Italy's Cities
Italy's Countryside
Scandinavia
Spain
Travel Extras

BLU-RAY

Celtic Charms
Eastern Europe Favorites
European Christmas
Italy Through the Back Door
Mediterranean Mosaic
Surprising Cities of Europe

PHRASE BOOKS & DICTIONARIES

French
French, Italian & German
German
Italian
Portuguese
Spanish

JOURNALS

Rick Steves' Pocket Travel Journal
Rick Steves' Travel Journal

APPS

Select Rick Steves guides are available as apps in the Apple App Store.

PLANNING MAPS

Britain, Ireland & London
Europe
France & Paris
Germany, Austria & Switzerland
Ireland
Italy
Spain & Portugal

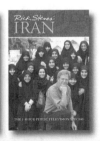

Avalon Travel
a member of the Perseus Books Group
1700 Fourth Street
Berkeley, CA 94710, USA

Printed in Canada by Friesens
First printing August 2011

Portions of this book were originally published in *Rick Steves' Mona Winks* © 2001, 1998,
1996, 1993, 1988 by Rick Steves and Gene Openshaw; and in *Rick Steves' France* © 2006,
2005, 2004, 2003, 2002 by Rick Steves and Steve Smith.

ISBN 978-1-61238-229-6

For the latest on Rick's lectures, books, tours, public radio show, and public television series,
contact Europe Through the Back Door, Box 2009, Edmonds, WA 98020, tel. 425/771-
8303, fax 425/771-0833, www.ricksteves.com, rick@ricksteves.com.

Europe Through the Back Door Reviewing Editors: Jennifer Madison Davis, Cathy
   McDonald
ETBD Editors: Tom Griffin, Gretchen Strauch, Cathy Lu
ETBD Managing Editor: Risa Laib
Avalon Travel Senior Editor & Series Manager: Madhu Prasher
Avalon Travel Project Editor: Kelly Lydick
Research Assistance: Cameron Hewitt, Gretchen Strauch, Elizabeth Wang
Copy Editor: Jennifer Malnick
Proofreader: Janet Walden
Indexer: Stephen Callahan
Production & Typesetting: McGuire Barber Design
Cover Design: Kimberly Glyder Design
Graphic Content Director: Laura VanDeventer
Maps and Graphics: David C. Hoerlein, Laura VanDeventer, Lauren Mills, Pat O'Connor,
   Barb Geisler, Mike Morgenfeld, Kat Bennett
Photography: Rick Steves, Dominic Bonuccelli, Gene Openshaw, Cameron Hewitt,
   Jennifer Hauseman, Gretchen Strauch, Laura VanDeventer, Bruce VanDeventer
Cover Photo: Rozenhoedkaai in Bruges © nagelestock.com/Alamy

ABOUT THE AUTHORS

RICK STEVES

Since 1973, Rick Steves has spent 100 days every year exploring Europe. Rick produces a public television series *(Rick Steves' Europe)*, a public radio show *(Travel with Rick Steves)*, and an app and podcast *(Rick Steves Audio Europe);* writes a bestselling series of guidebooks and a nationally syndicated newspaper column; organizes guided tours that take over ten thousand travelers to Europe annually; and offers an information-packed website (www.ricksteves.com). With the help of his hardworking staff of 80 at Europe Through the Back Door—in Edmonds, Washington, just north of Seattle—Rick's mission is to make European travel fun, affordable, and culturally enlightening for Americans.

GENE OPENSHAW

Gene Openshaw is a writer, composer, tour guide, and lecturer on art and history. Specializing in writing walking tours of Europe's cultural sights, Gene has co-authored ten of Rick's books and contributes to Rick's public television series. As a composer, Gene has written a full-length opera *(Matter)*, a violin sonata, and dozens of songs. He lives near Seattle with his daughter, and roots for the Mariners in good times and bad.